THE THIRD CITY

CHICAGO VISIONS AND REVISIONS

Edited by Carlo Rotella, Bill Savage, Carl Smith, and Robert B. Stepto

Also in the series:

THE WAGON AND OTHER STORIES FROM THE CITY
by Martin Preib

SOLDIER FIELD: A STADIUM AND ITS CITY
by Liam T. A. Ford

BARRIO: PHOTOGRAPHS FROM CHICAGO'S
PILSEN AND LITTLE VILLAGE
by Paul D'Amato

THE PLAN OF CHICAGO: DANIEL BURNHAM AND
THE REMAKING OF THE AMERICAN CITY
by Carl Smith

THE THIRD CITY

Chicago and American Urbanism

LARRY BENNETT

THE UNIVERSITY OF CHICAGO PRESS | CHICAGO AND LONDON

Larry Bennett is professor of political science at DePaul University. He is the author or coauthor of many articles and books, including *Neighborhood Politics: Chicago and Sheffield* and *It's Hardly Sportin': Stadiums, Neighborhoods, and the New Chicago.*

The University of Chicago Press, Chicago 60637
The University of Chicago Press, Ltd., London
© 2010 by The University of Chicago
All rights reserved. Published 2010
Printed in the United States of America

19 18 17 16 15 14 13 12 11 10   1 2 3 4 5

ISBN-13: 978-0-226-04293-0 (cloth)
ISBN-10: 0-226-04293-6 (cloth)

Library of Congress Cataloging-in-Publication Data

Bennett, Larry, 1950–
The third city : Chicago and American urbanism / Larry Bennett.
p. cm.
Includes bibliographical references and index.
ISBN-13: 978-0-226-04293-0 (cloth : alk. paper)
ISBN-10: 0-226-04293-6 (cloth : alk. paper) 1. Urban renewal—Illinois—Chicago.
2. Daley, Richard M. (Richard Michael), 1942– 3. Chicago (Ill.)—History. 4. City planning—Illinois—Chicago. 5. City and town life—Illinois—Chicago. 6. Sociology, Urban—Illinois—Chicago. 7. Neighborhoods—Illinois—Chicago. I. Title.
HT177.C5B44 2010
307.3′4160977311—dc22
2010002015

♾ The paper used in this publication meets the minimum requirements of the American National Standard for Information Sciences—Permanence of Paper for Printed Library Materials, ANSI Z39.48–1992.

For Susan Fainstein

CONTENTS

ACKNOWLEDGMENTS

I have been told that the origin of this book was a conversation between Greg Squires and Carl Smith. Greg is a friend of many years, and I thank him for mentioning me to Carl. Carl has become a friend and is also an imposing scholar, an astute editor, and a very funny man. I also want to thank Bill Savage and an anonymous reviewer who read the entire manuscript and offered very helpful commentary. At the University of Chicago Press, Robert Devens has offered consistent support and unwavering good humor. Thanks for both, Robert. Also at the press, Anne Summers Goldberg and Mary Gehl have skillfully guided logistics and text editing.

My understanding of Chicago—as well as many other things—has benefited from my interactions with several linked circles of scholars, activists, and colleagues. For most of the past decade, an evolving and at times rambunctious group of scholars, sometimes known as the Chicago Preskool, has convened to discuss both local and more general topics involving urban politics and policy. The mainstays of this group have been Dennis Judd, Terry Clark, and Dick Simpson. Partners in crime have included Bill Grimshaw, David Perry, Bonnie Lindstrom, Karen Mossberger, Mike Pagano, Robin Hambleton, and Evan McKenzie. Each of these colleagues has made contributions to our discussions that have been, in one way or another, incorporated into the argument of this book.

The link between the Preskool and the Uptown Summer Urban Studies Reading Group is Costas Spirou, the kind of friend and collaborator every frazzled academic should have. He and Jamie Smith have been heart and soul of the Uptown reading group, which has also included Fassil Demissie, Mike Maly, Rachel Weber, Janet Smith, Bill Sites, Michelle Boyd, Hugh Bartling, Julian Tysh, Jeff Edwards, Endy Zemenides, Jesse Mumm, and Stephanie Farmer. This younger group of mainly academics is just as sharp as the Preskool, and more appreciative of *vinho verde*. The hinge between the Uptown reading group and the Political Science Department at DePaul University is Cathy May. In my department I have been consistently challenged by the intellectual reach and commitment to teaching of Cathy, as well as of my old friends David Barnum, Pat Callahan, Rose Spalding, and Harry Wray. Mike Budde also belongs in this company, though he is more precisely characterized as semi-old. What I call the "new Chicago team" is linked to the Uptown reading group by Costas Spirou and Fassil Demissie. Its other members are John Koval, Roberta Garner, Michael Bennett, and Kiljoong Kim. Much in this book grows out of what I learned from the new Chicago team.

During the last fifteen years I have on several occasions worked with a circle of people either researching public housing in Chicago or advocating on behalf of Chicago Housing Authority residents. Janet Smith links this network to the Uptown reading group. It has been a great pleasure to work as well with Pat Wright and Adolph Reed. As to the advocates, I cannot easily express the depth of my admiration for Carol Steele, Bill Wilen, and the late Wardell Yotaghan.

The work of two undergraduate research assistants, Taylor Yeftich and Liza Getsinger, contributed mightily to chapters 5 and 6. Thanks Taylor and Liza, and Good Luck in life.

Closer to home I have come to rely on Alec Bennett's insights regarding cities, urban history, and historic preservation. To have a son who shares my enthusiasm for the nuances of place is foundational to my sense of personal satisfaction. Finally, I salute Gwyn Friend, untiring problem-solver, steadfast advocate, snappy dresser, and life partner.

THE THIRD CITY

Navy Pier became a great tourist attraction in the 1990s. Its Ferris wheel expresses the playfulness that distinguishes the Third City from Chicago's First and Second Cities.

ONE

THE THIRD CITY

CHICAGO IS THE most self-conscious of cities. In its origins it represented the dream of New York–based capital, a terminus for Great Lakes–borne commerce that would develop, in its own right, into the most formidable metropolis of the mid-continent.[1] In the aftermath of the Great Fire of 1871, the city's army of ambitious capitalists rebuilt it in a fashion that was grander than in its previous, short life as a frontier depot. By the last decade of the nineteenth century, the city's civic leadership was sufficiently self-assured to win for Chicago designation as host of the World's Columbian Exposition, an event commemorating Columbus's voyages to America at the end of the fifteenth century. To the dismay of one of the city's great artists, the architect Louis Sullivan, the Columbian Exposition's civic sponsors and committee of designers were not sufficiently self-assured to use the exhibition site to present a path-defining vision of city form and human settlement. Instead, the classically inspired, mammoth-scaled White City on the south lakefront seemed to embody the parvenu's quest for respect through emulation of his social betters.[2]

Chicago's self-consciousness is not simply a matter of maturing in the shadows of older, more worldly cities. In the early decades of the twentieth century, sociologists at the University of Chicago, led by a former journalist, Robert Park, embarked on a twofold quest to map the neighborhoods, people, and social intricacies of the city, and, in so doing, perfect a set of theories and analytical tools that could be applied to cities and urban development wherever metropolises were found. The title of what is probably Park's most influential piece of writing, "The City: Suggestions for the Investigation of Human Behavior in the Urban Environment" (1925), perfectly captures his ambitions for the nascent field of urban sociology: systematic investigation of human action in what was at that time presumed to be the emergent, typically behavior-shaping form of human habitation.[3]

Though the idea of scientific neutrality ruled the theorizing and observational methodologies of the early Chicago school sociologists, neutrality and what might be presumed as its associated values—even-tempered social discourse and the rational application of means to ends—were hardly characteristic of the city that was their object of study. The prairie depot of the 1830s and 1840s had grown to a metropolis of one million by 1890, and two million additional residents would be added to the city's streets, workplaces, and homes by the onset of the Great Depression. Chicago was a sprawling, vibrant industrial center, whose multinational population—Irish, German, Scandinavian, Polish, Italian, and a dozen smaller immigrant flows from southern and eastern Europe—on the best of days managed to coexist in an economically productive fashion, but on many bad days heeded the exhortations of ethnocentric political leaders and navigated the city's streets using a variety of means to avoid its myriad "others," or simply fell into intercommunal violence. The subject matter and titles of the early Chicago school of sociology monographs are direct evocations of this on-the-street social milieu: *The Gang* (1927), *The Ghetto* (1929), and *The Natural History of a Delinquent Career* (1931).[4]

Like many American cities of the early twentieth century, Chicago was the site of a deep-seated "civic war," pitting an older, largely Yankee-descended institutional leadership against an emergent, recently immigrant population of small proprietors, factory hands, neighborhood ethnic "nationalists," and upward-striving politicos.[5] The early urban sociologists were poised at the intersection of Chicago's clashing histories and worldviews, sharing with the retreating Yankees a quality of temperament and commitment to social amelioration while avidly recording the transgressions of the city's rising ethnic leadership and rank and file. At this point in Chicago's development there had emerged a clear divide between what might be called the normative city—a setting in which the execution of professionally ordained planning principles and the inculcation of citizenly virtues were presumed to be achievable—and the empirical city—a wild, unkempt place whose effect on its residents was just as likely to be demoralizing as salubrious.[6]

In the 1920s, the empirical Chicago asserted itself in a powerful fashion. The era of Prohibition coincided with the emergence of a complex underground economy devoted to satisfying the local craving for alcohol. Gangland figures found ready allies in Chicago's political parties, whose operatives had long joined electioneering and governance to economic self-aggrandizement. During this decade the city's Republican Party, led by the provocatively uncouth William Hale Thompson, established a standard of citywide venality and local favor-mongering on par with the misdeeds of any of the city's wrong-thinking, Catholic-leaning Democratic Party factions. In the wake of Thompson's three terms as mayor, the Cook County Democratic machine emerged and seemingly rendered permanent the scheming, look-out-for-Number One-style of politics that a generation previously had been the worst fear of the city's Yankees.[7]

Gang wars, intense ethnic and then racial competition, a politics defined by greed and aiming no higher than perpetuation in office: such was the Chicago that persisted in the early years following World War II. It was the particular brilliance of Richard J. Daley, Chicago's mayor from 1955 to 1976, to seize control of the empirical city and within a decade redefine the venal as the virtuous. Though Daley probably did not invent the expression, "good politics is good government" was the hallmark of at least the first decade of his mayoralty. Through his ability to centralize the Cook County Democratic Party and reinforce his party domination via the skillful distribution of government jobs, contracts, and various associated favors, Daley gave new life to the Democratic machine and achieved a considerable degree of national acclaim for his city.[8]

Nevertheless, Daley's Democratic machine of the 1950s and early 1960s foundered on the same shoals that broke the post–World War II civic calm of so many American cities: the flight of middle-class residents to the suburbs, the relocation of major employers to the suburbs and beyond, a vigorous local civil rights movement, and—growing from the confluence of the three preceding trends—a festering interracial quarrel over jobs and residential space. Chicago of the late 1960s was a city in turmoil, in part due to the "touching down" of national forces, such as Martin Luther King Jr.'s housing campaign of 1966, and in part due to the localized agonies associated with rapid, apparently ceaseless neighborhood racial transition. In quick succession, disasters such as the April 1968 West Side riots following King's assassination in Memphis, Tennessee, the August 1968 Democratic National Convention disturbances, and the Black Panther murders of December 1969 forced upon Chicagoans a new and heretofore uncharacteristic variety of self-consciousness.[9] Daley's "city that works" had suddenly crashed. In its place was a racially divided, economically crippled emblem of the soon-to-be-dubbed Rust Belt. Moreover, the attitudes expressed by Daley and his supporters—as they attempted to explain what had befallen Chicago—revealed a city leadership that was deeply provincial, and as such, seemingly incapable of comprehending the late twentieth century and its challenges.

Here is a personal anecdote that speaks—even in the face of these unwelcome developments—to the reach of the Richard J. Daley legend. Many years ago, and long before I became a Chicagoan, I found myself, or possibly had maneuvered to situate myself, in an undergraduate dormitory room with a half-dozen or so acquaintances. One of my company had grown up in the Chicago suburbs, and to my considerable surprise—even as Jimi Hendrix's "All Along the Watchtower" surged from the stereo speakers—proclaimed that the city's civil unrest of the previous weeks and months was in no way the doing of Mayor Daley. Rather, outside agitators had descended on Chicago, and what had occurred in April and August of 1968 was entirely their handiwork. At the time I was amazed at what I took to be my acquaintance's false consciousness. To this day, in the minds of many older Chicagoans, the image of Richard J. Daley in his political prime remains alive and unblemished by subsequent reflection.

Chicago's long 1960s climaxed in 1983 with Harold Washington's election as mayor. An African American and former Daley machine operative, Washington abandoned the regular Democratic Party as a member of the Illinois state legislature in the 1970s. He was drawn into the 1983 mayoral race by a coalition of black and neighborhood activists whose immediate target was the incumbent mayor, Jane Byrne, but whose dissatisfactions reached back to the Richard J. Daley era.[10] Washington, for his part, assembled an administration that sought to undercut the official Democratic Party, reinvigorate city government with an infusion of neighborhood organization veterans and academic experts, and chart an innovative policy course emphasizing public accountability, industrial retention, and neighborhood development.[11] The response of holdover Democratic Party loyalists in the City Council and elsewhere in the city and Cook County governments was a poisonous obstructionism.[12] Their call to arms was the incompetence supposedly demonstrated by the interlopers (often, but far from exclusively, African Americans) who had taken over the city government's executive branch. Amidst the rekindled racial antagonisms of the mid-1980s, a local civic organization issued a report asserting that the longstanding, purportedly effective working relationship among the city's political, business, and civic elites had been broken, and further wondered, at what cost to the city at large?[13] Over the next few years Chicago's new round of civic wars earned it the designation "Beirut by the Lake," a label reflecting Chicagoans' fears of inextricable racial / ethnic polarization coupled with a physically devastated cityscape.

And yet, the 1980s in Chicago are also frequently recalled as a time of elevated civic engagement—voting in municipal elections, for instance, increased dramatically—or, in parallel fashion, as the last time local politics were interesting. Some of this interesting upheaval was, of course, repellent, such as the street-corner fistfights so many of us observed on election day 1983. On the other hand, a Chicago comedian, Aaron Freeman, made his reputation by developing a skit in which the *Star Wars* principals Luke Skywalker and Darth Vader were embodied by Harold Washington and his chief City Council critic, Alderman Edward Vrdolyak. Across Chicago, citizens were entertained as well as enraged by this era's political strife. The art of political maneuvering is as central to Chicagoans' sense of their city as is pride in its commercial architecture. In retrospect, the Washington mayoralty increasingly looks like the apotheosis of a particular form of political / civic culture that is unlikely ever to return.

The shading of Chicago's self-consciousness has brightened in the last fifteen years. Another Daley—the great man's son, Richard M.—holds the mayoralty, and a burst of commercial and residential development has filled in many of the embarrassing holes that had been punched through the city's physical fabric by the consolidation of railroad operations, the departure of industry, and housing abandonment.[14] Like his father, as well as most mayors of note, Richard M. Daley is a great advocate of public works. In his two decades as chief executive, the younger Daley has rolled out a series of major physical projects: Millennium Park in the northwest corner of downtown Grant Park; the consolidation of a "Museum Campus" for the Field Museum of Natural History, the Shedd Aquarium, and the Adler Planetarium; and just south of the Field Museum, the futuristically recast Soldier Field, home of the Chicago Bears professional football franchise. For now, I will cut short the cataloging of Mayor Daley's public works accomplishments; in a subsequent chapter I examine in detail what might be the most consequential of all of Richard M. Daley's public works initiatives, the top-to-bottom reconstruction of the city's public housing developments. The impacts of Richard M. Daley's physical reshaping of central Chicago are such that sociologist Terry Nichols Clark of the University of Chicago has argued that the provision of urban amenities, if skillfully implemented, can become a crucial lever in stimulating a new era of central city growth both in Chicago and other American cities.[15]

As one can readily enough infer from Clark's premise, contemporary Chicago is less subject than it was twenty years ago to the self-consciousness of a Rust Belt city anticipating its demise. The 1990s were the City of Chicago's first decade of population increase since the 1940s. Nevertheless, even in the face of the mounting good news indicating an end-of-century turnaround in the city's fortunes, for many of the commentators on Chicago's local affairs there is a reluctance to give up its identity as a rough and tumble, political boss–dominated city. Consider, for example, this description of Chicago's political culture—penned in the early days of Richard M. Daley's mayoralty:

> [W]e are Chicagoans, and therefore prey to atavistic impulses. Ours is perhaps the only major city in the country that still expects its mayors to be tribal chieftains. Richard J. Daley was such a man, and so was Harold Washington. They were natural leaders, with followers who were loyal to the point of fanaticism. They would have run things even in a primitive society, although Lord knows they don't come much more primitive than Chicago.[16]

I grant the author of this commentary, journalist Ed Zotti, the right to compose satire, and in the wake of Chicago's contentious 1980s, "atavism" did seem to persist as an element of the city's political culture. But what I find particularly revealing about this assertion is how it extends the "framing" of Chicago's public life that had emerged at the outset of the twentieth century, when European immigrant hordes seemed to be overrunning the city, when the city's public institutions—at least in the eyes of more apocalyptic reformers—seemed to be tottering before a fall into some variety of tribalism, civil war, or anarchy.

This image of Chicago—a metropolis carved into ethnically defined neighborhood enclaves, its population craving iron-willed political leadership, the game of politics overshadowing the ends of politics—is such a powerful shaper of the city's sense of identity that many of its closest observers have failed to notice that in contemporary Chicago, what I call the "third city," is, in fact, emergent. This third city succeeds the first city, Chicago the sprawling industrial center, whose historical arc ran from the Civil War up to the

Great Depression, as well as the second city (not to be confused with A. J. Liebling's portrait of a backward, Potemkin village metropolis fated to a second-class emulation of the nation's metropolitan center, Manhattan[17]), the Rust Belt exemplar of the period from approximately 1950 to 1990. The hold on our collective and individual imaginations that is retained by Chicago's first and second cities is easy enough to understand. Those titans of empirical Chicago—William Hale Thompson, Al Capone, Richard J. Daley, even Jane Addams—negotiated a larger-than-life terrain that was curiously frontier-like in its capacity for producing sudden shifts in human fortune, for visiting prosperity or devastation on the deserving and undeserving alike. There is an awful grandeur to the story of Chicago's first and second cities. For many observers of contemporary Chicago it is tempting to recycle the past as present in a possibly unself-conscious quest to ward off the dread that we have been condemned to live in uninteresting times.

Contemporary Chicago is a tidier place than its first and second manifestations, but it is not less interesting. My aim is to look very closely at this third Chicago and to come to terms with it and its implications. The third city features a revitalized urban core, which at present coexists uncomfortably with a belt of very poor to working-class neighborhoods reaching west and south. The third city is home to a shifting population mix, including a very large segment drawn from Mexico; a smaller but significant immigrant stream from south and east Asia; a substantial population of middle-class professionals working in corporations, universities, and other "creative class" economic niches; and many thousands of "out" gays and lesbians. The third city is intensely conscious of Chicago's tempestuous history and erratically protective of the city's unique built environment. The third city is testing new approaches to neighborhood revitalization and the reform of public institutions.

The third city is also a work in progress, whose story is worth telling in its own right. Yet what makes the emergent Chicago of interest beyond its municipal boundaries, and for an audience in many cities, is once more the quality of self-consciousness animating the changes Chicagoans are bringing to their city. The "New Urbanist" architecture and site-planning characteristic of the Chicago Housing Authority's newly constructed "mixed-income" developments seeks to restore not just an idealized streetscape but also a particular understanding of neighborhood communalism. Mayor Richard M. Daley, while never directly expressing his ambition, clearly strives to fill the shoes of his determined father even as he portrays himself as an elected leader whose practice of governance somehow does not involve politics! Nevertheless, the current Mayor Daley's agenda is not simply a sleight of hand.

Bureaucratic transformation—and more fundamentally, the retooling of government services to reach new constituencies and support an evolving mix of business enterprises—is a hallmark of Richard M. Daley governance. Chicago's municipal government routinely invokes the idea of multiculturalism through its annual sponsorship of myriad neighborhood and ethnic festivals and as it "themes" local commercial strips as Greek, African American, Puerto Rican, or gay. How these willful blendings and distortions of history and how this highly self-conscious effort to shape a new city proceeds, represent a play of ideas and strategies that just might solidify into a new consensus on urbanism, local citizenship, and community formation. Certainly Richard M. Daley, members of his municipal administration, and many of his admirers presume that the contemporary Chicago-in-the-making is a prototype of successful urban reinvention. Closely examining Chicago's third city thus allows us to consider what metropolitan life across North America may well look like in the coming decades.

THE PANORAMIC CITY AND
THE CITY VIEWED FROM THE STREET

In the pages to come, I frequently shift my perspective from the very local—streets, groups of dwellings, debates over how to restore vitality to a neighborhood commercial strip—to a metropolitan scale and beyond. In so doing I employ and on occasion investigate perspectives that have been most forcefully, as well as elegantly, defined by two writers: Lewis Mumford and Jane Jacobs. It is my view that not only were Mumford and Jacobs the two most important interpreters of the American urban experience in the twentieth century but that their typical, respective "frames" for observing the city—the metropolitan scale or panoramic (Mumford) and the street level (Jacobs)—have, in practice, defined the basic analytical strategies employed by all observers of cities. But of course, perspective does not merely define a line of sight for viewing objects. The assumptions built into our chosen mode of viewing things further structure our substantive judgments of what we see and its meaning. For this reason, by both employing and critiquing the street-level and panoramic views of Chicago, I seek to assess some of the fundamental challenges—pertaining to social structure, the relationship between production and leisure activities, the role of governmental versus nongovernmental institutions, environmental quality and sustainability—that confront all great cities in the first years of the new millennium.

As many readers are no doubt aware, Jacobs and Mumford are usually considered to be the great intellectual antagonists among writers on the American city. This antagonism is in part a matter of their contrasting approaches to viewing the city—Jacobs from the sidewalk looking onto front doorsteps or along the street ahead, Mumford from some Olympian height, chronicling processes operating at a scale beyond the range of Jacobs's perspective. Aside from the matter of analytical perspective, Mumford responded to the publication of Jacobs's signal work, *The Death and Life of Great American Cities* (1961), with a withering review entitled "Mother Jacobs' Home Remedies."[18] For her part, Jacobs gave as good as she got, characterizing one of Mumford's books, *The Culture of Cities* (1938), as a "morbid and biased catalog of ills."[19]

In fact, the relationship between Jacobs and Mumford, both intellectually and as public figures, was rather more complicated than a simple antagonism. Jacobs—especially in her writing subsequent to *The Death and Life of Great American Cities*—developed analyses reaching far beyond her original point of reference, Hudson Street in lower Manhattan.[20] Mumford, for his part, was an informed commentator on buildings, site plans, and architectural detailing.[21] Moreover, Jacobs and Mumford, from the standpoints of career and intellectual stance, shared much ground. Neither earned an advanced degree in architecture or city planning. Both built their reputations as New York journalists, Jacobs as an editor at *Architectural Forum* for much of the 1950s and Mumford writing for a series of publications such as the long-expired arts journal the *Dial* and most memorably contributing "The Sky Line" column to the standard-bearer among arts weeklies, the *New Yorker*. In the years following World War II, Jacobs and Mumford were allied as persistent critics of New York City's development and highway czar, Robert Moses.[22]

More intriguingly, Jacobs and Mumford alike rejected even temperament as a prose strategy. Each was a passionate writer, ready with barbed judgments concerning the ideas, physical designs, and the authors of designs that earned their disapproval. Witness Mumford's comment, in his review of *The Death and Life of Great American Cities*, on the quality of the residential projects produced by the federal urban renewal program: "There is nothing wrong with these buildings except that, humanly speaking, they stink."[23] These sound like cruel words until one considers some of Jacobs's harsher tonalities. To mention one among many examples, consider her characterization of mid-twentieth-century city planning as "elaborately learned superstition," which she further likens to bloodletting.[24] Apart from the peculiarities of personality, what accounts for this harshness of judgment is, once again, a convergence in Jacobs's and Mumford's intellectual stances. Both were convinced of the profound importance of cities—as a particular type of social system, as virtually magical amalgams of physical form and social practice—in giving meaning, excitement, and in the best of cases, satisfaction, to the conduct of everyday human life. This is a conviction I share with Jacobs and Mumford.

Irrespective of the complicated relationships involving Jacobs's and Mumford's intellectual strategies and personal interactions, there are clear substantive divergences in their respective approaches to interpreting cities, and in particular their explanations of how urban social systems connect both with governmental institutions and deeper social values. Moreover, it is useful to highlight these contrasts given another striking aspect of the evolution in their intellectual dialogue: over the last generation, Jacobs's ideas have achieved a canonical status among presumably correct-thinking urbanists; while for the most part, Mumford's interpretation of the city has been assigned to the dustbin of bygone sagacity. By considering the shifts in value attached to Jacobs's and Mumford's intellectual capital, we can open some very interesting vistas onto the constellation of assumptions and working practices that are reshaping contemporary Chicago and cities across the United States.

For example, Jacobs's localist perspective—which is universally recognized as the foundation for her interpretation of the city at large—has typically been misconstrued in one key respect. Though many observers have pegged Jacobs as an advocate of the ethnic residential enclaves that were beginning to break apart in the early post–World War II era, her sense of what linked neighborhood residents had little to do with nationality- or religious-based communalism.[25] Witness the crucial vignette in part 1 of *The Death and Life of Great American Cities*, when Jacobs asks local merchant Bernie Jaffe—her neighborhood's "key holder" for out-of-town residents lending out their apartments—if he ever introduces his customers to one another. Jaffe's reply: "That would just not be advisable." By way of interpretation, Jacobs proposes that Jaffe boosts his business through the provision of informal services that exceed the expected range of merchant responsibilities. And if, resultantly, his street neighborhood is a more hospitable locale, then another advantage for his enterprise has been achieved. Jaffe serves the neighborhood, not as an expression of warm-hearted communalism, but due to an astute business sense. Or, as Jacobs observes just following this short essay on neighborhood "weak ties": "'Togetherness' is a fittingly nauseating name for an old idea in planning theory."[26]

Jacobs's aversions to professional planning and large-scale government initiatives, at first glance, represent more straightforward propositions. In the demonology that constitutes the first chapter of *The Death and Life of Great American Cities*, the visionary ideas and grand designs of Ebenezer Howard, Le Corbusier, and Daniel Burnham absorb the brunt of Jacobs's rhetorical attack, but in the remainder of the book—as she develops her complex, organic conception of street blocks, "districts," and the city at large—most of her criticism is directed at the centralizing tendencies of municipal bureaucrats and the fecklessness of federal administrators imposing large-scale policy models on unsuitable locales. Indeed, in Jacobs's later writing her skepticism of governmental action verges on antistatism:

> To develop in the first place . . . nations must have import-replacing cities [local economies producing for local consumption] and enough of them. Nothing else in their grab bags of economies suffices: not supply regions, not clearance regions, not regions workers abandon, not transplant economies, not artificial city regions, not stagnated cities. Yet to hold themselves together as systems, nations must drain their cities in favor of transactions of decline and must undercut volatile intercity trade in favor of supplying settlements that can't replace imports.[27]

From Mumford's perspective, this point of view might represent Jacobs's gravest intellectual error. As an urbanist, Mumford conceived of cities on a much grander geographic scale than did Jacobs, presuming that *regions* such as the New York metropolitan area, in order to remain habitable, needed to be conceptualized in an expansive fashion:

> Regional planning is concerned with provisions for the settlement of the country; and this settlement in turn implies a balanced use of resources and a balanced social life . . . [T]he regional planner seeks to establish new norms of city growth and to create a fresh pattern of regional and civic activities.[28]

Here I would note that Mumford's understanding of regionalism requires a strong governmental presence in order to define a balanced plan for regional economic and social life, as well as to insure environmental sustainability. To shift the emphasis to regulation, regional governance serves to prevent private development interests from producing an essentially inhospitable, environmentally unsustainable urban region.[29] Viewed in either light—and also granting Mumford's suspicion of political absolutists and technocrats—public action via government is an intrinsic feature of his regional vision.

Might it be the case that beyond the evident attractions of Jacobs's close-grained sense of locale and the cumulative benefits of seemingly quotidian, street-level human interactions, her intellectual stance especially resonates among a contemporary audience of architects and urbanists who presume that Mumford's benevolent state, his socially engineered vision of the balanced metropolis, were fleeting variants of the "modernist" effort to tame cities? If so, one must also recognize that lurking in the shadows of contemporary, Jacobs-inspired urbanism is a striking irony. Returning to the emergent Chicago, the third city is very much a joint product of entrepreneurialism and government action—government action via public works but also city planning cognizant of emerging trends in architecture and urban design, notably new urbanism. By way of more specific illustration, the community of academic researchers, planners, and policy experts seeking to reshape public housing in Chicago—seemingly without realizing it—concurrently exhaust themselves in praise of Jane Jacobs's wisdom even as their program of public housing reform—to recall Mumford's phraseology—"stinks" of social engineering.

I have come close to getting ahead of my narrative. We can best approach the third city, initially, by considering how the street-level and panoramic visions of urbanism have been expressed by a variety of Chicago observers, observers drawn to a particular subject but who have framed that subject in revealingly disparate ways. This traversal of sometimes overlapping, sometimes contrasting visions of Chicago also reveals the evolution of Chicago observers' self-consciousness—a self-consciousness often prone to finding in the present only a reformulation of the past, but on occasion able to identify the shape and meaning of the new. This exploration of Chicago "texts" provides the content of chapter 2.

In chapter 3 I examine the career and urbanistic philosophy of Richard M. Daley, the individual most closely associated with Chicago's renaissance since the 1990s. My particular emphasis in this discussion is parsing the local and the cosmopolitan sources of Daley's vision. There is a tendency in Chicago to root the aims and practices of all local politicians in the city's particular political culture; however, in the case of Daley I argue that much of his program is the outgrowth of trends in national policy as well as an emergent (and associated) philosophy of local governance that has been put into practice in a number of American cities. In chapter 4 I tackle one of the hardy perennials of urban analysis, the concept of neighborhood. The aim of this chapter, on the one hand, is to broadly trace the evolution of thinking about neighborhoods in American cities and, on the other, is to analyze what might be termed "the uses of neighborhood" as a tool in urban redevelopment. The latter portion of chapter 4 reconsiders one of Chicago's most persistent identities: the "city of neighborhoods."

Chapter 5 is a detailed inquiry growing out of several questions posed by the preceding chapter; specific subjects are the logic of public housing redevelopment in contemporary Chicago, the means that have been used to replan and rebuild local public housing communities, and the likely neighborhood impacts of this program of street-level redevelopment. In chapter 6 I draw on the lessons offered by contemporary Chicago and respond to the alternative scenarios represented by two recent, influential books: Richard Florida's *The Rise of the Creative Class* and Douglas Rae's *City: Urbanism and Its End*.[30] For simplicity's sake, at present I characterize Florida as the optimist and Rae the pessimist. Interrogating the arguments of Florida and Rae also opens up revealing insights in reference to the continued relevance of Lewis Mumford and Jane Jacobs as guides to understanding contemporary cities. The basic aim of this chapter, then, is to use Chicago's recent experience to explore the degree to which either the perspectives of Florida or Rae—or for that matter, those of Mumford or Jacobs—represent prescient accounts of future American urbanism, as well as, more broadly, whether or not we have reason to suppose that America can achieve a socially just, environmentally sustainable form of urbanism.

The corner of Chicago Avenue and Franklin Street. What was described by sociologist Harvey Zorbaugh in 1929 as "the gold coast and the slum" is now the gallery district known as River North.

TWO

RENDITIONS OF CHICAGO

BOTH SOURCE AND sign of Chicago's self-consciousness are the expansive literatures—sociological, city planning analyses, fiction, and journalism—that have sought to characterize the city. Within these respective streams of Chicago observation one finds both the panoramic and street-level framing of the city, as well as explicitly normative and empirical accounts of the city. Extensive reading in these literatures further reveals a complicated set of relationships cutting across these paired framing techniques. The easiest of these pairings to describe in the abstract is the polarity represented by the normative and empirical understandings of the city, the former presuming that social amelioration and physical improvements can yield a perfected city, the latter committed to describing the city "as it is."

At first glance, the polarity defined by the panoramic and street-level perspectives seems similarly straightforward, the first taking in the entirety of the city and the most prominent of its constituent elements (though sacrificing detail in favor of breadth of vision), the latter focusing on locale, specific sites, and the social processes at work in these sites. This contrast is true enough, but in most cases there is also a tendency for panoramic observers of the city to align themselves with some grouping of normative assumptions. In the case of Lewis Mumford, his panoramic depictions of metropolitan regions aimed to promote environmental sustainability and village-like local conviviality. One of Chicago's early, great panoramists, architect and city planner Daniel Burnham, envisioned a city of efficient transportation systems and imposing public spaces, a physical city capable of "cementing together the heterogeneous elements of our population, and . . . assimilating the million and a half people who are here now but were not here some fifteen years ago."[1] Conversely, the street-level perspective adopted by the many sociologists and novelists who have depicted "the language, habits, and daily routines" of "the South Side Irish, Southern blacks in Bronzeville, and Poles in the Milwaukee Avenue corridor" frequently aims for normatively unadorned, albeit "thick," description.[2] Yet the street-level perspective can be connected to normative concerns, as clearly demonstrated by Jane Jacobs. Beginning with apparently offhand observations of day-to-day sidewalk, park, and commercial space use, *The Death and Life of Great American Cities* evolves into a sophisticated presentation of how local entrepreneurialism, informal neighborly interactions, and dense streetscapes constitute the essential building blocks of urban vitality.

The inherent ambiguity of the street-level perspective is its capacity to serve two purposes, typically the presentation of the empirical city, but in some instances the elaboration of a normative vision. In turn, the power of the panoramic perspective—as we will observe, in particular, as we traverse Chicago planning documents—is dependent on the adequate apprehension of the empirical city. As a rule, city planners and their documents are attacked as *impractical*, promoting policies whose ends are beyond the reach of municipal leaders and their communities. In fact, just as often planning documents are willfully selective in their depiction of the actual city, and by way of selective engagement with the real, advance agendas that might otherwise generate substantial, empirical resistance.

In order to comprehend a city as complex as Chicago, one must employ both the panoramic and street-level perspectives. From the standpoint of proposing a *realistic* normative vision of the city, it is equally necessary to try to harmonize large-scale urban processes and systems—transportation networks, school systems, and the like—with local neighborhood circumstances and resident preferences. Inevitably, there is friction generated by the interplay of the panoramic and the street-level. The music so produced may be compositionally coherent, but there is likely to be some measure of dissonance, local streets widened in the interest of citywide traffic management, the "suboptimal" siting of some public facilities in lieu of demolishing a longstanding residential district.

Chicago is indeed one of the world's most observed cities, the locus of one of the main streams of city-directed social science research, the aesthetic workshop of numerous widely read novelists and journalists. For one wishing to come to terms with contemporary Chicago, the city's multiple literatures are a treasure. They allow the reader to pinpoint the sources of longstanding trends and to spot significant shifts in development. Moreover, though the typical sociologist, city planner, novelist, or journalist—as an observer of the city and producer of representations of the city—will be principally conversant with the stream of literature produced by his or her co-professionals, the cross-fertilization of Chicago literatures is also striking. In the words of literary scholar Carla Cappetti: "If one cannot properly understand the urban novels of James T. Farrell, Nelson Algren, and Richard Wright apart from the urban sociological studies that proceeded and accompanied them, it would be equally a mistake to ignore the literary and, specifically, the novelistic influences that the Chicago sociologists themselves derive from the early European and American literary tradition."[3]

Cappetti's obvious point is that a novelist such as James T. Farrell—or for that matter, sociologist Harvey Zorbaugh—developed a more acute sense of the empirical Chicago by reading "across literatures," and her book, *Writing Chicago: Modernism, Ethnography, and the Novel*, chronicles many such cross-fertilizations. However, over the long line of Chicago's twentieth century one can observe another consequence of the interactions between the streams of Chicago literature. Novelists surveying the work of urban sociologists can selectively mine the latter for empirical details or analytical metaphors that uphold their own preconceptions. Journalists can read fiction or sociological monographs and "discover" (and perhaps accept) a vision of Chicago that is as much a writerly construct as an empirical referent. In the pages to come I time and again note the acceptance and perpetuation of a series of Chicago tropes: a city of insular ethnic enclaves; a political arena whose permanent contestants are hard-nosed machine loyalists squaring off against high-minded, thin-shouldered reformers; a city whose plain-speaking and relentlessly *empirical* character was forged, in perpetuity, around 1900. We will both learn and unlearn from our traversal of Chicago school urban sociology, key city planning documents, recent fiction set in Chicago, and the journalism of Mike Royko. There is much to learn from these literatures that will assist our apprehension of the emergent Chicago, but we will also be on the lookout for strands of self-consciousness that mistake metaphor for description, that presume anything emergent must be an expression of an underlying, permanent, authentic Chicago.[4]

A NATURAL METROPOLIS

The Chicago school of urban sociology is the designation widely used to characterize the work of the group of sociologists who, beginning in the 1920s, devoted much of their professional energy to developing general sociological principles through the close examination of their home city. The central figure in setting the University of Chicago's Department of Sociology on its pioneering course was Robert Park, a late-blooming academic who before coming to Chicago had worked as a newspaper reporter and later as publicist for Booker T. Washington.[5] Among Park's noteworthy colleagues were Ernest Burgess, whose "concentric zone" map of urban development has been called "the most famous diagram in social science," and Louis Wirth, author of the still-read essay "Urbanism as a Way of Life."[6]

The ambitions of the Chicago school sociologists have been manifold, and the products of their research have included both panoramic depictions of the city's large-scale processes and dozens of "ethnographic" examinations of individual neighborhoods, the day-to-day rituals of tavern and diner regulars, and various "marginal" population groups. Although many of the leading figures among the Chicago school sociologists have lent their names and expertise to normatively inclined social welfare initiatives, as professional re-corders of social processes their overarching commitment has been to objective observation of the empirical city. The writings of the first generation of Chicago school sociologists played a formative role in shaping images of Chicago that emphasize the insularity of its ethnic neighborhoods as well as the inevitability of neighborhood transfor-mation in the face of overall city growth. However, in the years fol-lowing World War II, as growth processes in Chicago altered—for the first time, the central city lost population even as suburbs to the north, west, and south filled in—the Chicago school's naturalistic explanations of city growth and neighborhood change lost their ex-planatory power. Nevertheless, in the last decade a new group of scholars has reforged Chicago school propositions and methods, in so doing offering some very provocative depictions of the con-temporary city.

The original, professed ambition of the Chicago school sociolo-gists was the scientific investigation of the city, within which—as a collective or institutional phenomenon—many of the defining attri-butes of modern, industrial society could be observed. Accordingly, seminal Chicago school texts such as Park's "The City: Suggestions for the Investigation of Human Behavior in the Urban Environment" and Wirth's "Urbanism as a Way of Life" abound in references to cities around the world, both contemporary and historical.[7] And yet—as the Chicago school founders routinely acknowledged—their principal source of urban "data" was Chicago. The mix of urban generalities and Chicago specificity is nowhere more evident than in the different versions of Burgess's concentric zone map, one of which features a core zone identified as "The Loop," while an alternative rendering includes a meandering northwest/southeast line that is unidentified, but for any Chicagoan, can only be interpreted as the shoreline of Lake Michigan.[8] Describing "the city" as a characteristic form of modern human settlement was the unquestioned aim of the early Chicago school sociologists, but just as surely, what they often had in their mind's eye was a particular city: Chicago.

Park and his colleagues borrowed a number of analytical concepts from biology, and among sociologists "human ecology" emerged as the encompassing designation for these principles. Ernest Burgess's essay in the early Chicago school anthology, *The City*, which includes a series of his concentric zone diagrams, begins with this emphatic sentence: "The outstanding fact of modern society is the growth of great cities."[9] Powerful evidence of this fact was close at hand, Chicago having grown from a prairie outpost of 4,500 adventurers in 1840 to a perpetually clogged industrial metropolis of 2.7 million residents in 1920. Yet the sheer quantitative fact of population increase itself spoke very little to the routinely unsettling, *qualitative* experiences of cross-ethnic interactions within Chicago's neighborhoods, economic disturbances associated with a rapidly expanding—but also crisis-prone—industrial capitalism, and the institutional stresses of building and sustaining a functioning physical infrastructure. The city that was growing around the Chicago school sociologists was in many ways a chaotic mess, and they were quite sensitive to this qualitative fact.

If the city is presumed to be in various respects *like* a natural or ecological system, accounting for its messiness—seemingly haphazard patterns of land use, outbreaks of intercommunal violence, various indicators of personal and family pathology—becomes a principal challenge for the scientifically minded observer. In response, the Chicago school sociologists developed a formidable array of concepts that projected onto Chicago (and cities in general) an orderliness that could also accommodate much on-the-street disorderliness. Probably the most fundamental of these notions is "social disorganization": "a decrease in the influence of existing social rules of behavior on a group."[10] The concept was coined by W. I. Thomas and Florian Znaniecki, whose multivolume work *The Polish Peasant in Europe and America* (1918–20) is usually identified as the first major work of the Chicago school.[11] And as Thomas and Znaniecki's subject matter and title clearly communicate, the classic application of social disorganization was to European settlers in industrializing American cities. Cut off from the familial and village enforcers of good behavior in the "old country," disorganization was conceived as the transitional situation of recent arrivals to America who had yet to create their own or internalize preexisting modes of social control. A famous fictional harbinger of social disorganization is immigrant Jurgis Rudkus's personal descent (until rescued by socialism) in Upton Sinclair's *The Jungle* (1906).[12] Yet in spite of the horrific events and seemingly inexorable social forces that drove Rudkus's decline—as well as that of many of his real-life doubles—historian Alice O'Connor has noted that the processes of social disorganization as defined by the Chicago school were subject to a more mundane and socially congenial resolution: "family disorganization was not in and of itself a pathological development but a natural and temporary stage in the assimilation cycle."[13] In short, as immigrants—from Europe or from the American Deep South—settled into communities with emerging social institutions and expanding, conventional social networks, the mental disorders and social disruptions seemingly endemic to newly arrived urbanites would subside.

In his essay "The City: Suggestions for the Investigation of Human Behavior in the Urban Environment," Robert Park characterizes the city as "a mosaic of little worlds which touch but do not interpenetrate." The degree of local separateness that Park had in mind is revealed a few paragraphs later when he associates the term "moral region" with individual neighborhood areas.[14] In early Chicago school sociology, the urban neighborhood assumes a distinctly ambiguous character: on the one hand providing the familial, peer group, and institutional support for the assimilation process and on the other hand, and by way of exactly the same set of social groupings, sustaining a fair amount of interlocal and intergroup mistrust. This latter path of neighborhood influence indeed was viewed as contributing to the city's disorderliness, either by retarding the process of assimilation or by stimulating cross-ethnic strife and thereby producing gang and criminal activity.

And just how powerful could these localizing forces be? Park and his associates coined yet another term to describe local regions within the city: the "natural area," an "unplanned, natural product of the city's growth." In *The Gold Coast and the Slum* (1929), Harvey Zorbaugh elaborates:

> Within the limits of these broad zones and natural areas, competition, economic and cultural, segregates the population. There is no phenomenon more characteristic of city life, as contrasted with the life of the rural community or the village, than that of segregation . . . the great central business district, with its towering buildings and thronged streets; the railroads lined with smoking industries; slums and foreign colonies; the "bright light area" and the "red light district"; bleak areas of deteriorated dwellings, small businesses and "furnished rooms"; mile after mile of apartment houses; outlying districts of single homes and dormitory suburbs.[15]

Among the persistent images of Chicago is "city of neighborhoods," a trope further specifying that it is the social networks and institutions at the very local level within Chicago that shape its population's mental states and behaviors. This is a proposition that we can see emerge quite explicitly in the writings of Robert Park, Ernest Burgess, Harvey Zorbaugh, and the other early Chicago school sociologists.

Among the characteristic research strategies of early Chicago school sociologists was street-level analysis, narratives detailing the daily lives of skid row dwellers and neighborhood gang members, or close examinations of popular entertainment venues such as neighborhood dance halls. At the same time, Ernest Burgess, in particular, devoted great energy to mapping the entirety of Chicago; by the end of the 1920s, he had produced a "community area" map identifying seventy-five local communities across the city.[16] Burgess's community area map, in a slightly modified form, continues to structure popular perceptions of local neighborhood identity (Beverly, Austin, Uptown, and so forth) as well as numerous city planning and development initiatives.

Burgess was not the only early Chicago school sociologist with panoramic inclinations. The subject of Zorbaugh's *The Gold Coast and the Slum* is the extremely heterogeneous Near North Side of the city. A few years later, the even more ambitious *Black Metropolis*

(1945) by St. Clair Drake and Horace Cayton examined the entirety of the physically segregated but geographically expansive African American Chicago of the 1930s and early 1940s.[17] Echoing Burgess's emphasis on urban growth, per se, as a generator of many of the city's distinguishing features, Zorbaugh explains the particular dynamism of the Near North Side in this way: "The very march of the city, as commerce and industry push out from its center, encroaching upon residential neighborhoods, turning the population back upon itself, results in a physical instability and change which has significant implications for local life."[18]

Both *The Gold Coast and the Slum* and *Black Metropolis* combine panoramic perspective and street-level detailing, noting very local variations in residence and land use and even the geographic distributions of communal activities and organizations (for example, Drake and Cayton's maps of storefront church and social club participation densities).[19] In the case of Zorbaugh, however, his panoramic understanding of the city-scale growth processes gives way to the highly localized interpretation of the main forces shaping the lives of Chicagoans: "As one walks from the Drake Hotel and Lake Shore Drive west along Oak Street, through the world of the roominghouses, into the slum and the streets of the Italian Colony one has a sense of distance as between the Gold Coast and Little Hell—distance that is not geographical but social . . . And each little world is absorbed in its own affairs."[20] Actually, as historian Sam Bass Warner Jr. has noted, there is in Zorbaugh's account one exception to this forging of vision by the individual's particular "little world." Residents of the Gold Coast, and as such, the stewards of Chicago's principal business and cultural institutions, are the one group within the metropolis who can envision the entirety of the city, its populations, and the city's challenges. Given this privileged, panoramic vantage point, according to Zorbaugh, it will be in their hands to constructively shape the city's future.[21]

There was, however, another way of interpreting the city's ultralocalism. In the view of Saul Alinsky—well known as the founder of community organizing in the United States, but along the way a sociology student at the University of Chicago—local, seemingly parochial communities happened to be the wellspring of American democracy.[22] Alinsky's most influential book is *Reveille for Radicals* (1946), published a few years following his founding (with local resident Joe Meegan) of the Back of the Yards Neighborhood Council on Chicago's Near Southwest Side.[23] *Reveille for Radicals* is a fascinating text, described by Alinsky as his distillation of organizers' reports from the field, though in all likelihood much of its narrative is a recasting of his own experiences.[24] And "recasting" is just what Alinsky did: offering opaque designations of the communities discussed ("an eastern community," "Across the Tracks," and so forth) and peopling his narratives with both iconic protagonists ("Honest John," "Old Uncle Bill") and villains ("Tycoon Store," as well as the condescending attorneys "Van Snoot, Van Snoot, Van Snoot, and Snoot"). The book's explanation of community organizing renders all communities—whether small towns dominated by the mill or mine owner, or urban enclaves dominated by the packing houses—as subject to fundamentally similar economic and political power dynamics.

In sharp contrast to Zorbaugh's dismissal of neighborhood-level political efficacy ("local areas in the city cannot act"), Saul Alinsky proposed that the raw material from which social justice and democratic participation would be achieved, across the United States, could be found in community-level traditions and the fundamental decency of the "little guy."[25] To my knowledge, Alinsky never used the term "urban village," which was influentially adopted by sociologist Herbert Gans in the early 1960s, but it is a dominant theme of *Reveille for Radicals*.[26] The city's neighborhoods crucially shape Chicago and its inhabitants—though in Alinsky's mind, they are less distinguishable from small towns than his sociological mentors proposed—and the neighborhoods' communal character makes them prospective staging grounds for a reassertion of popular democracy. Even in contemporary Chicago, one seldom encounters a professional community organizer who does not endorse some version of this proposition.

In the years following World War II, neighborhood organizations across Chicago (several of them launched by Alinsky's Industrial Areas Foundation) tested the notion that "local areas can act," but they operated within a context of dramatically shifting urban growth dynamics.[27] The City of Chicago's population peaked around 1950, even as suburbanization was substantially expanding the physical reach of the metropolitan region and draining residents from central city neighborhoods. One of the early Chicago school's core ecological processes, "neighborhood invasion and succession," had in turn assumed a forbidding new guise. In its original formulation—as illustrated by Zorbaugh's depiction of the "march of the city"—the central city's growth drove the internal migration of land uses and populations, and thereby, neighborhood transformation. But with the era of suburbanization, business functions and well-off residents were hopscotching beyond the city, while within Chicago the African American South Side pushed farther south, east, and west into heretofore "white" neighborhoods. Coincidentally, a flood of newly arriving black southerners settled in West Side neighborhoods such as East and West Garfield Park, North Lawndale, and Austin.[28]

In the work of ethnographer Gerald Suttles, one observes a continuing effort to use ecological principles—premised by their collective, underlying assumption that there are "natural processes" driving urban change—to explain the tumultuous shifts in Chicago's demographic and neighborhood structure in the 1960s. Especially illustrative of the intellectual recalculations required to interpret changing circumstances by means of the ecological perspective is the collection of Suttles's essays, *The Social Construction of Communities* (1972). In the middle portion of this book Suttles discusses three varieties of local "community": "the defended neighborhood," "the expanding community of limited liability," and "the contrived community." Given events in Chicago during the 1950s and 1960s, the first and last of these community forms are of great interest.

In reference to the defended neighborhood, Suttles asserts that this type of enclave is, in fact, nothing new, that it had been observed by the first generation of Chicago school sociologists. Yet despite its longstanding character, the defended neighborhood, in Suttles's view, is not easy to specify with any precision: "All of these structural characteristics give the defended neighborhood an amorphous and indistinct appearance so long as we look for only a single bounded unit persisting through time. The defended neighborhood can expand or contract boundaries; it's [*sic*] activation is episodic; and the cohesion of its members is always qualified by alternative loyalties."[29] As a very abstract representation of the neighborhood-level complexities of racial transition, as well as of the programmatic and interpersonal challenges confronting community organizations in such neighborhoods, there is an *evocative* quality to Suttles's description. But it is also remarkably divorced from any direct representation of the specific array of forces—the opening up of a suburban "escape route" (with substantial federal government backing) for prosperous whites, the aggressive real estate practices that both promoted suburban living and sowed the seeds of resident dread at the prospect of neighborhood-level racial transition, the large-scale forces stalling economic upward mobility for many African Americans—driving contemporaneous efforts at neighborhood defense. More generally, Suttles's essay does not seem to recognize that defended neighborhoods, and more specifically, the neighborhood organization devoted to the protection of incumbent local resident (especially property owner) interests, was emerging as a characteristic feature of Chicago's local community structure.

Suttles's "contrived communities" are redevelopment areas, and in the instance of Chicago's Near South Side Douglas community area—the particular subject of this discussion—dominated by large-scale residential projects. By the late 1960s, Douglas included public housing developments as well as "private" residential areas that in some cases received substantial, indirect government assistance. Suttles specifically characterizes Douglas and the new developments within its bounds as an emergent form of residential community, though in fact, planned—and in a few cases, very large—central city residential developments had begun to appear in major U.S. cities before World War II.[30] The bulk of Suttles's discussion of Douglas focuses on organizational development, internal political dynamics, and the conspiratorial mindset gripping local residents as its redevelopment process played out.

These observations regarding residents' perceptions of their neighborhood and the unseen forces that were reshaping it are both interesting and of continued relevance to understanding conflict-beset neighborhoods, such as those undergoing rapid gentrification. But, as in the discussion of defended neighborhoods, Suttles's ecological preconceptions tend to find mystery in the straightforwardly comprehensible:

> Developers keep a close eye on one another, and the first to enter a particular area may start a trend quite apart from the fact that it may not subscribe to most advantageous economic usage of land. A fairly obvious example of this sort in Chicago and in the Douglas Park Community Area is the rather heavy concentration of public housing during the early stages of development. Lacking commercial bidders on land adjacent to inner city ghettos, government proceeded to use its own money to develop public housing, and once started, the placement of public housing made it difficult for city planners or private developers to consider the adjacent land for any purpose other than additional public housing. This process went so far in some areas of Chicago that it encroached on the lake front itself, which normally would have been reserved for more expensive housing.[31]

Yes, Suttles recognizes that the development process may be complicated by the interaction of public agencies, in this instance the Chicago Housing Authority (CHA) and private development interests, but in effect, he rests his analytical case by asserting that these interactions have distorted the natural processes that otherwise would have driven neighborhood change. Far more to the point, the concentration of public housing on Chicago's Near- and Mid-South Sides (including some desirable lakefront sites) was the result of explicit and much more clearly willful government determination: the combination of the Chicago City Council members' "veto" right in reference to public housing siting (which allowed white aldermen to block public housing construction within their wards), and the CHA's commitment to build spillover housing for African Americans displaced by ongoing, near-Loop redevelopment activities.[32] These historical "particulars" were surely familiar to Suttles (in 1966, a group of CHA residents had sued the public housing agency over its segregationist siting and tenant selection practices), but the public sector / private sector machinations that produced the South Side's seemingly incongruous land uses simply did not conform to the framing of neighborhood change processes assumed by the ecological model.

Suttles's work in the 1960s and 1970s reaffirmed the twin notions of localism and the primacy of naturalistic processes as the fundamental shapers of Chicago identities and neighborhood change. The most influential University of Chicago urban sociology in the 1980s and 1990s departed from the ethnographic tradition and tended to examine policy questions—such as the reputed emergence of an "urban underclass"—that transcended Chicago.[33] However, a recent spate of books by younger sociologists has renewed the Chicago school's ethnographic tradition. *Black Picket Fences*, by Mary Pattillo, *American Project*, by Sudhir Venkatesh, and *Heat Wave* by Eric Klinenberg offer both instructive evidence of the continuing reach of Chicago school understandings and striking new insights on Chicago as a city.

Of these three studies, Pattillo's *Black Picket Fences* can be most readily connected to the long line of Chicago school neighborhood and ethnographic research. Pattillo's geographic focus is "Groveland," a fictitious designation for the South Side Avalon Park community area. Her book's sociological focus is African American social stratification, and in particular the threats to middle-class life posed by the proximity of low-income enclaves such as "Treelawn." The masking of neighborhood identity is a trademark of Chicago school research, but more substantively, Pattillo, early on, notes that she will examine the "ecological context" structuring the lives and neighborhood of her Groveland subjects.[34] Accordingly, Pattillo's discussion of local crime begins with a preface on social disorganization. *Black Picket Fences* is notably "old school" in one other way:

two of the chapters are presented as first-person narratives offered by their respective subjects. Such first-person accounts were a staple of early Chicago school ethnographic research.

Yet in several crucial respects, *Black Picket Fences* moves beyond the framing of locale and local life characteristic of preceding Chicago school sociologists. In the first instance, Groveland and its residents live in a clearly delineated postindustrial Chicago, a city whose heyday as a manufacturing center—and correspondingly, as a city offering African Americans plentiful economic opportunities in blue-collar occupations—has long passed. And here is the core of Pattillo's analysis: how a neighborhood's residents, who have achieved a middle-class standard of living, respond to economic and social threats to their material position and social standing. In practice, there is little that Grovelanders can do about the sources of their economic concerns, but the social threat posed by adjoining neighborhoods—declining property values as the result of spreading disinvestment, declining standards of youth behavior as young Grovelanders succumb to the "ghetto trance"—is the object of multiple responses.[35] The latter include the extremely protective measures that parents (or grandparents) sometimes adopt to insulate younger children from unwholesome influences, but also the guarded tolerance of local criminals such as drug traffickers, so long as their activities are directed *outside* Groveland. Overarching these localistic practices is the larger popular culture and its African American–directed (and overlapping) subcomponents of sports partisanship, sports-themed apparel, hip-hop, and "gangsterism." Most young Grovelanders adopt some portion of the consumer menu represented by these products and enthusiasms, and for some of these younger people, downward social mobility—and geographically speaking, the migration from Groveland to Treelawn—is the result.

Mary Pattillo situates neighborhood stresses within a realistically contemporary urban and economic/consumerist context. Moreover, her discussion of "street" versus "decent" behavioral norms—and the gradations of actual behavior strung between these poles—illuminates the complicated impacts of economic restructuring, social class identification, and the varying consumer mindsets of Chicago African Americans.[36] The experience of their neighborhood grounds much of the worldview and action of Pattillo's Grovelanders, but the larger world and its enticements likewise shape character while destabilizing day-to-day communal relations.

Sudhir Venkatesh's *American Project* is the product of several years of doctoral fieldwork conducted at another South Side location, the CHA's Robert Taylor Homes. Venkatesh does not mask the identity of Robert Taylor Homes, though he does disguise the identities of his local sources. In one sense, Venkatesh's perspective carries on a longstanding Chicago school tradition: the examination of "problem" urban communities. However, in Venkatesh's account, the factors principally complicating the day-to-day lives of Robert Taylor Homes residents in the early 1990s were emergent shifts in national and local public housing policy. One does not read in Venkatesh's account the naturalistic explanation of neighborhood forces that typified early Chicago school sociology.

Given the horrific reputation that had been achieved by the Robert Taylor Homes as early as the 1970s, a striking feature of Venkatesh's narrative is the degree of local loyalty expressed by many of the development's residents. Venkatesh also documents a moral/behavioral ambiguity that mirrors the "don't ask, don't tell" attitude adopted by many law-abiding Grovelanders in the face of local drug trafficking:

> LAC [the Robert Taylor Homes resident governance council] officers justified their actions . . . "It was your job, if you was on LAC you had to know everything going on, and people selling stuff, trying to do their little hustle, you had to keep it under control, that was your job." Although some leaders suggest that they intervened only to the degree that hustling affected the quality of life of their constituents, nearly all LAC officers admitted some payoffs from their tenants and others who hustled in their jurisdiction. Certainly, many felt the need to oversee hustling as a way to protect themselves against accusations by the CHA that they were unfit to govern.[37]

The Robert Taylor Homes that Venkatesh describes is an unequivocally impoverished, crime-riddled neighborhood, and the origins of
its local misery reach back decades. Overscaled—with 4,415 apartments in 28 high-rise towers—and otherwise poorly designed in
the first place, Robert Taylor Homes' internal management had collapsed by the late 1960s. And from the 1970s, deindustrialization
emasculated the neighborhood economies of Chicago's Near- and
Mid-South Sides.

The substitute economy of the Robert Taylor Homes increasingly depended on underground entrepreneurship (various forms
of ad hoc retailing and service provision) that was frequently illegal
(most obviously, the drug trade). By the early 1990s, the early phases
of crisis-oriented public housing policy had emerged—such as the
CHA's short-lived and resident-alienating "clean sweep" anti-crime
campaign—and if anything, these new policy initiatives made life in
Robert Taylor Homes even more unbearable. Venkatesh's narrative
also brings to light another notable parallel to Pattillo's Groveland
research. Discussing the worldview of drug-marketing gang members, he observes, "Gang activity . . . is a life that is not far afield
of the classic rags-to-riches American success stories, particularly
the idealized organized crime narratives in which immigrants rise
above their slums but remain closely wed to people living there."[38]
As such, Venkatesh's most provocative insight may be his suggestion
that—quite to the contrary of contemporary "underclass" discourse
with its emphasis on the social isolation of the very poor—mainstream, media-defined cultural values were an important source of
identity- and value-formation for young Robert Taylor Homes residents.

Unlike Pattillo and Venkatesh, sociologist Eric Klinenberg did
not do his graduate work at the University of Chicago. Nevertheless, *Heat Wave*, his "social autopsy" of the catastrophic health crisis
produced in Chicago by a mid-July 1995 temperature spike (derived
from his University of California, Berkeley, doctoral dissertation) is
directly engaged with Chicago school theoretical perspectives:

This analysis . . . breaks from the school's traditional approach to the issue of *social isolation in the city,* one of the key concerns of American sociology. For while the early Chicago school urbanists emphasized the isolation of different regions in the metropolis, here I treat the city as a complex social system of integrated institutions that touch *and* interpenetrate in a variety of ways.[39]

With specific reference to early conceptions of the isolated urbanite, such as Robert Park's discussion of the "marginal man," Klinenberg's interpretation of the city proposes that most urbanites are indeed quite connected with their fellow citizens and neighbors, as well as a variety of institutions. Among the research questions posed by Klinenberg regarding the 1995 heat wave's five hundred–plus death toll is how to account for the social isolation that appeared to characterize the lives of the many elderly, often single men whose deaths were disproportionate among the July 1995 fatalities. Klinenberg's line of analysis inverts the traditional perspective, by proposing that social integration is the condition typifying the lives of urban dwellers.

In yet another way, the Chicago school's legacy shapes *Heat Wave's* presentation. One of the book's key chapters is entitled "Race, Place, and Vulnerability: Urban Neighborhoods and the Ecology of Support," in which Klinenberg presents a neighborhood contrast between a "high-death" *community area* (yes, one of Burgess's original seventy-five), North Lawndale, and a low-death community area, South Lawndale (these days, more commonly known as Little Village).[40] The former is a largely African American, low-income area, undermined over the years by a series of economic setbacks. South Lawndale, which directly adjoins North Lawndale, though a poor community, is also a major port of entry for Mexican immigrants to Chicago. Indeed, South Lawndale's 26th Street commercial strip is one of the busiest neighborhood shopping districts in the city. The focus of Klinenberg's neighborhood comparison is the paradox presented by the two community areas' divergent fatality rates in mid-July 1995 (North Lawndale, 40 per 1,000; South Lawndale, 4 per 1,000 residents). Klinenberg touches on a variety of factors, such as contrasting patterns of family networking and church affiliation, but his central argument is derived directly from Jane Jacobs: with the thinning out of North Lawndale's population and the associated thinning out of its housing stock and commercial thoroughfares, routine street life, such as local shopping and out-of-doors "neighboring," has largely disappeared. South Lawndale, by contrast, features active street life, especially along its 26th Street spine. In effect, the physical density that has been retained by South Lawndale is a crucial factor supporting the density of local community relationships. These dense social networks meant that few poor, ill, or elderly South Lawndale residents were overlooked by neighbors and kin in mid-July 1995.

Klinenberg also examines how new trends in municipal service delivery—aimed at cost cutting and often involving interagency reassignments of responsibility or "contracting out" with private vendors—inhibited quick response to the 1995 heat crisis. In a parallel fashion, he documents the halting, often misdirected news reporting of the heat wave, which variously designated the unfolding events as a wearying but unremarkable summer temperature spike (producing, for example, above-average lakefront crowds), a "natural disaster" (rather than a meteorological anomaly colliding with a breakdown in emergency services), and a universal calamity (that was affecting all local population groups more or less equally).[41] Ultimately, this discussion underscores just how unfixed and variable the *empirical city* actually is. For the vast majority of urbanites, apprehending their cities is an idiosyncratic process involving direct experience, use of presumably authoritative sources such as daily newspapers and local television and radio news coverage, and conversation-borne information gleaned from friends, neighbors, and other acquaintances. The city that urbanites typically *know* is a pastiche of impressions and information, and as such, often something quite at variance with any unequivocal standard of "objective reality." Ironically, Eric Klinenberg observes that in July 1995, just such confusions also clouded the judgment of professionals in Chicago's city government and major news-gathering organizations.

THE PLANNERS' DRIFT TOWARD THE EMPIRICAL

During the past half-century, various Chicago municipal administrations, as well as a succession of prominent civic organizations, have issued planning documents intended to analyze contemporaneous city problems and offer projections of an improved, future Chicago. These planning reports have rarely failed to include reverential allusions to the 1909 *Plan of Chicago* and its principal author, Daniel Burnham. As a rule, the producers of these more recent documents also manage to work into their analyses some reference to the master planner and architect's famous dictum: "Make no little plans." By rhetorically linking their work to this most renowned of American city plans—which has been described by historian Mel Scott as a "milestone . . . particularly in its proposals for regional roadways, forest preserves, and lakeshore parks and beaches"— Burnham's successors have staked a claim to the normative ground first occupied a century ago by Burnham and his civic sponsors.[42] The ongoing history of the *Plan of Chicago* as a civic totem is bound to a particular sense of conflict between the normative and empirical Chicago. There are some observers, such as Burnham's biographer, Thomas S. Hines, who argue that the Burnham vision in fact exercised significant influence on subsequent Chicago development: "Though facing inevitable alterations over the long span of its enactment, Burnham's Chicago Plan formed the basic outlines of the city's development and expansion in the twentieth century."[43] There are, however, dissenters from this view, such as journalist James Krohe Jr.: "So universally is Chicago identified with the physical inheritance of the *Plan* . . . that it comes as a surprise to learn how little of what Burnham proposed was ever actually built."[44]

The release of new city planning documents in Chicago invariably produces press commentary to the effect that high-minded but naive idealists once again are challenging the entrenched practices of parochially minded politicians and market-driven entrepreneurs. Yet in truth, an examination of the more noteworthy Chicago city planning documents issued between the mid-1950s and the early 2000s reveals that, to a considerable degree, the normative city imagined in the earliest of these reports, the "Development Plan for the Central Area of Chicago" (1958) has become the empirical city presented in the last of this sequence, the "Chicago Central Area Plan" (2003).[45]

The trail of ideas connecting the central area plans of 1958 and 2003 is in other respects also fascinating. We will observe, for instance, the growing acceptance of street-level analysis, not to the exclusion of the panoramic perspective, which seems intrinsic to large-scale planning exercises, but as an increasingly invoked means of specifying the day-to-day human impacts of planning initiatives. From a substantive standpoint, there is an implicit dialogue running through this sequence of documents centering on how postindustrial Chicago might be distilled from the empirical, industrial Chicago of midcentury. Indeed, as we consider the most recent of these planning documents—*Chicago Metropolis 2020* (1998)[46] and the "Chicago Central Area Plan" (2003)—it will be evident that they function not just as projections onto the future, but also as *ratifications* of the emergent empirical city.

Chicago city planning was not in abeyance during the decades between the publication of the Burnham plan and the release of the Department of City Planning's "Development Plan for the Central Area of Chicago." In conjunction with the preparation of the Burnham plan, the Chicago Plan Commission had been created to shepherd the implementation of Burnham's recommendations. During the World War II years a second-generation Chicago Plan Commission—its precursor having been absorbed by the city government a few years previously—released a series of reports examining various elements of Chicago's physical infrastructure.[47] In 1958, the Department of City Planning was a newly formed municipal agency, and recently elected mayor Richard J. Daley was advancing a mammoth program of public works aimed at revitalizing central Chicago.

Unlike the *Plan of Chicago*, the "Development Plan for the Central Area of Chicago" is not the product of what might be termed a grand civic enterprise. In a letter prefacing the main text, commissioner of city planning Ira Bach notes that this publication was produced in less than a year, and unlike many of the city's subsequent planning documents, the central area plan acknowledges the contributions of just a handful of private citizens and nongovernmental organizations. It is, however, a document that claims Daniel Burnham's vision as one of its touchstones: "In the spirit of Burnham's 'make no little plans' this Plan for Chicago seeks to embrace the highest standards and to give to the people a program which will make Chicago one of the most desirable cities in the world in which to live and work."[48]

The most striking element of the "Development Plan for the Central Area of Chicago" is its assessment of mid-twentieth-century Chicago's changing character. In this document one encounters an unambiguously postindustrial vision. Chicago's Loop is characterized as the "central commercial center," and in effect, the plan proposes that downtown Chicago will become a command and control center for corporate and governmental institutions. Apart from these core functions, the document also promotes the siting of a new University of Illinois campus on the Near South Side, anticipates a residential population of 50,000 (including "housing for all income levels," [26]) in the Loop and adjoining areas, and devotes considerable attention to new park and lakefront recreational projects. There is little mention of near-downtown industrial enterprises, which in just a few sentences are exiled to the city's Near West Side.

The plan places much emphasis on downtown beautification. The summary comment regarding the civic center complex to be developed at the north end of the Loop is quite telling (as well as self-consciously competitive): "An aesthetic environment would be created which would not be rivaled by any American city" (16). Even more suggestive of the planners' vision is the series of graphic renderings previewing the appearance of the central Chicago to come. "The New Residential Environment" (25) is the most arresting of these, in which the viewer observes modernist, curtain-wall buildings in the background, a large plaza with trees and other plantings in the middle ground, and well-dressed groups of diners at outdoor café tables in the foreground. The single waiter in this image appears to be wearing a tuxedo. The development plan's Chicago is benignly futuristic: glistening, modernist buildings; efficient and carefree mobility, whether by foot, car, or mass transit; environmental purity (the grime and aural chaos of industrial Chicago only a memory). As such, the "Development Plan for the Central Area of Chicago" lays the groundwork for a peaceful transition to a new urban reality. Political scientist Joel Rast has argued that this is precisely what is wrong with its vision. Based on the presumption that industrial Chicago was already a historical artifact, subsequent municipal actions actually contributed to the decline and withdrawal of otherwise prospering, centrally located industrial enterprises.[49] Yet if a prime flaw of the "Development Plan for the Central Area of Chicago" is its failure to acknowledge the transitional uncertainties of the 1950s, a jarring discordance between the normative and empirical is to be found in the "Chicago 21" plan of 1973.[50]

For a decade between the early 1960s and early 1970s, City of Chicago planners worked on a new "comprehensive plan," initially producing a statement of "basic policies" in 1964. Over the next several years, sixteen "development area" studies of particular sections of the city were released.[51] The last of the development area reports—entitled "Chicago 21: A Plan for the Central Area Communities"—appeared in June 1973. "Chicago 21" is unquestionably the most controversial of the city's post–World War II planning documents. This is in part a function of its timing. By 1973, Mayor Richard J. Daley's political reach and personal vitality were in decline. Relatedly, the controversies attendant to the city's civil rights movement of the 1960s and growing displeasure across Chicago at the impact of the city's many redevelopment initiatives in those years, produced a wave of grassroots consternation in the face of the civic agenda revealed in "Chicago 21."[52]

The published version of this planning analysis is curiously presented, prefaced with a letter by Mayor Daley, yet bearing no specific indication of authorship. In the mind of the *Chicago Tribune*'s Paul Gapp, however, there was no uncertainty regarding the provenance of "Chicago 21." In an article entitled "Power Elite Drafts City Master Plan," Gapp reported that what was then the city's leading down-town business association, the Chicago Central Area Committee, had hired the prominent architectural firm, Skidmore, Owings & Merrill, to draft "Chicago 21" and that "city officials, from Mayor Daley on down, have been kept closely informed."[53] For the purposes of public consumption, "Chicago 21" was characterized as a collab-oration between municipal government and the Chicago Central Area Committee.[54] In some respects, "Chicago 21" is simply a carry-over of the benign futurism of the "Development Plan for the Cen-tral Area of Chicago." Its pictorial rendering of a new Chicago, just like its predecessor, emphasizes modernist architecture, open space, and extensive recreational facilities.

"Chicago 21" also proposes that the new central Chicago will have a much larger residential population, and it is this prognostication that generated much of the initial negative commentary on the plan. Community activists in areas such as Pilsen (southwest of the Loop), as well as the Near West and Northwest Sides, viewed "Chicago 21" as a blueprint for placing high-end residential enclaves in histori-cally working-class, near-downtown neighborhoods. This appre-hensive response was, in part, grounded in the realities of how the municipal government had been proceeding with its ongoing rede-velopment program. In addition, "Chicago 21" is a masterpiece of suspicious phrasing and pseudoscientific planning argot. At various points, its tone is also strikingly defensive: "Access to the Central Business District by alternative modes is superior to that in most large cities. Yet because of misconceptions concerning transit ser-vice and safety which reduce the level of ridership on that system, expressways are congested during rush hours" (7).

"Chicago 21," much more than the "Development Plan for the Central Area of Chicago," is filled with the organic metaphors— "the City's . . . heart" (iii), the "heart and nerve center of the metro-politan region" (87), "life support systems of the city" (10)—that his-torian Robert Fogelson notes have long been the staple of central city elites seeking to fend off the threats posed by encroaching slums and suburban commercial competition. According to Fogelson, such phrasing expresses the principle of "spatial harmony" between the interests of downtown property owners and the businesses and residents of outlying areas.[55] In effect, if the heart of the city is not saved, then the whole body will expire. These linguistic maneuvers did not distract the critics of "Chicago 21," who were undoubtedly no more comforted by the document's insistent reference to central area "communities" or its thirteen-category assessment of these communities (20). The latter exercise determined that the prosperous Gold Coast / Streeterville area was awash in "community assets" (ten of thirteen items), while the scoring of immigrant / working-class neighborhoods such as Chinatown and Pilsen was dominated by items requiring unspecified "improvement" or "major effort."

Like the Burnham plan, "Chicago 21" has generated much subsequent debate over the scope of its impacts on the empirical city. One line of interpretation proposes that the burst of residential development that swept central Chicago in the 1990s is a direct result of steps taken to implement "Chicago 21."[56] However, twenty years elapsed between the release of "Chicago 21" and the Near West- and Near South Side development boom, and in the years from the mid-1970s until the dawn of the 1990s Chicago's municipal administrations were preoccupied with crisis management, and in the case of the Harold Washington mayoralty, quite evidently pursuing an alternative policy of economic and inner-city redevelopment.

The "Chicago Development Plan 1984," or as it was also called, "Chicago Works Together," is a product of the Washington mayoralty. Among post–World War II Chicago planning reports, it is unique in its emphasis on supporting key sectors of the city's industrial economy. The presentation of "Chicago Works Together" is resolutely street-level, the majority of its pages devoted to profiling particular development initiatives. Released a year following Washington's election as mayor in the spring of 1983, "Chicago Works Together" makes no effort to present itself as a grand civic enterprise, though a considerable amount of city government / civic and grassroots consultation contributed to its production. As a municipally authorized planning report, the format of "Chicago Works Together" is in several respects startlingly unconventional. It is graced with neither photographs nor other graphic renderings of the city to come. It includes but one map. It is also blunt in its assessment of Chicago's economic health in the early 1980s, noting that there were 218,000 unemployed Chicagoans ("two-thirds of whom were minority") and that 123,500 jobs had been lost between 1972 and 1981. Its summation of this catalog of economic ills: "These are bleak and troubling statistics, numbers which indicate an immense amount of human hardship and deprivation."[57]

"Chicago Works Together" devotes one-quarter of its pages to a detailed discussion of "goals, policies, and programs." Put briefly, the five overarching goals are (1) an economic development focus on job creation, (2) "balanced growth" between the downtown and outlying neighborhoods but also across economic sectors, (3) a neighborhood economic development emphasis, (4) municipal and private sector assistance for neighborhoods, and (5) pursuit of state, regional, and national government support for the foregoing goals. Unlike conventional comprehensive planning documents—such as "Chicago 21"—whose policy mandates tend to be derived from unexamined first principles, the empirical "sources" of "Chicago Works Together" can be clearly specified: twenty years of deindustrialization, a longer record of very spotty local urban redevelopment activity, and the recent election of an insurgent African American mayor.

Grounded in empirical Chicago's shaky social and economic condition of the early 1980s, "Chicago Works Together" sought to guide actual municipal action. Most of its text is devoted to discussing fifty-seven "programs" and thirty "projects" that would receive the attention of Washington's city government. Among the latter were initiatives as modest as two eighteen-unit, affordable-to-moderate income housing developments on the West and South Sides of the city (Lockwood Terrace [43] and Winneconna Park [46], respectively). By dispensing with the panoramic views and optimistic rhetoric of conventional plans, "Chicago Works Together" was viewed by some as failing the Burnham test, as such, offering no "magic to stir men's blood." One member of Chicago's city council responded to the plan's release with this comment: "What's new about any of this? It's a drop in the bucket; much ado about nothing."[58] Alderman Edward Burke's words also underline the aggravated political resentments dividing the Washington administration and its critics on the city council and among the city's longstanding Democratic Party leaders.[59]

Among the city's post–World War II planning documents, "Chicago Works Together" is notably transitional in its agenda, framing of issues, and tone, "looking back" in the sense of promoting industrial development and "looking ahead" via its highly localized, street-level program of action. The last pair of planning documents that I examine, *Chicago Metropolis 2020* and the "Chicago Central Area Plan" of 2003, are products of Chicago's new urban reality. During the 1990s, the City of Chicago experienced a net gain in residents for the first time since the 1940–50 census cycle, and Chicago's downtown and near-downtown neighborhoods experienced a boom in residential and commercial investment. Yet all was not well across the city. Unemployment and poverty rates remained very high on the city's South and West Sides. Nor were city services such as public education and police protection beyond reproach. Nevertheless, many Chicagoans perceived the 1990s as a decade during which the city reversed the declining fortunes of the preceding quarter-century.

Chicago Metropolis 2020, which was released to the public in November 1998, is a grand-scale planning report attributed to an individual author, Elmer Johnson, a former corporate executive.[60] Johnson's work was supported by a longstanding business organization, the Commercial Club, which indeed is the group that had sponsored the Burnham plan. *Chicago Metropolis 2020* very clearly is conceived as a successor to that landmark document. In the foreword by historian Donald Miller, Burnham and the 1909 *Plan of Chicago* enter the discussion within the first half-page. The document includes three appendices, the first of which is "The Story of the Plan of 1909." The muted harvest tones of *Chicago Metropolis 2020*'s illustrations and charts also echo the most striking visual feature of the Burnham plan, Jules Guerin's hand-drawn art. It is also the exemplar of the grand civic enterprise. A series of study committees, each composed of leading business and civic figures, forwarded recommendations to Elmer Johnson. An implementing organization—somewhat confusingly, also known as Chicago Metropolis 2020—has been created to promote the plan's recommendations.[61]

In one important respect, *Chicago Metropolis 2020* amplifies the vision of the Burnham plan. Much more than its famous precursor, *Chicago Metropolis 2020* truly is a regional plan, couching much of its analysis in the presumption that region-wide benefits can be produced through governmental reorganization, innovative public service delivery, environmentally conscious transportation and land-use planning, and socially responsible corporate practices. For example, Elmer Johnson explains how the interests of the inner-city poor, prosperous Gold Coasters, the working-class residents of outlying Chicago neighborhoods and inner suburbs, and the middle-class homeowners of Wilmette, Oak Park, and Olympia Fields converge: "More than ever, regions compete against other regions. Our region competes with practically every sizeable metropolis in the nation, and increasingly in the world, based on the quality of life we offer our residents and the quality of business environment we hold out to employers."[62] Furthermore, it is the aim of this plan to promote policy innovations that will insure Chicago's place as "one of the ten or fifteen great metropolitan centers of the world economic order that is emerging."[63]

Chicago Metropolis 2020's specific recommendations number in the dozens, many of which involve the kinds of physical and public works improvements often found in comprehensive plans: transit-centered development along corridors radiating from the center of the region, consolidation of commercial rail facilities, and the like. However, the plan gives equal weight to promoting innovation in metropolitan governance and the improvement of crucial public services, notably education. Though its recommendations are keyed to a panoramic, metropolitan-scale viewpoint, *Chicago Metropolis 2020*'s underlying logic does reveal a family resemblance to "Chicago Works Together." The latter was more comfortable advocating municipal leadership in policy innovation (often at the very small scale); *Chicago Metropolis 2020* is friendly to both the private sector and public / private partnership. But like "Chicago Works Together," *Chicago Metropolis 2020* is prepared to acknowledge local imperfections: "Benefits to the majority have been accompanied by serious costs, borne mostly by those living in distressed areas of the central city and in the worst-off suburbs."[64] Ultimately, both documents view economic growth as a public good to the degree that its benefits are broadly distributed, and over the long run, both seek to promote upward mobility for less prosperous city / metropolitan residents.

The "Chicago Central Area Plan" trumps *Chicago Metropolis 2020's* cautious optimism with a mighty blast of central city triumphalism. The "Chicago Central Area Plan" is a lineal descendant of the "Development Plan for the Central Area of Chicago" and "Chicago 21," like the former mainly a product of the city government, more approximating the latter in its ambitious scope. There is also a crucial thematic link between the "Chicago Central Area Plan" and *Chicago Metropolis 2020*, which is the presumption of Chicago's prominence as a node in the network of global cities:

> Chicago will retain its role as one of the world's great crossroads cities, attracting businesses, residents and visitors internationally. Its Central Area will be a preeminent international meeting place, easily accessible from major destinations around the globe via expanded O'Hare International and Midway Airports. Chicago's Central Area will remain the dominant business center in the interior of the United States.[65]

The "Chicago Central Area Plan" joins this conceptualization of "global Chicago" with a series of other "visions," notably "hometown Chicago" and "green Chicago." The former encapsulates the advantages of central Chicago as a residential site, in particular due to the variety of cultural and recreational amenities accessible in and near the Loop. "Green Chicago"—a notion aligned with the personal commitments of Mayor Richard M. Daley—speaks once again to the central city's environmental amenities but also proposes that Chicago is becoming a "model of sustainability" and pioneer in "green technologies."

This most recent plan's variety of benign futurism arrives with a contemporary twist. Computer-enhanced photographs comprise much of its illustrative material, which, given the Day-Glo hues of these images, present a city—absent overcast skies, rain, or snow— that is not especially consistent with Chicago's often grim meteorological realities. Among the most characteristic images to be observed in this document are the several "dense mixed use corridors" whose paths will expand Chicago's downtown, but which will also serve as local retail and service axes for adjoining commercial or residential districts. These corridors include LaSalle and Halsted streets running north / south and Chicago Avenue, Randolph Street, and Roosevelt Road running west from the Loop and lakefront (48). This expansion of the Loop is, of course, perfectly consistent with the expectations of "Chicago 21," but in the new "Central Area Plan," Jane Jacobs's prescriptions (and even the adoption of her terminology) are frequent. "Diversity," walkability, and maintenance of a "critical density" are among the principles associated with this corridor-oriented development vision.

Yet the most revealing feature of the "Central Area Plan" may be its carefully indirect presentation of a significant, street-level change in the empirical Chicago. In its "district recommendations" for the Near North area, there is no mention whatsoever of the CHA's (at one time 3,500-unit) Cabrini-Green development, although the plan does speak of the Near North Redevelopment Initiative, the city government's preferred designation for the mixed-income neighborhood intended to replace Cabrini-Green (123). Though previous downtown-directed planning documents largely steered clear of public housing's troubling details, at the least, the existence of such residential areas was acknowledged. For example, in reference to Cabrini-Green, "Chicago 21" exhorts city officials to "foster a new sense of community through a broad range of improved social and public services paired with self-help and new home ownership programs" (43). This recipe, of course, was boilerplate, but in the "Chicago Central Area Plan," other than the indirect reference to Cabrini-Green, the only discussion of public housing is a single-sentence allusion to the Near South Side Hilliard and Ickes complexes (133). In tandem with the on-the-street demolition, redevelopment, and even renaming of public housing neighborhoods, the "Central Area Plan" presents an image of the Loop and its environs that is at once, Jacobsian, and for those who can afford its shopping venues and residences, credibly benign and increasingly empirical.

TERMINUS, POINT OF DEPARTURE, AND NODE

Chicago attained the status of noteworthy literary subject in 1872, when the Reverend E. P. Roe recalled the events of the previous year's devastating urban conflagration in his novel bearing the conspicuously allusive title, *Barriers Burned Away*.[66] In the final decades of the nineteenth century a torrent of Chicago-centered literature was produced. English urban historian Asa Briggs refers to Chicago as the world's "shock city" during this period, and indeed, the city's shocking population and geographic expansion, its daring architecture, and its teeming industrial districts all were subject to extensive nonfiction reportage, as well as serving as base material for poetry, short stories, and novels.[67] In 1893 alone, the World's Columbian Exposition brought millions of visitors to Chicago and yielded copious commentary.[68] Critic Carl Smith notes that in the works of Frank Norris (*The Pit*) and Theodore Dreiser (*Sister Carrie* and *The Titan*) the reader encounters depictions of Chicago's industrialized cityscape that are thoroughly ambivalent: on the one hand registering perplexity at the exploitation of workers and degradation of the physical environment, and on the other describing with some enthusiasm the dynamic creativity of local captains of industry and their technological processes.[69]

Across the first half of the twentieth century, Chicago's capacity to shock diminished, but even so, a group of writers who have been called "neighborhood novelists"—notably James T. Farrell, Richard Wright, and Nelson Algren—produced an influential body of

work focusing on the daily traumas of Chicago's inner-city working class.[70] Given the cross-fertilizations between these novelists
and the Chicago school sociologists, one is tempted to label Farrell,
Wright, and Algren street-level empiricists, though anyone who has
wrestled with the latter's extended passages of hallucinogenic lyri-
cism recognizes in Algren's writing a prose that is, at most, unevenly
empirical.

There is, however, an unequivocal typification of Farrell, Wright,
and Algren that provides a baseline for considering how some contemporary novelists are presenting Chicago. For the early-twentieth-
century neighborhood novelists, Chicago was a terminus, a horrific
dead end allowing no escape route for their fictional subjects. Yet
with the arrival of midcentury, the perception of Chicago as a terminal industrial hell gives way to another framing of the city and its
residents. In the work of Saul Bellow, notably his picaresque novel,
The Adventures of Augie March (1953), the reader still finds a grimy,
industrial-age Chicago, but for the ambitious, adaptable, and lucky
Augie March, his fatherless household and degraded neighborhood
are but points of departure. In one sense, as Martin Amis put its, *The
Adventures of Augie March* is "a surrealist catalogue of apprentice-
ships": "During the course of the novel Augie becomes (in order) a
handbill-distributor, a paperboy, a dimestore packer, a news-vendor,
a Christmas extra in a toy department, a flower-deliverer, a butler,
a shoe salesman, a saddle-shop floorwalker, a hawker of rubberized
paint, a dog-washer, a book-swiper, a coalyard helper, a housing sur-
veyor, a union organizer, an animal trainer, a gambler, a literary re-
searcher, a salesman of business machines, a sailor, and a middle-
man of a war profiteer."[71] In parallel fashion, Augie March's Chicago
is an expansive place with multiple links to the world beyond. Long
before his great trek to Mexico, which encompasses several chapters midway through the *Adventures*, Augie has visited, lived in, or
adopted the mores of downtown Chicago, scholastically stamped
Hyde Park, the north suburbs, and such ports-of-call as Muskegon
and St. Joseph, Michigan. The contrast with the closed-in lives of
Algren's characters is unmistakable. In *The Man with the Golden*

Arm (1949), for example, Frankie Majcinek is nearly as place-fixed as his physically disabled wife Sophie. Late in the novel, his improvised flight to an African American neighborhood south of his Division Street apartment is presented as a gauntlet-like ordeal, even though Frankie has traveled no more than a mile or two.[72] Unlike Augie March, but very much like Farrell's Lonigan clan and Richard Wright's Bigger Thomas, Frankie Majcinek is physically trapped in an implacable Chicago.

In three recently published novels set in mid- to late-twentieth-century Chicago, characteristic themes in Chicago fiction such as the shaping force of ethnicity and neighborhood life are treated in ways that offer suggestive insights on the emergent, empirical Chicago of the late twentieth century. Chicago novelist Michael Raleigh presents *In the Castle of the Flynns* (2002) as a memoir of the mid-1950s.[73] The novel's narrator, Daniel Dorsey, recalls the years just following his parents' premature deaths when he lived with his maternal grandparents. The North Side setting of the book—near the old Riverview amusement park at the intersection of Belmont, Clybourn, and Western avenues—is presented with considerable care, and as in the neighborhood fiction of the 1930s and 1940s, ethnic identity and practices are recurring subjects. However, though the Flynn and Dorsey families may devote much energy to discussing their Irish heritage and most of them are regular if not inspired parish congregants, young Daniel's new neighborhood is not an Irish enclave, nor is it crisscrossed with the hyper-localized, ethnically determined turf-marking given so much attention both by the early Chicago school sociologists and the neighborhood novelists. Indeed, probably the most striking feature of Dorsey's recollections is the accessibility of the larger city. Daniel's grandfather, a former transit worker, does not hesitate to bring his youthful charge with him as he takes advantage of his pensioner's free rides on trains and buses. Near the book's close, Daniel's cousin Matt runs away from his parents' residence, taking refuge near Lake Michigan in Lincoln Park. The family's adults are overwrought by the little boy's (Matt has not reached his tenth birthday) disappearance, but within several hours

Daniel and one of his uncles are able to locate the dirty but otherwise unscathed Matt still lingering in the large city park.

As an adult revisiting this earlier time in his life, Daniel's attitude is bittersweet. Though he has departed the old neighborhood, Daniel does not consider himself to have accomplished much in his own life. Many of the family members he has described have died, none having made a significant mark in the world. Nevertheless, the neighborhood and city he evokes, both in terms of security and openness, are quite distinguishable from the hemmed-in working-class environments of Farrell, Wright, and Algren. There is a family resemblance between Raleigh's North Side of the 1950s and the neighborhood novelists' interwar Chicago, but even for the modestly achieving Daniel Dorsey, the neighborhood has not been a terminus.

In Ward Just's *An Unfinished Season* (2004) the main action occurs at the outset of the 1950s (that is, two or three years earlier than *In the Castle of the Flynns*). Just has written more than a dozen novels, many of them set in Washington, D.C., and involving characters playing some role in national affairs. He is, however, a native of Waukegan, Illinois, to the north of Chicago, where as a young journalist he worked on the newspaper owned by his family. Just's account in *An Unfinished Season* of the end of Wilson Ravan's teenage years (with a coda presenting a middle-aged Ravan still endeavoring to come to terms with the disturbing events from that earlier time) is organized in four parts: "Quarterday," "The Debutante's Archipelago," "The King of Chicago," and "Famagusta." Quarterday is the exurban community in which Ravan's family lives. In the spring and summer of his senior year in high school Wilson participates in a round of coming-out parties for affluent, north suburban (in local parlance, North Shore) girls, as such, "the debutante's archipelago." For Wilson, this season of parties yields a girlfriend, Aurora Brule, whose father is a prominent Chicago psychiatrist. In subsequent weeks the young king of Chicago spends many hours in the company of Aurora's worldly family while working a summer job with a Chicago daily newspaper. The unanticipated conclusion to this section of the novel gives way to a brief sequence of events—and considerable self-scrutiny by an older Wilson Ravan. This final section of the novel is set in Famagusta, Cyprus.

Just has structured his action in such a way that the geographic expansion of Wilson Ravan's experience is coterminous with his emotional development, and within this line of growth, the experience of Chicago—a North Side jazz club and its coterie of characters, the exotically cosmopolitan Brules, a hard-nosed and emphatically uncivic newsroom—is an important right of passage. Like Raleigh, Just carefully details a series of specific locales around the city. As the reader observes Wilson Ravan's unforeseen jolt from wide-eyed adolescence—following the suicide of Aurora Brule's father, an event that has not receded to Ravan's "dead past" even many years later—Just presents a young "bon vivant by night, workingman by day" initially capable of only the sketchiest understanding of the personalities and events in which he has been, for a short time, enmeshed. In one instance, Just makes this point by way of Chicago's complicated physical and social geography, sending the drunk Wilson into a threatening (and to him, unknown—"the newspaper's writ did not run in that neighborhood") ethnic enclave somewhere on the city's West Side where he nearly comes to blows with a group of local men. Wilson Ravan—formerly of Quarterday, newly of Chicago—may consider himself a bon vivant, but in fact, he is a narrowly experienced youth whose achievement of thoughtful maturity lies years in the future.

As Just draws his narrative to a close, these thoughts run through Wilson Ravan's mind:

> In Famagusta there were remains of Egyptians, Greeks, Macedonians, Venetians, Genoese, Ottomans, and British. I imagined that within a short distance of where I sat there were reminders of all the visitors, a fallen column, a cobbled street or a ruined bathhouse, a stable or a square, and of course the lost ships of sea. Substitute memory for architecture and human beings resembled cities. People came into your life without warning, stayed awhile, and went away, always leaving something of themselves behind, a look, a word, a phrase, a gesture.[74]

By likening the physical evolution of cities to the maturation of human beings, Just underlines the evocative nature of particular physical spaces, as well as the glancing, often random quality of accumulating experience and insight. The antecedent of this elaborate metaphor is a convincing presentation of the empirical Chicago of the 1950s, whose scale and complexity defy the immediate grasp of Just's teenage protagonist. Nevertheless, the frequently incomprehensible Chicago experienced by young Wilson Ravan is a doorway opening out onto the world beyond. Not an end of experience, it is instead a point of departure.

Far more than *In the Castle of the Flynns* or *An Unfinished Season*, Bayo Ojikutu's first novel, *47th Street Black* (2003), evokes the work of Farrell, Wright, and Algren.[75] As in *Native Son* or *The Man with the Golden Arm*, the leading characters are social marginals, the locales are physical wastelands, and the ambassadors of conventional authority—neighborhood pastors, Chicago police officers—are debased. However, the sources of Ojikutu's fiction transcend Chicago and its literary heritage. The novel's presentation of the criminal careers of J. C. Rose and Mookie King owes much of its nihilistic force to contemporary inner-city "gangster" cinema: *Boyz n the Hood* and the multitude of like melodramas it has spawned. In the case of J. C.—the more introspective of the two principals—his periodic dreams and morbidly psychedelic recollections draw on the sensory and verbal distortions of magical realism.

Just as crucial to the evocative power of *47th Street Black* as Ojikutu's rendering of J. C. and Mookie, their eroding friendship (over two decades from the mid-1960s into the 1980s) and the sequence of physical confrontations, subterranean deals, and incarcerations driving the novel's plot is the presentation of locale. At the novel's outset—in the late 1960s—47th Street, on the city's South Side, is a run-down commercial thoroughfare that nevertheless continues to function as a communal crossroad for Chicago African Americans. As the next two decades unfold, the physical thinning out of 47th Street's structures coincides with the growing desperation of its habitués, notably the wino and seer known as 47th Street Black. Upwardly mobile African Americans are moving to the south and east, to the neighborhoods adjoining Stony Island Avenue, and smart criminals like Mookie King follow the money.

Bayo Ojikutu's rendering of these trends is convincingly empirical, though he eschews the structural causalities—deindustrialization, property disinvestment, municipal service deterioration—that the sociologist would bring to analyzing processes of neighborhood rise and fall. Human perfidy fuels the decline of Ojikutu's 47th Street. Of much greater interest to the novelist are shifting modes of ethnic and racial interaction. Mookie and J. C. thrive, in large part, due to the withdrawal of Italian mobsters from the direct participation in the South Side rackets. As this withdrawal occurs, older identity boundaries are blurred: Mookie, though not given to congenial relations with his Italian American mentors, nonetheless aspires to be a "gangster" rather than a "nigger"; young gangster Tony Ricci is enthralled by soul music, but more to the point, by black women.

The action of *47th Street Black* is resolved by a crime whose import lies in its cyclicality. The nephew of now-dead Mookie King attempts to assassinate J. C. Rose, who had arranged his old friend's murder. Neither J. C. nor Mookie can escape their lineage and environment; one must suppose that a new round of misdirected aspiration and intracommunal war will decimate the upcoming generation of South Side gangsters. Though this denouement is suitably Algrenesque, Bayo Ojikutu has coincidentally offered a fictional account of neighborhood change (as opposed to stasis), as well as a city of slippery (rather than fixed) ethnic / racial identities. Ojikutu's 47th Street is not quite a terminus—indeed, during the novel's final chapters rumors of its gentrification have begun to circulate—but at least for J. C. and Mookie, departure is blocked by the still-formidable strictures of racism in league with their particular failure to imagine a mobility path other than the one they have projected onto their Italian American patrons.

For native Kansan Sara Paretsky, Chicago has served as a terminus, but one offering rich artistic possibilities. Her series of V. I. Warshawski detective novels, which has spanned more than two decades, offers a knowing and often detailed account of Chicago's shifting cityscape, demography, and popular image. V. I. Warshawski's Chicago is, at once, a very plausible rendering of the empirical city and a sly reworking of some of its previous literary incarnations. Also embedded in the details of the Warshawski life that is revealed "across" the individual novels' narratives is a very astute interpretation of 1960s Chicago, its conflicts, and its legacy.

Among the pleasures of the V. I. Warshawski novels are Paretsky's concise, evocative sketches of the physical city. Here V. I. is driving along the lakefront to her childhood neighborhood on the city's far South Side:

> At Seventy-ninth Street the lake disappeared abruptly. The weed-choked yards surrounding the giant USX South Works stretched away to the east, filling the mile or so of land between road and water. In the distance, pylons, gantries, and towers loomed through the smoke-hung February air. Not the land of high-rises and beaches anymore, but landfill and worn-out factories.[76]

V. I.'s investigations routinely take her to some of the city's most destitute neighborhoods, but in her pursuit of schemers, hitmen, and witnesses she traverses the whole cloth of Chicago's social and geographic fabric. In the following quick sketch of a physical locale, Paretsky introduces the reader to the privileged material circumstances as well as the sense of entitlement achieved by one of V. I.'s acquaintances: "at five I set out for her Lincoln Park town house, one of those three-story jobs on Cleveland where every brick has been sand-blasted and the woodwork refinished so it glows warmly."[77]

The physical, social, and economic gaps separating, among others, Lincoln Park gentrifiers and laid-off, South Side factory hands (and just as routinely, suburban mansion owners versus inner-city walk-up apartment dwellers) are a defining attribute of Paretsky's Chicago. Also notably empirical are, over the course of the Warshawski series, such changes of circumstance as the detective's office move from a decrepit commercial building in the Loop (subsequently demolished and replaced by a new, and for V. I., unaffordable office tower) to a loft office in recently glamorized Bucktown, a mile or so northwest of the Loop:

> I miss being downtown, where the bulk of my business lies, but I'm only 10 minutes away by L or car. The warehouse has a parking lot, which I couldn't offer clients before. And a lot of the queries I used to have to do on foot—trudging from the Department of Motor Vehicles to Social Security to the Recorder of Deeds—I can handle right in my office by dialing up the Web.[78]

Most days, Warshawski is automobile-dependent. Without her car, she could not conduct her metropolis-spanning investigations, which are often impeded by setbacks such as car breakdowns, accidents, and the occasional detonation. V. I. Warshawski is constantly driving, and by journeying to so many points of the metropolis's geography she attains a kind of panoramic perspective, which, as such, allows her to link the complex strands of action and association radiating from particular criminal incidents. Conversely, what often isolates her most downtrodden clients, witnesses to crime, or their acquaintances is the physical challenge confronting anyone who attempts to traverse Chicago locales without access to an automobile. These include characters such the elderly Zerlina Ramsay, of *Burn Marks*, who must take three buses to travel between an apartment on the West Side and V. I.'s office in the Loop, and the deceased Nicola Aguinaldo, of *Hard Time*, who in life could spend but a few hours each week with her own child due to her punishing, transit-dependent commute between north-side Uptown and the western suburbs where she worked as a nanny.

V. I. Warshawski is an unrelentingly blunt speaker, and her creator, Sara Paretsky, offers a seemingly unadorned portrayal of Chicago. Yet in both small and large ways Paretsky draws on the work of Chicago literary forebears. At times, this engagement with preceding Chicago writers is amusingly inconsequential, as in the *Blood Shot* chapter, "Humboldt's Gift," whose title is borrowed from one of Saul Bellow's novels. Here is the final sentence of that chapter: "We left as quickly as we could, but it seemed I could hear that maniacal bellow all the way to the lobby."[79] In other instances, Paretsky's evocation of literary precursors substantively shapes character and action. The thoughts of V. I. Warshawski, a native of working-class, far South Side Chicago, regularly turn to events of her childhood, notably the early deaths of her parents. Though V. I. is independent-minded to a fault, a reasonably successful professional (having worked as an attorney before becoming a private investigator), and an unflinching feminist, she also retains a modicum of guilt for leaving the old neighborhood, and in turn, not becoming the kind of girl her parents had wished to raise. As for the parents—her mother Gabriella, an Italian immigrant, her father Tony, a Chicago police officer—their lives are remembered as if drawn from the pages of one of the neighborhood novelists. Here is an account, from *Killing Orders*, of their meeting:

> He was a policeman. Rosa [Gabriella's sister] had thrown Gabriella out on the street, an immigrant with minimal English. My mother, who always had more courage than common sense, was trying to make a living doing the only thing she knew: singing. Unfortunately, none of the Milwaukee Avenue bars where she auditioned liked Puccini or Verdi and my father rescued her one day from a group of men who were trying to force her to strip.[80]

Not only are the details willfully Algrenesque—economic deprivation, family strife, barroom excess—but Paretsky has also placed the events on Milwaukee Avenue, the site of much of the action in Nelson Algren's fiction.

One of the recurring characters in the Warshawski series—Chicago police lieutenant Bobby Mallory, a contemporary and friend of V. I.'s late father—functions as an infuriating substitute parent. He routinely involves himself in her investigations, typically by way of inept interrogations and seldom fails to remind V. I. that she ought to have settled down, married, and produced "happy healthy babies." Unlike V. I.'s father, who was a Polish policeman "in an all-Irish world," Mallory has moved up the police hierarchy. The Chicago that

he continues to inhabit emphasizes unflagging loyalty to one's police colleagues and political sponsors and presumes that those who
hold power in the city ought to be obeyed. Such views are anathema
to V. I. In effect, her efforts to expose those who hold political and
corporate power in contemporary Chicago, as well as her ongoing
disputes with Bobby Mallory over neighborhood, departmental, and
ethnic allegiances, or the appropriate role of women, revisit various
of the social cleavages that divided Chicago in the 1960s.

It was in 1966 that the young Sara Paretsky, raised in the rural
Midwest, had her first serious encounter with Chicago, by way of the
Chicago Presbytery's "Summer in Service" program. Working for a
church-affiliated neighborhood day camp program on the Southwest Side, and in close proximity to that era's black/white residential
frontier, Paretsky observed "people [who] . . . stayed close to home.
Many of the children had never seen the city, had not even gone
downtown to view the lights and candles at Christmas." The youthful Sara Paretsky, one might say, found herself in the midst of Bobby
Mallory's Chicago. And indeed, Paretsky's memoir of this time expresses a discordant bundle of feelings: on the one hand a sense of
gratitude for the kindness of local residents, including the family
who provided her a temporary home that summer, on the other disapproval of their seemingly ready acceptance of racial stereotypes.
Certainly, Bobby Mallory's amalgam of surface geniality, unmistakable affection for V. I. as the daughter of a departed colleague,
and unblinking acceptance of social injustice bears a close resemblance to Paretsky's recollection of West Englewood residents whose
"domestic virtues" coexisted with "public hates."[81] As for V. I. Warshawski, her crime-solving, which tends to include in equal measure a commitment to identifying specific perpetrators and a determination to expose the misdeeds of local power-holders, expresses
an egalitarian ideal that cannot be assimilated by Bobby Mallory's
normative framing of his city.

If in the V. I. Warshawski novels we observe the divide between
an older, European immigrant–defined, neighborhood-focused
Chicago and a more cosmopolitan, socially diverse successor to that

city—a divide that approximates the social fault lines some observers attribute to the decline of industrial Chicago, and which others have linked to the breakdown of a pre-1960s social consensus[82]—the work of Aleksandar Hemon directly fuses the immigrant experience with a very contemporary sense of Chicago's global character. Hemon's *Nowhere Man* (2002) is a resolutely fragmentary account of the early life of Jozef Pronek, a character whose experiences and personality at times seem to merge with those of other characters in the novel. Even given this book's many plot ambiguities, there are these certain incidents strung along *Nowhere Man's* narrative line. A native of Sarajevo, Pronek immigrates to Chicago in the early 1990s. In Chicago, Pronek casts about for work and while canvassing for Greenpeace, meets a young woman, Rachel, who becomes his girlfriend.

The Chicago experienced by Jozef Pronek—as well as by the shadowy narrator who relates much of the book's action—is palpably grubby. Here is Hemon's rendering of a North Side neighborhood visited by Pronek in the process of performing one of his transitory jobs: "The houses all looked the same, as if they were made in the same lousy factory, but the lawns were different: some were trimmed and orderly like a soccer pitch, some had strewn litter, little heaps of dog turd, and wet leaves raked together." The city's grubbiness is as much a matter of language, notably imperfect English usage, as untidy streets and semi-respectable occupations. In the novel's initial episode, the narrator travels from his apartment to a job interview in the suburbs (at a language school, where he encounters Jozef Pronek). Along the way, the narrator notices one after another mangled rendering of English, such as this handwritten note on a tree, which begins "I LOST MASCULINE DOG, THIS COCTAIL SPANIEL AND HIS NAME LUCKY BOY." A bit later, a broken soft drink machine sports this taped-on message: "NO WORKING."[83]

Hemon—born in Sarajevo and an involuntary immigrant to Chicago when he was unable to return from a visit in 1992—describes a city of new immigrants, not the older Chicago of ethnic neighborhoods and associated social institutions. His characters are often social isolates. His principal concerns are geographic dislocation and the disruption of individuals' lives when they are suddenly, unpredictably pulled from one locale to another. Given these emotional and artistic preoccupations, the significance of Chicago within Hemon's novel rests in its simultaneous separation from and connection to other places. Sometimes this is rendered as a matter of similarity linking seemingly disparate locales, as when a character recalls: "We compared Chicago and Sarajevo, how lovingly ugly they were, and how unlovingly parochial."[84] Hemon locates his disjointed narrative in various settings: Chicago, Sarajevo, Kiev, Shanghai. Chicago's importance is due to its place within a globe-spanning network of cities, its particular niche a matter of past immigrant flows (Eastern Europeans continuing to navigate extended family networks), its international transportation linkages (notably O'Hare Airport), and a lingering reputation as a metropolis offering a plenitude of opportunities to earn quick, off-the-ledger cash. For Hemon's itinerant characters, Chicago is neither a terminus nor a point of departure. It is instead a prominent urban node within an increasingly linked, urbanized globe.

Aleksandar Hemon's Chicago is a global city, but not for the reasons that local boosters usually tout, such as emerging "new economy" business functions, a wealth of arts institutions, Lake Michigan's beauty and on-shore leisure amenities, or its concentration of noteworthy architecture. Hemon's global Chicago is a creature of international immigration, and in particular, its contemporary form of contingent, cross-border movement. Newcomers to Chicago from Sarajevo, Mexico, or east Asia may not only countenance a return to their home lands, they can very readily maintain contacts with friends and past neighbors in these places. Indeed, these immigrants may not come to Chicago, or for that matter to the United States, in order to become Americans. They are thrust into new places, such as Chicago, and make use of (and find meaning in) these places as they can.

MIKE ROYKO'S AUTHENTIC CHICAGO

In the foreword to the first collection of columnist Mike Royko's essays published following his death in 1997, friend and fellow writer Studs Terkel characterizes Royko's work in this way: "It was the 'real' of Chicago—and metaphorically of our society—that Royko searched out."[85] For nearly thirty-five years, Royko was the Chicago "voice" most recognizable to both local and national readers. An omnivorous interpreter of Chicago politics, personalities, and social mores, whose *Chicago Daily News* pieces were nationally syndicated by the late 1960s, Royko reached a huge audience, sustaining throughout his career a writing persona constituted of equal parts no-nonsense egalitarianism, irreverent satire bordering on the juvenile, and plain-speaking Chicagoan's-view-of-the-world. Royko's artfulness in presenting this persona was such that he was early dubbed an authentic Chicagoan as well as skilled journalist, or as the *Daily News* introduced his column in September 1963, "He thinks, talks, and writes in Chicagoese."[86] The corollary of Royko's status as authentic local voice was that his presentation of Chicago could be considered, as Studs Terkel suggests, a depiction of the real Chicago.

Mike Royko's Chicago, like the other renditions of Chicago I have examined, can be connected to the conditions of the empirical city that he encountered, but Royko's work is also stamped by personal predispositions, borrowings from fellow interpreters of the city, and habitual compositional strategies. Royko's persona, as the plainspoken representative Chicagoan, or at least, the representative of a very typical kind of Chicagoan, meant that more than other interpreters of the city, his characterization of Chicago is often accepted as true to life. Even the Chicago recorded by the Chicago school sociologists, for all their commitment to empiricism, is a city whose description is mediated by periodic doses of social science theory. Royko's claim to verisimilitude was, ultimately, bound up with the notion that in a down-to-earth metropolis such as Chicago, his lack of pretense—his abhorrence of all theory—made his presentation of the city closest to the grain of reality.

Yet as one reads through Royko's thousands of daily columns—as well as his single sustained composition, *Boss: Richard J. Daley of Chicago*—one soon enough can identify a thematic palette that colors Royko's main concerns as a local observer. The most important shadings within this palette, no doubt, were derived by Royko from his sense of Chicago's reality, but over the course of his life as a writer, these shadings also became Royko's interpretive filters as he confronted new situations to be assessed and written up. By the end of his career as a columnist, Royko's apprehension of the city was increasingly retrospective. As embodiments of the city he construed as the authentic Chicago, Royko made peace with old political adversaries and more generally sought to fix an image of Chicago—as the ceaselessly grasping, inherently parochial metropolis—that was still plausible in the 1950s and 1960s, but not especially attuned to the empirical Chicago of the 1990s.

The principal shading to Royko's interpretive palette is the formative influence of neighborhoods. Here is Royko, in the column he wrote following Richard J. Daley's death, interpreting some of the late mayor's most fundamental motivations:

> Daley was a product of the neighborhoods and he reflected it in many good ways—loyalty to the family, neighbors, old buddies, and the corner grocer . . . But there are other sides to Chicago neighborhoods—suspicion of outsiders, intolerance toward the unconventional, bigotry, and bullying. That was Daley, too. As he proved over and over again, he didn't trust outsiders, whether they were longhairs against the war, black preachers against segregation, reformers against his machine, or community groups against his policies.[87]

Years earlier, having characterized Daley as a "small-town boy," Royko sketched this half-satirical neighborhood geography:

> The neighborhood-towns were part of larger ethnic states. To the north of the Loop was Germany. To the northwest Poland. To the west were Italy and Israel. To the southwest were Bohemia and Lithuania. And to the south was Ireland . . . Here and there were outlying colonies, with Poles also on the South Side, and Irish up north.[88]

Royko qualifies this latter description by noting that the city's network of neighborhoods still conformed to these boundaries "as late as the 1950s," but over the next quarter-century he never quite gave up on this sense of Chicago as its core identity. He sprinkled his columns with seemingly inexplicable dialogue, especially as uttered by his fictive sidekick, Slats Grobnik: "'Wherejagettum,' I hissed. 'Gynatruck cameroun' sellnum,' he hissed."[89] In Royko's Chicago, "Chicagoese" was a language of dialects, with neighborhood the prime shaper of individuals' lingo. Characterizing himself as an "amateur anthropologist," Royko further specified a series of human "types" to be found among Chicagoans, which again, are a function of neighborhood environment: "I was familiar with the ways of Two-Flat Man, Bungalow Man, Tavern Man, and all of the other species that form the general classification of Neighborhood Man." In a column he wrote in the early 1980s, Royko lampooned himself taking on a new identity, "High-Rise Man."[90]

Yet as Royko's comment regarding the passing of the ethnically inflected neighborhood mosaic during the 1950s reveals, in the empirical Chicago of the 1960s and 1970s, that older geography was breaking apart. One clue as to the source of its demise is to be found in the tour de force introductory chapter of *Boss*, in which Royko guides the reader through a typical day in the life of Mayor Richard J. Daley. Briefly leaving the mayor at midday to observe the lunchtime companions of the city council floor leader—Thomas Keane, a protégé of Daley who, in the lore of Chicago politics, settled for second-tier political influence in order to amass a material fortune—Royko notes that "he lunches each day with a clique of high-rise real estate developers."[91] Keane's coconspirators are not simply real estate developers, nor even "high-end" or "luxury" real estate developers. In Royko's mind, a crucial aspect of new real estate development's threat to the older city was the incursion of tall buildings into the street-level Chicago of bungalows, two-flats, parish churches, and corner taverns.

Several chapters later, and in reference to Richard J. Daley, Royko describes the threat to the neighborhoods in a somewhat different fashion: "His vision of the city was . . . downtown first. Revitalize the Loop and nearby commercial areas and the rest of the city will follow."[92] In this rendering of the downtown / neighborhood cleavage, the risk to the latter is principally due to municipal inattention and resource starvation. In effect, Royko is proposing that Richard J. Daley's single-minded focus on rebuilding the Loop will induce him to betray the neighborhoods. Royko's commentary on development trends in the 1960s, and of the political machinations that sustained them, had a substantial impact on local political discourse and practice. By politicizing the interpretation of redevelopment initiatives, Royko contributed a key rhetorical strand to the campaigns of Chicago neighborhood activists for many years to come.[93]

Another characteristic Royko presentational strategy is to adopt the role of the informed insider who is able to comprehend and lead the reader through the subterranean structures that drive the city's visible life. There is a long tradition of this kind of urban exposé, including the work of nineteenth-century European novelists such as Dickens, Gaskell, Balzac, and Zola, and in the United States, among crusading Progressive era journalists such as Jacob Riis (*How the Other Half Lives*, 1890) and Lincoln Steffens (*The Shame of the Cities*, 1904). *Boss*'s first chapter is filled with insider material. Royko visits Richard J. Daley's residence on South Lowe Avenue, commenting on the mayor's personal pastimes and noting which of the mayor's associates are granted access to his home and the rituals of Daley family domesticity. In an analogous tour of the mayor's office on the fifth floor of Chicago's city hall, Royko describes the office suite's layout and decor, explains the functions of the different rooms, and reports on Richard J. Daley's working routines.

Royko's *Daily News* column of May 31, 1974, "How This City Really 'Works,'" typifies his insider's view of Chicago. The article's subject is a small-scale landlord, John Karpowicz, whose Near Northwest Side apartment building, in spite of his best efforts, had recently been condemned by the city government. The tale of Karpowicz's downfall is complicated, involving neighborhood change and the rise of gang activity on nearby blocks, but most tellingly, an apparent pullback of local policing. The withdrawal of the police, according to

Karpowicz's understanding of events, has been dictated by "somebody downtown." Royko does not seek to identify who that "somebody" might have been, but his column closes with the suggestion that real estate interests may well have influenced officeholders, who in turn diverted city services in anticipation of developers stepping forward with plans for neighborhood revitalization.[94]

The most interesting twist to Royko's use of the insider perspective is his assessment of how fully Mayor Daley—himself an insider, and evidently a persistent collector of information regarding the city's workings—may or may not have understood his own city. On the one hand, Richard J. Daley is presumed to personally monitor every employee hired by the city government: "Nobody goes to work for the city, and that includes governmental bodies that are not under the mayor, without Daley's knowing about it. He must see every name because a person becomes more than an employee: he joins the political Machine." Nor are Daley's efforts to observe his city simply a matter of overseeing patronage workers:

> His police department's intelligence-gathering division gets bigger and bigger, its network of infiltrators, informers, and spies creating massive files on dissenters, street gangs, political enemies, newsmen, radicals, liberals, and anyone else who might be working against him. If one of his aides or handpicked officeholders is shacking up with a woman, he will know it.[95]

Yet at the same time, Daley is the captive of his daily routine, and so far as one can tell, of subordinates seeking to shield the mayor from some of the city's less uplifting sights and circumstances. His limousine ride to work each morning is routed so as to avoid the badly deteriorated areas to the north and east of Bridgeport, the neighborhood that has been his lifelong home. Whereas in the 1950s Daley had concluded his ride to work at some distance from city hall, walking west across the Loop the last several blocks, by the late 1960s (in order to avoid street confrontations) he is driven directly to his first stop downtown, St. Peter's Church.

Richard J. Daley's pursuit of a comprehensive, panoramic understanding of Chicago is only partially successful, and as such, is the source of a deeper paradox. To what degree did the mayor control events in his city, or were his actions better understood as reactive to events and the initiatives of others? Much of *Boss*'s chapter 7 focuses on Daley's relationship to the civil rights movement. Early in this chapter Daley is quoted as asserting "we do not have segregation in Chicago." Two pages later, Royko relates the thoughts of a local activist, who accuses Daley of "passive hypocrisy," adding, "He could have prevented all the trouble. He could have controlled his own people."[96] On the surface, this is a straightforward recounting of contradictory perspectives, but if one considers how Royko has otherwise framed his narrative, straightforwardness gives way to considerable ambiguity. Was Daley simply lying when he commented that Chicago was not segregated, or had his increasingly insulated mayoral routine, coupled with the reassuring words of aides anxious not to bring discordant news to their leader, deceived him as to the degree of local segregation, to say nothing of the depth of African American alienation? "Passive hypocrisy"—a term Royko quotes—is itself a slippery turn of phrase, and the explanation offered by Royko's informant, John Walsh, is at the least questionable. Is it not possible that Daley feared "his own people" would reject him if he appeared overly conciliatory to civil rights leaders such as Martin Luther King Jr.?

A few pages further in this chapter, Royko observes that "the black vote was easily controlled," but he also quotes one of Daley's subordinates to this effect: "The more blacks picketed [school superintendent Benjamin] Willis, the more popular he [Willis] became among the whites. If Daley gave in, the whites would have been mad."[97] In this instance, the prospect of Daley's losing support among his white constituents is acknowledged. But what of his presumed "control" of the black vote? Here it is unclear whether Royko is referring to Democratic Party electoral manipulations that could deliver African American votes to Daley even if underlying African

American support for the mayor was negligible; or is Royko proposing—quite at odds with his book's main line of argument—that there continued to be substantial black support for Mayor Daley? Given the extraordinary circumstances of the 1960s, multiple interpretations of events and of Mayor Daley's actions are not surprising. Nevertheless, in chapter 7 of *Boss*, and elsewhere in this book and his columns, Royko's plain-speaking style—report the information provided by sources using their own words, present narratives as unembellished sequences of events, and avoid undue interpretation of either of the foregoing—seems to work against a coherent explanation of complex political situations. Moreover, Royko's most sustained interpretation of Daley, that of the all-knowing, all-responsible czar of his city, has become the standard recollection of "the Boss." That the details of Royko's presentation of Richard J. Daley do not really square with this master image is rarely noted.

In Royko's Chicago—as well as the world at large as he saw it—a crucial social marker is the division between plain-speaking, down-to-earth people and sophisticates. However, sophisticates do not simply talk and live differently from rank-and-file Chicagoans. As often as not, their sophistication is a facade erected in order to disguise their own inauspicious roots. In contrast to the authenticity of the average Chicagoan, sophisticates are typically self-inflated as well as self-deluded. This distinction is hilariously articulated in one of Royko's columns from the 1960s, "It Wasn't Our 'Clout' She Stole, But a Counterfeit," in which the Chicago reporter (via telephone) confronts a *Vogue* magazine editor for misusing a crucial Chicago expression, "clout" (defined by Royko as "influence—usually political—with somebody who can do you some good"). The unmistakable sign—in all likelihood just as Royko heard it—of the *Vogue* editor's trumped up sophistication is her tendency to stretch the pronunciation of words such as "everyone" and "everybody" ("EV-er-eeee-body"). For his part, Royko cannot help but speculate as to biographical (probable birthplace: Iowa or Nebraska) and sartorial ("I mentally bet myself that she was wearing a hat and boots while she worked and that she used to smoke with a cigarette holder, when it was fashionable.") details that solidify his perception that he is dealing with a vacuous snob.[98] Ultimately, the *Vogue* editor terminates the conversation by slamming down the phone receiver, presumably unable to accept either that she has misused such an *au courant* expression, or for that matter, that a New York magazine editor would ever borrow cultural capital from the bleak and featureless Midwest.

Of course, there are Chicago sophisticates, notably the local high-rise men and women whose use of "pidgin French" is noted by Royko. He associated the emergence of this new Chicago type with the enveloping cultural influence of cities such as San Francisco and New York, portrayed in his column "San-Fran-York on the Lake" from the 1960s as mainly a matter of modish consumer preferences.[99] Yet as late as Richard J. Daley's death in 1976, Royko continued to hold out for Chicago as a distinctive city (as opposed to the same pair of cities whose insidious, hip consumerism had been depicted years previously as threatening Chicago authenticity): "Maybe New York will let porn and massage parlors spread like fast-food franchises, and maybe San Francisco will welcome gay cops. But Chicago is still a square town."[100] In this cataloging of urban particularities, Royko reproduces the logic of his thinking about the old neighborhood order: each "town" had its distinctive population, cultural norms, and even language.

Royko's ability to mimic the vocal inflections of his subject, and from this base material, extrapolate a seemingly comprehensive statement of the subject's worldview, is crucial to his portrayal of Richard J. Daley in *Boss*. In chapter 1, as Royko follows the mayor through his daily round of activities, he initially sprinkles the text with brief extracts of the mayor's own words. In reference to *Robert's Rules of Order*, Royko reports Daley's comment that it was "the greatest book ever written." Just previously Royko has recalled one of Daley's rants directed at critics on the city council: "It is easy to criticize . . . to find fault . . . but where are your programs . . . where are your ideas . . ." Royko is introducing the reader to Mayor Daley, and also to Mayor Daley's view of his city. Yet as the chapter 1 narrative proceeds, Royko's presentation of Daley takes a subtle turn:

The limousine passes Comiskey Park, where his beloved Sox play ball. He goes to Wrigley Field, too, but only to be seen. The Sox are his team. He can walk to the ball park from the house. At least he used to be able to walk there. Today it's not the same. A person can't walk anywhere. Maybe someday he'll build a big superstadium for all the teams, better than any other city's. Maybe on the Lake Front. Let the conservationists moan. It will be good for business, drawing conventioneers from hotels, and near an expressway so people in the suburbs can drive in. With lots of parking space for them, and bright lights so they can walk. Some day, if there's time, he might just build it.[101]

Royko has begun this paragraph by specifying one more cluster of incidents in the sequence of journeys, meetings, and public occasions constituting this day in the life of Richard J. Daley. But by mid-paragraph he is no longer offering a plausible though invented sequence of events. Instead, he imagines the mayor's thoughts—not by finding illustrative quotations—but by stringing together a series of thought-like statements composed in a fashion that reflects Richard J. Daley's characteristic vocal inflections. Mike Royko's portrayals of Richard J. Daley, and of Richard J. Daley's city—often praised for their unblemished realism—are constructed with materials to a considerable degree derived from the writer's imagination.

Royko's vocalization of his subjects' varying perspectives was most effective when he reported on discordant events such as civil rights conflict and neighborhood racial change in the 1960s. In "The Welcome Wagon Didn't Come," his subject was the family of Alice and Charlie Roberts, African Americans whose white Southwest Side neighbors could not accept them as fellow pursuers of "part of the American dream."[102] Much of "Kids Say the Darndest Things" incorporates descriptions of West Side rioting composed by elementary school students, several of which note that Chicago police had themselves carried off liquor and other merchandise from neighborhood business establishments. Royko closes this column by quoting a string of bureaucratic obfuscations, evidently offered in response to reporters' inquiries regarding police behavior: "There . . . have been reports of instances where shop owners requested police assistance to help remove merchandise from the shops . . . There's nothing definite. Just complaints and stories." Royko's summary sentence is abruptly ironic: "Those seventh-grade kids do tell some stories."[103] At his best, Royko communicated the uncertainties associated with social conflict by vocalizing multiple perspectives, often finding in misunderstanding (or asymmetrical understanding) a telling insight. Many years later, during the impassioned mayoral election of 1983, Royko offered this assessment of Harold Washington: "He is a smart, witty, politically savvy old pro. He is far more understanding of the fears and fantasies of Chicago whites than we are of the frustrations of Chicago blacks."[104]

Yet as the decades passed, Royko's palette of interpretive techniques seemed to limit his capacity for appreciating new developments in his city. He increasingly devoted himself to memorial columns: for departed friends such as Nelson Algren, for frequent subjects such as Richard J. Daley, or for iconic Chicagoans such as George Halas, longtime coach of the Chicago Bears. Royko often used these essays to speak wistfully of a bygone city. By 1988, Royko could write a column beginning in this fashion: "There is something almost eerie about the similarities between the year 1955—a milestone in Chicago's political history—and this year, which could be another milestone." His subjects are Richard J. Daley and Richard M. Daley, the latter soon to be elected mayor. Royko closes his column in his typically pithy way: "It's like déjà vu all over again."[105] In this instance, though, his punch line is a recycled expression popularly attributed to former baseball player Yogi Berra. And in reference to the classic Royko technique of turning conventional wisdom on its head, here he has affirmed conventional wisdom and presented the son as reincarnation of his father.

In his foreword to *One More Time: The Best of Mike Royko*, Studs Terkel asserts that Mike Royko "discomfited the powerful."[106] In his later years this was not so clearly the case. For example, in Royko's column marking Richard J. Daley's death (which was added to *Boss* as an introduction when a new paperback edition was issued in 1988) he seems to come to terms with his old nemesis:

There are those who believed Daley could have risen above politics to statesmanship had he embraced the idealistic causes of the 1960s rather than obstructing them. Had he used his unique power to lead us toward brotherhood and understanding, they say, he would have achieved greatness. Sure he would have. But to have expected that response from Daley was as realistic as asking Cragin, Bridgeport, Marquette Park, or any other Chicago neighborhood to celebrate Brotherhood Week by having Jeff Fort [a well-known local gang leader] to dinner. If Daley was reactionary and stubborn, he was in perfect harmony with his town.[107]

If anyone should be discomfited by this passage, it would be surviving liberal critics of Richard J. Daley. Moreover, Royko poses but two alternative courses of action, either platitudinous acceptance of social change and harmonious evolution, or ostrich-like opposition to any form of social amelioration. This is not an especially sophisticated explanation of how real political leadership works, and one also finds in this rendering of Daley and his city an almost Algrenesque determinism. As a white Chicagoan—born and bred in a city of small "towns" and ethnic "states"—Daley could not have acted other than in the way that he did.

Another such "making peace" column appeared about a year before Royko's death. Its title expresses its central claim, "Rostenkowski's Sin Was Not Changing with the Times," and in this essay Royko employs one of his most characteristic techniques—a quick sketch of the unfortunate circumstances of a rank and file Chicagoan, "Mary" (a latter-day John Karpowicz or Alice Roberts)—to illustrate the unrecognized virtues of the disgraced congressman Dan Rostenkowski. In this instance, Rostenkowski had assisted Mary in getting admitted to a hospital where she could receive overdue surgery. Royko credits Rostenkowski with "using his political muscle to help people out" and further likens Rostenkowski to another Democratic Party stalwart, alderman Vito Marzullo, "who usually placed one or two young lawyers in city or county patronage jobs." In turn, these lawyers "came to Vito's ward office and handled legal chores for low-income people from the neighborhood."[108] No doubt, Rostenkowski made a signal contribution to Mary's well-being, and it is surely the case that some number of Marzullo's constituents were materially benefited by the free counsel of his gratefully reciprocative young attorneys.

But is this all there is to consider in reckoning whether or not Dan Rostenkowski has been an effective, responsible public official? Certainly, when Royko examined Richard J. Daley in the 1960s he observed a devoted family man as well as a politician who prided himself in helping individuals. But in that earlier time Royko noted that this ethos of individual helping was a mixed virtue. It existed in uneasy relation to another aspect of the elder Daley's style of politics: the inattention to individuals who were unknown by him (and as such, would be passed over by city agency personnel officers in favor of ward organization-connected job applicants); the politically "unconnected" constituencies (whose neighborhood might be in the way of a major public works projects). The younger Royko did not criticize the Democratic Party or Mayor Daley because they were miserly in doling out favors—quite the contrary, favors fueled their conduct of politics—but because their sense of private virtue precluded their developing an awareness of broader social responsibility. The older Mike Royko finds in Dan Rostenkowski a politician whose manner and day-to-day practices recall the vexing, exciting city of his youth. At the end of his writing life Royko had redefined what was empirical and not altogether admirable about an earlier Chicago as both endangered and normative.

A CITY OF PERSISTENT THEMES

Like all great cities, Chicago is a city of persistent themes. The circulation of these themes allows newcomers and visitors to form a concise, comprehensible sense of an otherwise unknowable environment. For stand-up comedians and journalists, the embroidering of these themes can also be a useful creative technique. Traced to their sources, these themes often can be related to the empirical city, though the empirical city in question may be fifty years past.

Many of Chicago's persistent themes—"the city of neighborhoods," a city of broad-shouldered straight talkers, a city in which "reform" perpetually wars with "the machine"—have their sources in the city's rich history of sociological observation. Seldom noted, but of crucial importance to the perpetuation of local themes, is the cross-fertilization of urban observations: creative writers finding inspiration, subject matter, or apt metaphors in social science monographs; city planners discerning in older visual images of the city a template for projecting the future. Likewise underappreciated is how such cross-fertilized, persistently restated themes—in the minds of some observers—*become* the empirical city.

In the preceding pages I have examined four strands of Chicago commentary, and in so doing have extracted some persistent themes, explored their varying relationship to the evolving city of the last half-century, and found, among them, some important insights in reference to the emerging, empirical Chicago. If there is a core Chicago theme, it is the Chicago of parochial, ethnically rooted neighborhoods. Though race has replaced ethnicity as the preeminent, individualizing social marker across Chicago, contemporary research on Chicago neighborhoods still bears traces of the original Chicago school view of neighborhood localism. Among race-conscious neighborhood researchers such as Mary Pattillo, Sudhir Venkatesh, and Eric Klinenberg, the application of a decades-old research strategy to the contemporary city's neighborhood life—in varying ways, and often indirectly—confronts a core dilemma: as the emergence of racially *and* economically homogenous ghettoes supersedes an older geography of ethnic neighborhoods, is the larger city's apparatus of longstanding functional relationships fatally compromised?

And yet, the "black and white Chicago" of the 1960s some time ago gave way to a new racial/ethnic/immigrant reality. Chicago's Latino population—overwhelmingly of Mexican descent—in all likelihood will numerically surpass African Americans within a generation, and other "new immigrations" from east Asia and central Europe are dotting the cityscape with emergent residential enclaves and ethnic business districts. I will not speculate on how this new ethnic / immigrant overlay—onto a racially stamped cityscape that itself overlaid the old ethnic mosaic—will further redefine Chicago, other than to note that presumptions of the city's neighborhood *parochiality*, given current trends, ought to be viewed with some skepticism.

A seemingly more coherent rendition of Chicago has been the panoramic normativeness of its city planners, whose presentations have typically imagined a sleek, well-ordered, postindustrial metropolis. Although the texts of "Chicago Works Together" and various of the Chicago Metropolis 2020 organization's planning documents have deviated from this tendency, over a period of six decades the content of the planners' metropolis has been remarkably consistent. The most recently issued of the documents that I have discussed, the "Chicago Central Area Plan" of 2003, represents a highly suggestive end point to this series: on the one hand, describing neighborhood development strategies by way of an overtly Jacobsian vocabulary; on the other hand, erasing from consideration (and from visual representation) discordant cityscapes such as public housing developments. Moreover, as one moves from the earliest of these documents, the "Development Plan for the Central Area of Chicago" (1958), to the most recent "Central Area Plan," the vision offered moves from the largely normative—that is, the *projection* of a postindustrial urban order onto what was still a heavily industrial city—to a generally empirical rendering of a transformed central city.

Each of the strands of Chicago commentary that I have discussed engages with the most fundamental reshaper of Chicago since the 1950s, its wrenching and highly ambiguous transformation from an industrial to postindustrial metropolis. Among the most dramatic consequences of this transformation has been growing economic inequality, as, in particular, Chicago's unionized, manufacturing workforce has diminished. In a physical sense, the classic marker of this human inequality has been the contrast between Chicago's Loop and the city's outlying neighborhoods. Not only did Mike Royko make repeated reference to this striking physical dichotomy, many of insurgent mayoral candidate Harold Washington's supporters in 1983 viewed his campaign as a crusade of the neglected neighborhoods versus the prosperous, *modernist* downtown. Since the 1980s, the physical reach of Chicago's downtown has been markedly extended. And quite ironically, the look of the enlarged downtown—at the behest of planners espousing new urbanist principles, through the work of trend-conscious developers—has in many respects emulated the features of Chicago's older, outlying neighborhoods. This strategy of physical redevelopment has not, so far, reduced social inequality, but it has undercut the characteristic visual marker of a venerable and widely employed trope of Chicago commentary.

Left unresolved by this traversal of Chicago commentaries is the question of intention versus process. That is, to what degree can we attribute the emergent Chicago to the vision, plans, and action of civic leaders, politicians, and technocrats? It is certainly plausible to contend that we are observing a process of urban transformation mainly driven by a globalizing economy and the working out of local market—notably, real estate—forces. In the next three chapters I address this quandary, first by examining the two-decade mayoralty of Richard M. Daley, and subsequently by considering how Chicago's new, central city neighborhoods are being developed.

Central Station is a recently developed neighborhood just southeast of the Loop and home to Mayor Richard M. Daley.

THREE

THE MAYOR AMONG HIS PEERS

FROM MID-MAY INTO early July 2006, four members of Mayor Richard M. Daley's administration were defendants in a federal criminal trial alleging that they had exercised insider political influence to place Daley campaign workers in city government jobs. U.S. attorneys argued that the actions of the four Daley appointees violated a court-mandated settlement to litigation filed during the Richard J. Daley mayoralty. This settlement, popularly known as the Shakman decree—commemorating Michael Shakman, the attorney who had originally sued the elder Daley—in effect bans patronage hiring for the vast majority of Chicago city government jobs. In a variety of ways, Chicagoans who followed the legal proceedings in mid-2006 were carried back to the Richard J. Daley era. Three of the four defendants resided in the Near South Side Eleventh Ward, Richard J. Daley's original power base. The most prominent of the defendants, Robert Sorich, who had headed a mayoral unit called the Office of Intergovernmental Affairs, was identified by the *Chicago Tribune* as the son of "the official photographer for the late Mayor Richard J. Daley."[1]

Yet in other respects the prosecution of Robert Sorich, Timothy McCarthy, Patrick Slattery, and John Sullivan revealed a new world of Chicago electoral politics. For example, the "blessed lists" of preferred job applicants Robert Sorich was accused of circulating among city agency personnel officers were composed of individuals affiliated with political groups such as the Hispanic Democratic Organization (HDO) and the Coalition for Better Government. In the Richard J. Daley era and before, patronage hiring was the domain of the Democratic Party's fifty ward committeemen, whose neighborhood-focused electoral operations used access to city hall for two essential purposes: to generate the array of favors, waivers, and other special considerations used to maintain a hold on local electorates and to access government jobs for the precinct captains and other electoral workers who were the street-level agents of Democratic Party largesse.

In contrast to the geographically fixed ward organization system, Richard M. Daley campaigns have mobilized racially or ethnically defined groups—such as the HDO and the Coalition for Better Government (identified during the Sorich et al. trial as a "white ethnic" operation)—to campaign in "pockets" of the city where a particular racial or ethnic group predominates.[2] As such, HDO activists and their fellow Daley political workers drop into particular neighborhoods, glean votes, and depart. They do not engage in the ongoing political party organization / constituent interactions once considered essential to cementing voter loyalty. And ironically, defense attorneys even argued that the efforts by Sorich and his codefendants to reward, for example, HDO activists with city jobs represented an informal mode of affirmative action.

To some degree, such claims by the defense in this case must be viewed as desperate gambits to gild the less savory practices of Richard M. Daley's electoral operation. Nevertheless, the reader of press accounts of the Sorich et al. trial also encountered, both among Sorich prosecutors and reporters covering these events, an insistence on interpreting the actions of Sorich, McCarthy, Slattery, and Sullivan as evidence of Chicago's continued dominance by a political machine. In his closing remarks to the jury, one of the U.S. attorneys asserted, "This machine doesn't have any brakes. That's you. It's time to say enough."[3] On the eve of the trial, John Kass of the *Chicago Tribune* wrote a column entitled "Boss' Son Rebuilt Machine in Own Image."[4] Among political commentators, little attention was given to a plausible, alternative proposition: that while politically motivated manipulation of municipal resources continues in Chicago, new political structures aimed at reaching the city's shifting electorate have in recent years quietly taken root. Thoroughly unacknowledged was a related point: that Chicago's continued status as a "one-party" city is not, of itself, proof that it is dominated by a "machine," at least as the latter has long been defined.

The trial of Robert Sorich and his associates was an outgrowth of a Daley administration scandal that had been publicized, initially, by the *Chicago Sun-Times* in early 2004.[5] This administration embarrassment—which has come to be known as the Hired Truck scandal—according to federal prosecutors, involved city personnel soliciting campaign contributions and personal financial kickbacks from trucking companies seeking to do business with city government agencies. As described in one of the indictments of Hired Truck Program (HTP) participants, this initiative "provided certain City operating departments with a mechanism to use trucking services on an as-needed basis to complete construction and operating obligations. Participating HTP trucking companies were hired by the City and provided equipment and operators to the respective City operating departments to perform specific tasks."[6] A press account, in parallel fashion, characterized the Hired Truck Program as "alleviating the need for city trucks and drivers that would be used for only part of the year."[7]

In one sense, the Hired Truck scandal can be viewed as a particular example of a general phenomenon the Chicago press has labeled "pinstripe patronage," favorable treatment for well-connected city hall insiders, as well as the business associates of city officials. Apart from its alliterative allure, pinstripe patronage also serves to connect contemporary political practice in Chicago with its presumed machine heritage, even though, in this instance, the "patronage" being distributed is city contracts—many worth hundreds of thousands or even millions of dollars—as opposed to the twenty thousand– to thirty thousand–dollar annual price tag of a city job in Richard J. Daley's heyday. Like the 2006 prosecution of Robert Sorich and his associates, there is another way of interpreting the Hired Truck Program: as a cost-saving measure intended to reduce city government expenditures associated with maintaining a large, permanent fleet of heavy hauling equipment. Moreover, as is the case with various other initiatives of Richard M. Daley's administration, the city government had attempted to use this "contracting out" venture to support racial minority- and female-headed Chicago businesses.[8]

Press and popular discussion of the city hall hiring and Hired Truck scandals during Richard M. Daley's fourth full term as mayor usually portrayed ongoing problems of corruption in Chicago as direct outgrowths of the city's heritage of machine politics. Given the personalities involved, some with evident connections to the Richard J. Daley era, and practices revealed, which could be construed as extensions of old-style Chicago politics, this discovery of the undead past continuing to assert itself was probably inevitable. In the case of some commentators, binding contemporary Chicago to its roguish, romantic past is just what it takes to establish one's credentials as an authentic Chicagologist. Neglected by most commentary on the city hall hiring trial and the misadventures of the Hired Truck Program were intimations of new forces reshaping Chicago politics, and in particular, the administration of Richard M. Daley. Although the typical framing of contemporary Chicago politics begins with the article of faith that Richard M. Daley must be assessed in reference to his larger-than-life father, just as relevant to understanding the programs and politics of the second Mayor Daley are the strategies, initiatives, and legacies of a group of his contemporaries who transformed mayoral practice in the 1990s. These peers of Richard M. Daley include Stephen Goldsmith, John Norquist, Ed Rendell, Rudolph Giuliani, and Richard Riordan.

A SHORT HISTORY OF MAYORING

In the minds of most Americans, the office of mayor is undoubtedly likened to the U.S. presidency, though of course the scope of authority exercised by the municipal chief executive is much more limited than the president's executive reach. What most rank-and-file citizens do not realize is that just as the actual influence exercised by presidents—as a class of governmental officeholder—has flowed and ebbed over time, so have the political stature and influence of mayors—as a group—fluctuated. However, unlike the layperson's history of the United States, whose early decades are punctuated by the exploits of presumably strong chief executives—Washington, Jefferson, Madison, Jackson—there are very few remembered mayors before 1900. In the words of urban historian Jon Teaford, "In 1800 a visitor to Philadelphia or New York City would have discovered municipal power concentrated in the city council, or board of aldermen; the municipal legislature was virtually the government of these cities. One hundred years later an observer of America's major cities would have found the aldermen and city councils objects of disdain and ridicule, stripped of their former powers and inferior to the mayor and executive commissioners in their authority to determine basic municipal policy."[9]

The era of memorable mayors began at the end of the nineteenth century, when urban reform advocates—seeking among other things to more clearly specify accountability in municipal administration and increase day-to-day efficiency of operations—sought the reallocation of authority in city government. As a result of city charter revision, the large and sometimes bicameral legislative branch of city governments shrank in size, while executive powers and the duration of mayoral terms were increased. In reference to executive powers, mayors often became the dominant figure shaping the municipal budget; they were usually able to exercise some degree of agency oversight through expanded powers of appointment, as well. The details of charter revision and enhanced mayoral power varied from city to city, but as historian Martin Schiesl emphasizes in *The Politics of Efficiency*, his history of late-nineteenth-century municipal reform, growing executive power was also a function of more ambitious individuals seeking the office of mayor. Schiesl's account of "strengthening the executive" combines two elements—structural reforms giving mayors the opportunity to exercise broader governmental influence—and mayors such as Carter Harrison I (Chicago), Seth Low (Brooklyn), and Hazen Pingree (Detroit) determined to use mayoral authority to transform municipal governance.[10]

The emergence of empowered mayors around 1900 did not guarantee that individuals holding the office would be either wise or effective, and the annals of many American cities were subsequently checkered by the misadventures of "scoundrel mayors" such as James Michael Curley (Boston), "Beau James" Walker (New York)—that rarity among failed mayors, who actually fled the country before his second four-year term was completed—and Chicago's own William Hale Thompson.[11] The Great Depression also yielded a cohort of heroic mayors, figures such as Detroit's Frank Murphy and New York's Fiorello La Guardia who are widely viewed as instrumental in their cities' safely navigating the economic crisis of the 1930s.[12]

During the first two decades following World War II, American cities were jolted by immense social disruptions and an array of new public policies. The postwar economic boom; middle-class Americans' linked infatuations with physical mobility, the car, and the single-family home; and various federal government initiatives collectively unleashed the pent-up rush to the suburbs that had been postponed during the crisis decades of the 1930s and 1940s. Within central cities, neighborhood deterioration seemed to accelerate even as racial transition clearly occurred, but coincidentally, the federal urban renewal and interstate highway programs offered the opportunity to stem neighborhood deterioration and modernize core area infrastructure. Big city mayors were typically at the center of these efforts. Writing in 1964, political scientist Robert Salisbury described a "new convergence" of political power in cities:

> It is headed, and sometimes led, by the elected chief executive of the city, the mayor. Included in the coalition are two principal active groupings, locally oriented economic interests and the professional workers in technical city-related programs. Both these groupings are sources of initiative for programs that involve major allocations of resources, both public and private. Associated with the coalition, also, are whatever groups constitute the popular vote-base of the mayor's electoral success.[13]

The presumed centrality of mayoral leadership in the execution of post–World War II urban redevelopment is reflected in this characterization of the urban renewal program in New Haven, Connecticut, as offered by Jeanne R. Lowe in her widely read book, *Cities in a Race with Time* (1967): "Richard C. Lee is the first Mayor in the country to have made urban renewal the cornerstone of his city's administration as well as of his political career. Under Lee, New Haven has done things that many other cities have just talked about or dabbled in."[14] In effect, the salvation of New Haven rested on the shoulders of the federal urban renewal program, whose success in turn, rested on the shoulders of Mayor Lee. Recalling this era, and identifying Richard Lee as one of its "prototype mayors," political scientist Peter Eisinger adds, "They excelled in grantsmanship, and they understood how to use city hall as a bully pulpit in their efforts to bridge racial and class divisions."[15] Yes, Lee excelled at winning federal aid for New Haven, and John Lindsay of New York famously used the mayoralty as a progressive "bully pulpit," but as a group, this generation of postwar activist mayors has been judged a failure. Within a few years of his departure from Gracie Mansion, John Lindsay's city had fallen into fiscal default. In his book assessing the performance of some of America's best-known mayors, historian Melvin Holli offers this terse review of a pair of Lindsay's contemporaries, Detroit's Jerome Cavanagh and Cleveland's Carl Stokes: "two promising political high-flyers who were grounded by grim and ugly urban riots."[16] Even the achievements of the widely praised and repeatedly reelected Richard C. Lee have, with time, been downgraded. In his compendious account of New Haven's decline across the twentieth century, *City: Urbanism and Its End*, a sympathetic Douglas Rae charges Lee with noble overreaching: "By setting out to re-create a region in which firms and families pressed inward on the central city, seeking out opportunities to produce, sell, and live in the middle of New Haven, Dick Lee had set himself against history . . . Lee had addressed a project of social engineering that no government on any scale has to my knowledge managed to fulfill."[17]

The consensus view of the activist post–World War II mayors is that their ambitions soared beyond the capacity of their municipal administrations, their grasp of day-to-day governmental operations was weak to nonexistent, and in most cases, they were blindsided by the intensified racial polarization of the late 1960s. Moreover, mayors such as Cavanagh, Lee, Lindsay, and Stokes presided over cities that were also badly punished by deindustrialization and the associated geographic and economic restructurings of the 1970s and 1980s. Yet in the face of the declining fortunes of East Coast and Midwest industrial centers, a new vision of municipal governance and mayoral craft began to form. By the late 1970s, a former Lindsay administration official, E. S. Savas, emerged as a persistent advocate of public service privatization, a strategy Savas argued would contribute both to governmental cost saving and improvement in the quality of service delivery.[18] Although Savas initially seemed like a voice in the wilderness—and various municipalities' early experiments in privatization produced modest results—by the late 1980s a more broadly framed reinterpretation of municipal governance problems and prospects coalesced. In 1992, a journalist, David Osborne, and former municipal administrator, Ted Gaebler—who pointedly asserted that "we believe deeply in government"—published their highly influential *Reinventing Government.* This book is thick with examples of municipal innovation, but its essential arguments can be discerned in this introductory summary:

> Most entrepreneurial governments promote *competition* between service providers. They *empower* citizens by pushing control out of the bureaucracy, into the community. They measure the performance of their agencies, focusing not on inputs but on *outcomes.* They are driven by their goals—their *missions*—not by their rules and regulations. They define their clients as *customers*, and offer them choices—between schools, between training programs, between housing options ... And they focus not simply on providing public services, but on *catalyzing* all sectors—public, private, and voluntary—into action to solve their community's problems.[19]

During the 1990s, Osborne and Gaebler's gospel of restructured service delivery, close attention to performance measures, and citizen (customer)-focused action was vigorously and persistently asserted in the pages of *Governing* magazine, one of Congressional Quarterly, Inc.'s publications, which regularly ran articles by David Osborne. Many issues of *Governing* featured profiles of new-style mayors such as John Norquist (Milwaukee), Stephen Goldsmith (Indianapolis), and Dennis Archer (Detroit), and these articles invariably praised initiatives aimed at simplifying bureaucratic regulations, reorganizing welfare services, or otherwise enhancing the local "business climate."[20]

The 1990s also coincided with the "comeback" of many central cities, which in some cases—such as Chicago—added population for the first time in decades, while in other urban centers, notable quality of life improvements were achieved. Among the latter, New York City's remarkable downturn in murders—and reported criminal activity in general—was exemplary.[21] Quite a debate could be generated by the following paradox: did the comeback of major cities "make" successful mayors, or did effective mayors play a significant role in improving their cities? Judged by the proliferation of books by these mayors—or those chronicling their achievements—one has to suppose that the latter contention has the wider endorsement.[22] Among the mayor-authored books published during the 1990s, Stephen Goldsmith's *The Twenty-First Century City* and John Norquist's *The Wealth of Cities* are especially suggestive. Goldsmith, a Republican who led Indianapolis's government from 1992 to 2000, devotes much of his book to discussing how "marketization" of municipal services can improve cities. Yet linked to this emphasis on improving governmental efficiency is a distinctly moralistic cast of mind:

> The family is the fundamental unit of every successful society. But for the past thirty-plus years, government has consistently undermined this source of public virtue. Government has taken money away from families through ever-increasing taxes and then perversely used some of the revenues on programs that actively discourage poor Americans from forming families. [23]

Goldsmith thus presents himself as an unusual variety of municipal chief executive, on the one hand a "policy wonk" determined to cut city government costs, yet on the other, a crusader for rank-and-file Indianapolis families.

In contrast to the apocalyptic tone discernible in *The Twenty-First Century City*—at one point Goldsmith discusses neighborhood conflicts pitting property owners against "superpredators"—Norquist, in *The Wealth of Cities*, writes as a knowing connoisseur of cities.[24] Many of his arguments directly parallel Goldsmith's: federal fiscal aid has often harmed cities; service privatization can improve performance; a healthy local economy is the prerequisite for achieving a prosperous, commodious city. Yet as Norquist wraps up his narrative, *The Wealth of Cities* takes on a theme, urban design, that is nowhere to be found in Goldsmith's book. Norquist is a proponent of new urbanism, and even of one of new urbanism's most controversial projects, the Disney Corporation–founded Celebration, Florida: "Celebration . . . features a traditional main street, with three-story commercial buildings close to the street, and residential areas, with houses built close together and trees for shade. Celebration is so popular that homeowners are being chosen from a waiting list via lottery." Norquist, by espousing the return to "real neighborhoods" and "real cities," without directly criticizing predecessors such as Richard Lee and John Lindsay, exposes another divide separating the mayors of the 1960s and 1990s.[25] While the earlier generation unquestioningly accepted the proclaimed benefits of revitalization through urban renewal—and as such, the modernist reworking of the city fabric—new-style mayors such as John Norquist, as well as Richard M. Daley, are more likely to prefer traditionalist architectural and public space planning strategies.

In this account of resurgent cities and resurgent mayoring in the 1990s, I have not yet discussed some of the figures who might most evidently be considered Richard M. Daley's peers, Rudolph Giuliani (New York), Ed Rendell (Philadelphia), and Richard Riordan (Los Angeles). These mayors, in addition to the leaders of smaller cities such as Goldsmith and Norquist, all participated in national organizations such as the U.S. Conference of Mayors and in various ways engaged in on-the-job "insight-sharing." For example, Giuliani biographer Fred Siegel notes that Ed Rendell was invited to address a transition workshop for New York City agency heads in the weeks following Giuliani's election as mayor in 1993.[26] The mayoring challenges of very large cities like New York, Philadelphia, Los Angeles, and Chicago are distinctive, and it is in reference to these particular challenges that I think the most interesting commonality linking Giuliani, Rendell, Riordan, and Daley can be identified.

All have straddled conventional political boundaries during their careers, most especially during their terms as mayor. Even as he adopted a highly moralistic attitude in reference to crime control and welfare reform, Giuliani was sympathetic to pro-choice and gay rights advocacy. Giuliani also consulted Democratic Party–affiliated political advisors, and in 1994 he endorsed Mario Cuomo, the Democratic Party candidate for governor of New York. In many ways Ed Rendell has more closely fit the profile of loyal Democrat, but probably his greatest political triumph as mayor of Philadelphia was holding the line on salaries and fringe benefits for city workers, a heavily Democratic constituent group. Like Giuliani, Republican Richard Riordan depended on a number of political operatives drawn from the ranks of the Democratic Party. Political scientist Raphael Sonenshein further notes that Riordan "had little affection for the municipal government, whether its elected officials or its permanent employees. He wanted the sway that a CEO might have in a corporation . . . His real feeling of being an outsider at city hall hurt him when it was time to get something done, but was well received by the public."[27] Interestingly, although each of these mayors—like Richard M. Daley—regularly asserted his nonpartisanship, Giuliani, Rendell, and Riordan were often abrasive public figures. Siegel's description of Giuliani as an "immoderate centrist" is an apt characterization. Giuliani, Rendell, and Riordan often won political victories by out-flanking municipal bureaucracies and by surprising political opponents. Their policy positions sometimes defied conventional expectations, and very often, their successes were a function of redefining what the public expected from municipal government.

CHICAGO'S SECOND MAYOR DALEY

Richard M. Daley was not from the start the son of a famous mayor. Born in 1942, he was nearing his thirteenth birthday when Richard J. Daley defeated Robert Merriam in the general election of April 5, 1955. The younger Richard Daley grew up in the Bridgeport neighborhood, the lifelong home of his parents. Richard M. left Chicago to attend Providence College, but he soon returned, completing his bachelor's degree at DePaul University. He also earned a law degree from DePaul. The younger Daley won his first elective office in 1969, when he was chosen as a delegate to the convention writing a new state constitution for Illinois.[28] For most of the 1970s Daley served as a senator in the Illinois General Assembly. As a state legislator, Daley was not universally admired. In 1977, *Chicago* magazine published an article—based on a survey of twenty state capitol insiders—identifying the ten best and worst members of the General Assembly. Richard M. Daley was ranked among the ten worst. The profile of Daley appearing in this article describes him as "shrewd" but also "shark-like."[29]

Mayor Richard M. Daley regularly asserts his nonpartisanship, so it is of some interest that he served as Eleventh Ward Democratic Party committeeman for a few years following his father's death. However, by 1980 Daley found himself in the unlikely position of running against the Democratic Party's endorsed candidate in the primary election for Cook County state's attorney. In this race, Chicago Mayor Jane Byrne had backed another young politician with deep family roots in the Democratic Party, Fourteenth Ward alderman Ed Burke. Daley defeated Burke, won the general election, and was reelected state's attorney in 1984 and 1988. During the 1980s Daley also suffered the only electoral defeat of his political career, finishing a close third in the three-way Democratic mayoral primary of 1983, won by Harold Washington. Daley's failure to win the mayoralty in 1983 was not an unmitigated political setback. Campaigning as a "moderate, good government reformer," he won the endorsement of some prominent Democrats who had previously op-

posed his father.[30] He also distanced himself from the racially po-
larizing rhetoric of some of the more vociferous anti-Washington
Democrats.

In 1989 Daley defeated the incumbent mayor, Eugene Sawyer—
selected by the city council to serve as interim mayor following Harold Washington's sudden death in late 1987—in the "special election"
primary, then triumphed over Ed Vrdolyak (until recently a Democrat, running as the Republican Party nominee) and Timothy Evans
(qualifying for the election as the standard-bearer of the short-lived
Harold Washington Party) in the general election. Daley has been
reelected mayor in 1991, 1995, 1999, 2003, and 2007. His original voting base was a "white/brown" coalition of working-class Democratic
Party loyalists and Latinos, and until the mid-1990s there were recurring efforts by African American activists to rejuvenate the "Harold Washington coalition" and unite behind an African American
candidate for mayor.[31] In fact, over the span of Daley's five reelection
campaigns he has substantially increased his support among black
voters. Until the emergence in 2004 of the series of corruption scandals that have substantially tarnished his administration, the one
sign of Richard M. Daley political weakness was his declining ability
to mobilize the electorate. Like his father, Richard M. Daley has been
an incumbent whose reelection victories have combined impressive
winning percentages and diminished voter turnouts. In the younger
Daley's "landslide" election of 2007 he drew two hundred thousand
votes fewer than in his special election victory of 1989.

Richard M. Daley by all accounts has been a consummate political leader. Apart from his string of election victories, he has reas-
serted mayoral control over what had been, in the 1980s, a very fractious city council. He has also extended mayoral influence over the
city's many non-municipal service-providing agencies, including the
Chicago Public Schools, the Chicago Housing Authority, the Chicago Transit Authority, and the Chicago Park District. The national
press has frequently and favorably commented on his record, and a
variety of governmental, civic, and environmental groups have hon-
ored him. The latter have included the U.S. Conference of Mayors,

the National Trust for Historic Preservation, and the National Arbor Day Foundation. In designating Daley as a Public Official of the Year for 1997, *Governing* editor Alan Ehrenhalt commented: "He has been patient and skillful in mastering the details of local government, and remarkably creative in devising pragmatic solutions to the most complex problems."[32] As such, Richard M. Daley fits comfortably among the ranks of the pragmatic municipal chief executives who emerged in the 1990s, a group Peter Eisinger has called the "post-federal" era mayors.

Though Eisinger's characterization of new-style mayors—which is of a piece with *Governing*'s paean to Richard M. Daley—plays down their commitment to a broad social vision in favor of emphasizing their "mastering . . . details," the Richard M. Daley administration, over time, has advanced a discernible and far-from-timid mayoral program. The three fundamental components of this program include promotion of Chicago as a global city, the reorganization of a variety of municipal and independent agency service functions, and social inclusivity at the elite level.

The Daley administration's promotion of Chicago as a global or "world-class city"—as articulated in the most general sense—is in no way a striking or innovative policy preference. One only needs to recall the wide-eyed Flint, Michigan, officials who were interviewed by Michael Moore in *Roger and Me* (1989) to recognize that the dream of postindustrial transcendence to the friendly skies of mass tourism and the "leisure economy" is an impulse driving many municipal leaders. The Daley administration, nevertheless, has pursued this goal in a reasonably strategic fashion. Efforts to expand both O'Hare Airport and the downtown McCormick Place convention complex seek to build on demonstrated Chicago assets: geographic and transportation network "centrality," and extensive facilities to support trade shows and conventions. The Daley administration's redevelopment of Navy Pier at the northeastern end of the downtown area and the creation of the Millennium Park complex have forged two powerful tourist magnets. Likewise, the Chicago bid to host the 2016 Olympic Games—very clearly a Daley administration / civic elite collaboration—attempted to highlight Chicago's international prominence by way of a low-cost physical development program.[33]

Less dramatically, but possibly more consequentially, Richard M. Daley city planners have implemented numerous small-scale infrastructure and beautification improvements, speeded up approval processes, and reimagined local neighborhood identities in such a fashion so as to add momentum to the ongoing industrial to commercial / residential transformation of the city's Near West and Near South Sides. So far, the gentrification of these areas has engendered relatively little neighborhood resistance. From the standpoint of Chicago's image as a global city, this expanded cityscape of "upscale boutiques and stylish restaurants" represents both a talent-drawing amenity and a marker of Chicago's progressive, postindustrial character.[34]

Richard M. Daley has also been an aggressive reorganizer of local government bureaucracies. In 1995, he won state legislation enabling him to replace the school board and top administration at the Chicago Public Schools (CPS). As new CEO of the CPS, Daley selected Paul Vallas, who had previously served as his budget director. Vallas pulled back authority from the parent-dominated local school councils (elected to govern each Chicago public school), moved to standardize the curriculum, and pushed hard for improvement in student performance on academic achievement tests. Mayor Daley, in turn, poured immense resources into a program of school construction and rehabilitation. Since the mid-1990s Chicago school system standardized test performance has generally moved upward— though slowly and unevenly across testing areas—and in June 2004, Daley and CPS CEO Arne Duncan, Vallas's successor in the post, announced Renaissance 2010, a plan to close poorly performing schools and to replace them with a hundred new schools, many of which are independent charter schools.[35]

No less sweeping has been Daley's makeover of the Chicago Housing Authority (CHA). Following the U.S. Department of Housing and Urban Development's takeover of the CHA between 1995 and 1999, Daley appointees initiated an agency restructuring called the Plan for Transformation, which aims to reduce the number of local public housing units from approximately forty thousand to twenty-five thousand (with ten thousand units reserved for senior citizens), rehabilitate or build anew each of those twenty-five thousand units, turn over day-to-day property management and social service provision to private vendors, and site most public housing in mixed-income developments. As a rule, these mixed-income developments adhere to a one-third / one-third / one-third proportioning of public housing, affordable housing (mainly rental, some for sale), and market-rate housing.[36]

The CHA's track record in implementing the Plan for Transformation has been very mixed. At some developments, resident acceptance of the new CHA vision has been forthcoming, at other developments—including the famous Cabrini-Green complex on the Near North Side—there has been substantial resident resistance. One of the most significant "process" challenges involved in a planning effort of this magnitude is resident relocation, both temporary moves as developments are rebuilt and permanent relocations from public housing. On both counts, the CHA's performance has been poor. At developments such as the ABLA Homes on the Near West Side, planning and project execution have spanned more than a decade, during which time the inconveniences visited upon residents have been extraordinary. For former public housing residents across the city, CHA-contracted relocation services have been very spotty. The findings of researchers who have examined where former CHA residents have found new places to live are disturbingly unequivocal: in overwhelmingly African American neighborhoods nearly as poor as the public housing communities from which they departed.[37]

Richard M. Daley's other major public service reorganization has been within the city government. In 1994 the police department implemented a citywide program of community policing known as the Chicago Alternative Policing Strategy (CAPS). The CAPS initiative has put more patrol officers onto Chicago's sidewalks, and via nearly three hundred monthly "beat" meetings brings together police personnel and community residents to discuss local crime-related issues. During the later 1990s and into the 2000s, Chicago's crime rate has paralleled the pattern of decline achieved in many cities. The Daley administration has not hesitated to attribute the local decline to the effective implementation of CAPS.[38]

The third component of the Daley program is elite social inclusivity. As mayor, Richard M. Daley has routinely filled important administrative positions with Latinos, African Americans, and women. Although his 1989 voting base included few African Americans, Daley has worked hard since that time to solidify his relationship with leading black political figures such as the late John Stroger, who until mid-2006 was president of the Cook County Board of Commissioners. Daley has also cultivated the city's business and civic leadership, which for its part, has been warmly grateful to the mayor for Chicago's resurgent reputation. And not least, in a stunning departure from his father's politics, Richard M. Daley has courted formerly marginal constituencies, such as gay rights and environmental activists. Richard M. Daley most strikingly distinguishes himself from his father—in terms of worldview, his sense of the city, and his coalition-building inclinations—through his appearances at the annual Gay Pride Parade.

Nevertheless, the current Mayor Daley's approach to social inclusivity is a matter of communication and consultation at the elite level. In a 1999 assessment of Daley's record, journalist David Moberg observed: "The mayor has done everything he could to discourage any popular involvement in civic affairs that would compromise his hold on power. Despite preserving many of the reforms that emerged during Harold Washington's brief tenure, he has largely rejected Washington's belief in community participation in planning and implementing public policy."[39] Daley planners, in effect, have dictated the terms of public housing redevelopment, and since the mayor's asserting his control of the Chicago Public Schools in 1995, there has been a substantial erosion of influence exercised by the neighborhood-based, elected local school councils. Even the mayor's admirers agree that he is a reclusive decision maker who relies on the advice of a handful of close advisors. In short, Daley promotes Chicago as a prospective home and workplace for all, though as the chief executive he has depended on a very narrow stream of local information gathering, expertise, and counsel.

The preceding is a fair assessment of the basic features of the Richard M. Daley program, but in its retrospectiveness, this description has also exaggerated the program's coherence and the degree of rationalistic forethought that shaped it. Daley's candidacy in 1989 was described as a "cautious, scripted campaign," and his April 1989 inaugural address was brief though richly platitudinous:

> Our common opponents are crime and ignorance, waste and fraud, poverty and disease, hatred and discrimination. And we either rise up as one city and make the special effort required to meet these challenges, or sit back and watch Chicago decline. As one who loves Chicago, I'm ready to make that special effort—and to ask everyone in our city to do the same. Business as usual is a prescription for failure. The old ways of doing things simply aren't adequate to cope with the new challenges we face. In times of limited resources, government must be more creative and productive than ever before. We must do a better job with the resources we have.[40]

In a subsequent passage—which was also the only section of the speech addressing a specific local government function—Daley turned to Chicago's public schools. Education reform, of course, has become a signature Richard M. Daley initiative, but his crucial move in this policy area—which was to seek state government approval for reorganizing the CPS—would wait for another six years, following his reelection to a second four-year term as mayor. In the pages to follow, I attempt to explain how Richard M. Daley's program emerged, and in so doing, link his mayoralty both to recent trends in American mayoral practice, as well as to some unique and more individualistic sources.

RICHARD M. DALEY RECONSIDERED

A generation ago political scientist John W. Kingdon published a book entitled *Agendas, Alternatives, and Public Policies* in which he offered a "loose, messy" decision-making model as a more realistic alternative to "the tight, orderly process that a rational approach specifies." Even my unadorned summary of Richard M. Daley's main initiatives projects a degree of rationality onto the processes of policy selection that is at odds with reality. In this reconsideration of Daley's program—intended to more fully account for how his mayoralty has evolved and to link his mayoral practice to the broader strategy of municipal leadership that emerged across the United States in the 1990s—I propose an interpretive framework that is loosely drawn from Kingdon's triad of public agenda sources: "problems, policies, and politics."[41]

The Richard M. Daley administration's approach to governing Chicago bears the mark of five shaping forces. These forces are a mixed bag, but also represent a constellation of influences structuring the action of any big-city mayor: broad-scale economic and social conditions; the mayor's personal inclinations as a municipal leader; opportunities presented by emerging situations or trends in public policy; the laundry list of prospective projects (usually physical projects) circulating among local elites and begging the mayor's attention; and what I term "politically usable policies" that emerge as priorities due to their strategic constituent appeal. As we walk through this funhouse of potential action, I believe we can begin to understand more readily both the coherencies and incoherencies of the Daley program, even as we also gain a deeper sense of why his particular program emerged.

In terms of understanding the main threads of Richard M. Daley programmatic action, the simplest of the five shaping forces to identify are the pair of basic structural conditions looming over both Chicago and his nascent mayoralty in 1989. The first of these was the massive economic restructuring that had undermined Chicago's industrial economy since the 1960s. The second was carryover racial polarization, initially produced by the city's wrenching neighborhood transitions and the politics of civil rights activism and resistance in the 1960s, then reignited during the election of 1983 and the subsequent Harold Washington mayoralty.

In reference to economic restructuring, with the exception of Harold Washington—an outlier not just among the ranks of Chicago chief executives—the dream of every Chicago mayor running back to Richard J. Daley has been the transformation of central Chicago into a more formidable corporate management district and upscale residential enclave. This reworking of the central city's physical environment has been promoted both to compensate for the decline of the manufacturing economy and to boost the Loop and its environs as generators of tax revenue. In effect, local leaders since the 1950s have sought what is literally unspeakable in the proud city of Chicago, the *Manhattanization* of the Loop and the adjoining Near North, West, and South Sides. Richard M. Daley's contribution to the achievement of this dream—apart from holding the mayoralty at a time when the real estate market was moving very briskly along a parallel course—has been to skillfully use public works to environmentally enhance central Chicago and deploy an array of planning tools intended to lubricate private investment. Mayor Daley's efforts to expand O'Hare Airport and the McCormick Place convention complex likewise have sought to boost Chicago advantages as a transportation node and tourist / trade show destination.

Traditional infrastructure and central city development initiatives have not been Richard M. Daley's only gambit to economically reposition Chicago. In the early years of the current decade his unrealized CivicNet project sought to improve Internet access throughout Chicago, and his administration has also sought to strategically protect portions of the city's remaining industrial economy.[42] Nevertheless, in terms of resources committed and publicity generated, not just the rebuilding, but more grandly, the reimagining of central Chicago has grown out of Richard M. Daley's particular approach to his city's long line of economic transformation running back to the 1960s.

Also attuned to conditions originating in the 1960s has been Richard M. Daley's commitment to elite social inclusivity. I must run ahead of my narrative for a moment to observe that Richard M.

Daley is not a "political natural" in the sense of embracing crowds and seizing opportunities to speak extemporaneously. Yet recognizing the racially divided electorate of the 1980s—and more fundamentally, Chicago's unresolved social conflicts dating from the 1960s—Daley has moved to co-opt key figures representing various dissident constituencies, notably African Americans and anti–Richard J. Daley "independent" Democrats. He has also reached out to the city's corporate and civic leadership while cultivating new constituencies such as gays and environmentalists. Daley is not a "warm" politician in the manner of a Harold Washington or Fiorello La Guardia, but through high-level consultation and careful observance of the city's civic protocols he has projected the image of a publicly attentive, if not personally accessible, chief executive.

Then there are Richard M. Daley's personal inclinations as mayor, which admittedly constitute an amorphous subject for analysis. Nevertheless, various of the mayor's biographical details do permit a plausible explanation of one of his administration's most persistent commitments, its diversified campaign of civic beautification. My plausible accounting for this Daley inclination begins by noting his coming of age during the 1960s, and more pertinently, during the latter half of his father's administration. In these years the Chicago cityscape was badly damaged: by civil unrest that destroyed hundreds of buildings along major South Side and West Side commercial corridors; by fires, housing abandonment, and demolitions in many residential areas; by deferred maintenance of public structures such as schools, transit stations, and most notably, public housing developments.[43]

Given the proprietorial mindset that Richard M. Daley seems to have inherited from his late father, his persistence in repairing—or rebuilding more grandly—basic infrastructure such as roadways, bridges, schools, libraries, and parks buildings brings to mind the heir to a once-opulent estate who aspires to restore its past glory. Moreover, Daley has determined that there is an economic payoff to urban beautification. The following comment to the Chicago Greening Symposium in 2002 makes the point quite succinctly: "The nice thing is, if you improve the quality of life for the people who live in your city, you will end up attracting new people and new employers."[44] Other factors that surely have stoked Daley's commitment to physically restore Chicago include his mingling with the likes of John Norquist at U.S. Conference of Mayors events, as well as his extensive world travels. Unlike his father, the younger Mayor Daley is a geographic and urban cosmopolitan.

And lastly, regarding Daley the beautifier: among the striking elements of the Richard M. Daley beautification campaign are the multitude of small-scale physical improvements one observes across Chicago. Much press coverage has been devoted to Daley's big projects such as Millennium Park, but for rank-and-file Chicagoans, the mayor's most lasting contribution to physical Chicago has been through sidewalk bicycle rack installations, the planting of perennial flowers and shrubs in previously neglected traffic islands, the rebuilding of neighborhood public libraries, and the like. Daley's urban design inclinations are Jacobsian, typically street-level in their impact. They represent the kinds of small-scale physical improvements one can well imagine occurring to a rider gazing from the rear window of an automobile, the vantage point from which Richard M. Daley most frequently views his city.

Richard M. Daley has also been an opportunistic mayoral leader, responding in imaginative ways to unforeseen situations or even programmatic setbacks. Political scientist Joel Rast has proposed that the Daley administration's re-engagement with a previously dismissed policy option—neighborhood economic development, which was viewed initially as too closely associated with Harold Washington's administration—was just such an opportunistic policy selection. Having experienced the political undoing of several large-scale public works proposals, notably a South Side airport plan and a near-Loop casino project, and having suffered through the embarrassing "Loop flood" of 1992 (when tunnels running beneath downtown office towers filled with water escaping from the main channel of the Chicago River), Daley and his planners determined that basic infrastructure improvements should be given greater attention.[45]

Though community policing in Chicago is repeatedly invoked as a mayoral initiative, it was in fact a grassroots movement—the Chicago Alliance for Neighborhood Safety—that first promoted intensified street patrolling and closer cooperation between the police department and neighborhood residents.[46] The Daley administration has certainly been a leader in promoting public school and public housing restructuring, but these are also policy areas in which there had been years of national debate preceding the advent of local action.[47] Once more, it bears mentioning that Richard M. Daley has been an active participant in national organizations whose agendas have, in part, been directed to discussion of just such policy innovations.

Similarly opportunistic was the series of long-term lease / management agreements negotiated by the Daley administration and private vendors between 2005 and 2008. In each instance, the leasing of a major municipal asset—a South Side toll highway, Midway Airport, city government–owned parking garages and parking meters— promised to earn huge advance payments for the city government. For instance, the first of these agreements, which transferred management of the Chicago Skyway toll road to a Spanish-Australian business consortium for a period of ninety-nine years, added $1.83 billion to the Daley administration's coffers.[48] However, the latter pair of these arrangements—involving Midway Airport and the city's parking meters—appear to have been negotiated in some haste, in part to provide a quick fiscal fix for the city government. Having agreed in the fall of 2008 to take over the management of Midway Airport, by April 2009 the Midway Investment and Development Corporation accepted a sizable financial penalty and cancelled its contract with the city government. Coincidentally, the early weeks of the private vendor's oversight of Chicago's parking meters were tempestuous, generating charges that the vendor was unprepared to take on its new job. Local resident consternation was amplified by steep increases in parking meter charges imposed by Chicago Parking Meters, LLC.[49]

In the years to come, Chicago's many visitors will principally celebrate Richard M. Daley's accomplishments as an urban builder. In central Chicago, his term in office has coincided most notably with the following achievements: the redevelopment of Navy Pier as a tourist / entertainment attraction, the reconstruction of Wacker Drive paralleling the main and south branches of the Chicago River, the development of Millennium Park, the rerouting of Lake Shore Drive (which permits uninterrupted pedestrian movement between the Field Museum, Shedd Aquarium, and Adler Planetarium—the area now known as the Museum Campus), the rebuilding of Soldier Field, and several expansions of McCormick Place. The Daley administration has won much praise for seeing these projects through to completion (though McCormick Place might be viewed as ever-expanding), but the roots of several of these initiatives preceded Daley's mayoralty. Plans to convert the then-derelict Navy Pier into a public promenade date from the 1980s.[50] During the same years, the Chicago Bears National Football League franchise, Soldier Field's principal tenant, began lobbying for a stadium upgrade.[51] Historian Timothy Gilfoyle, in his account of the creation of Millennium Park, notes that even this public works extravaganza—which is so closely identified with Richard M. Daley—grew out of earlier efforts by several of Chicago's civic notables to create a "Lakefront Gardens" performing arts complex.[52]

There is, however, an overriding "logic" that has yielded this clustering of public works initiatives, and which is unquestionably attributable to Richard M. Daley. In a fashion that mimics the approach to civic enhancement—if not invariably the classically inspired architectural monumentality—associated with the early-twentieth-century City Beautiful movement, Daley has devoted billions of dollars to dignifying those portions of his city most accessible to visitors, but which might also be considered a civic common ground for Chicagoans. And judging by the popularity of these sites, this effort to create a memorable civic gathering place for all Chicago has been successful. For Richard M. Daley—personally speaking—there is good reason to suppose that this mammoth program of civic refurbishment is also a satisfying exercise in erasing physical reminders of Chicago's sad decline in the 1960s and 1970s.

In short, Richard M. Daley the urban builder has pursued a course of action that has general sources—the dreams of nearly all ambitious mayors include large-scale public works accomplishments—but is also reflective of his proprietorial view of Chicago, and as well, effective opportunism. Practically speaking, the Daley public works program has involved picking a group of projects—several of which were already in the civic / municipal "pipeline"—and bringing them to fruition. This taking on and completing initiatives that antedate one's administration is a characteristic feature of successful public works execution, but it is a form of action not limited to infrastructure and public buildings. Richard M. Daley's movement into public school reform, from the standpoints of political action and policy choice, has followed an analogous course. Toward the end of Harold Washington's mayoralty, parent groups, a civic / business alliance known as Chicago United, and a few members of the mayor's administration began to promote an overhaul of the CPS. Ironically, the fruit of their work was state legislation passed in 1989 that dramatically *decentralized* CPS operations by vesting new powers in the local school councils. Daley's "takeover" of the CPS in 1995, in one sense, carried on reform efforts that had begun in the previous decade, even as, in another sense, these reforms were reversed by Paul Vallas's recentralization of CPS decision making.[53]

If Rudolph Giuliani can be characterized as an immoderate centrist, the equivalent designation for Richard M. Daley might be eccentric relativist. Among Daley's arsenal of politically usable policy stances has been a bewildering series of "moral issue" endorsements: neighborhood referenda to authorize "problem" tavern closures, official recognition of same-sex marriages, online identification of sex offenders.[54] There appears to be little philosophical coherence to Daley's expressed commitments on these matters, but there is a discernible political logic. Over the course of his two-decade mayoralty, Daley has persistently sought to broaden his initially white / brown electoral (and as such, racially / ethnically inflected) coalition. This strategy has involved reaching out to African American ministers, who are often vigorous proponents of strict moral standards, and it has also involved catering to Chicago's substantial gay population. It is a strategy that clearly incorporates some of the mayor's particular inclinations, especially his support of urban bicycling and various "green" measures such as rooftop gardens. Each of these constituencies—socially conservative African Americans, gays and lesbians, outdoors enthusiasts, and environmentalists—represents a relatively small increment of support for the mayor, but conjoined they have allowed Richard M. Daley to expand his constituency base well beyond his initial, narrower voting coalition.

Undoubtedly the most encompassing of Richard M. Daley's politically usable policies has been his personal identification with managerial innovation. Apart from the real policy reorientations evident in the Chicago Public Schools, Chicago Housing Authority, and the police department, Daley has steadfastly presented himself as a mayor above politics. As he explained to a reporter in 1994: "If I had to worry about my election, I'd never make a decision here and my role is to make decisions. I don't consume this political stuff . . . I'm not a political junkie. [Working in government] is where you get things done."[55] It has been many years since Daley served as Eleventh Ward Democratic committeeman, and as a rule, he has adopted a neutral pose in the face of internal Democratic Party disputes. Yet it is also evident that Daley's posture as manager rather than politician has served a useful political purpose. Until the spate of corruption scandals rocked his administration in 2004, Daley routinely deflected criticism by asserting that efficiency and calculation of the public good were his first—and only—executive considerations. The following is his response to criticism that had been directed at the CPS in early 2006:

There is nothing wrong with people giving me their ideas, whether Congressman [Luis] Gutierrez or you or anyone else . . . That is what you do as a public official. You listen. You take their criticism, you take their evaluation . . . I had the vision, I had the will and I had the character to do it, and the courage . . . I said we are going to make a difference, and there has been a difference. I am the only mayor in the United States who would take that political responsibility. Every other mayor ran out left and right.[56]

In this articulation by Daley of his own aims and means, executive wisdom and courage are contrasted with the small-minded carping that is the presumed stock and trade of politicians, such as Congressman Gutierrez.

RICHARD M. DALEY, HIS ADMIRERS, AND HIS CRITICS

The markers of Richard M. Daley's success as mayor are numerous: five reelection victories, citations by a variety of local and national civic organizations, and more subtly, the near-absence of sustained political opposition since the mid-1990s. Daley's tenure as mayor is also widely associated with a reversal of Chicago's fortunes. Between 1990 and 2000, the city's population expanded for the first time since the 1940–50 census period. Correspondingly, beginning in the mid-1990s Chicago's crime rate entered a period of sustained decline. From approximately the same point in time, the standardized test performance of Chicago public school students inched upward. Less certain is whether Daley's decision making has been instrumental in substantively expanding Chicago's economy and improving its quality of life, or whether the evident improvements revealed by measures such as crime rate and student performance have projected a favorable aura onto Daley, thereby ordaining him as a successful mayor.

Although Richard M. Daley is not a beloved public figure, he is widely admired. The most prosaic, but also in all likelihood, the most widely shared favorable sentiment derives from the visible improvements in Chicago's physical environment over the last twenty years. And as I have previously noted, this involves both large-scale initiatives such as Millennium Park, as well as countless median-strip plantings, neighborhood playground refurbishings, and commercial strip improvements. Even civic leaders who might well view Daley as having stolen some of their benevolent thunder endorse his accomplishments. George Ranney Jr.—a leading figure in the Chicago Metropolis 2020 organization and a proponent of the discarded Lakefront Gardens proposal—reacted in this fashion to the opening of Millennium Park: "We are just full of admiration for Millennium Park. It's a quantum improvement over what we dreamed of all those years ago."⁵⁷

Daley's admirers also characterize him as a unifying figure, a mayor for all Chicagoans. This is a curious notion, given his public awkwardness and periodic eruptions of vindictive fury. During the mid-1990s, Daley's relationship with Illinois governor Jim Edgar was highly acrimonious, particularly as the two officials sparred over whether or not a small air terminal at the southeast corner of Grant Park, Meigs Field, would continue operations. It was the mayor's intention to convert the Meigs Field site to a public open space. This dispute was ultimately terminated—for want of a better expression—by Daley's sending a group of bulldozers to Meigs Field, which "dug six huge 'X' marks into the lone runway, putting the little lakefront airport out of commission in a move clearly meant to be permanent."⁵⁸ The Meigs Field assault was unannounced and conducted under the cover of darkness, at approximately midnight on a Sunday evening in late March 2003. Nevertheless, Daley clearly has been a civic stabilizer, if not quite a conciliator. As one business leader pithily observed to journalist James Atlas in 1996: "He saved the city."⁵⁹ Chicago's salvation, according to this line of reasoning, has grown out of Daley's ability to defuse the intense racial polarization of the 1980s, and more generally, restore the city's national and international reputation.

As I have noted, Richard M. Daley has also won praise as a diligent and creative public manager. This, of course, has been the source of *Governing* magazine's longstanding admiration for Daley.

Among Daley's most expansive local admirers is sociologist Terry Nichols Clark, who attributes to Daley and appointees such as Paul Vallas and Forrest Claypool (head of the Chicago Park District in the mid-1990s) a transformative impact on Chicago governance and service delivery:

> This is the core of reform in Chicago and other cities. The political enemy is clientelism or patronage, which reformers seek to replace. These are usually replaced with public goods that are shared widely across a geographic area, ideally the entire city, such as clean air, environmental improvements, and governance procedures open and accessible to all (not just the politically connected).[60]

Obviously, the city hall hiring scandals dating from 2004 suggest that under Richard M. Daley, patronage hiring has not been quite the "political enemy" Clark supposed it was. Daley, for his part—as the revelations of insider favoritism have multiplied—has taken pains to recast his image as a public manager. In the early years of his mayoralty, Daley allowed reporters enough access to his day-to-day routines to impress on them the image of the tireless executive (according to James Atlas, "He claims to only need three or four hours of sleep.") willing to devote himself to the most mundane of administrative tasks (Richard H. Roeder characterized him as "a mayor . . . who familiarizes himself with arcane Building Department procedures").[61] Here is Richard M. Daley on Richard M. Daley in 2004, responding to inquiries by a journalist examining then-breaking corruption stories: "I wish I could be on top of every detail. I'm aware that the prevailing perception is that I am. Obviously, in an organization as large and multilayered as city government, that's impossible."[62]

Ultimately, Daley's success as Chicago's administrator-in-chief does not appear to be a function of anything particularly distinctive in his management style, or even of an uncanny knowledge of municipal arcana. The mayor has elicited strong performance from many subordinates due to some fairly unfashionable executive strengths: a strong hold on the local electorate, which produces the widely shared presumption that the man at the top will be in charge so long as he wants to be, and ruthlessness in punishing subordinates in the wake of publicized performance breakdowns. It is noteworthy that Richard M. Daley's approach to managing city services has also been the source of some of the most pointed criticisms of his administration. In chapter 2, I discussed sociologist Eric Klinenberg's analysis of social services privatization and the marginalization of emergency services within the police and fire departments, in light of the heat wave–provoked public health disaster of July 1995. Another sociologist, David Pellow, in his study of Chicago's since-terminated "blue-bag" recycling program, *Garbage Wars*, reaches a series of conclusions that are directly analogous to Klinenberg's. Chicago's recycling rate stalled at well below 10 percent, and the private firm that was in charge of the blue-bag program from its initiation in 1995, Waste Management, Inc., is poorly regarded both in terms of its environmental record and labor / management practices. In effect, quite like the municipal government's privatization of social services, favorable publicity for presumably cutting edge management practice—that is, contracting with private vendors— masked underlying performance deficiencies.[63]

The most typical criticism of Richard M. Daley follows the line of argument offered by journalist John Kass, that the younger Mayor Daley rules by means of a political machine, though one whose features have in one way or another been updated. In the early 1990s, political scientist William Grimshaw attempted to capture the old / new elements of Richard M. Daley's politics by characterizing him as a practitioner of "machine politics, reform style."[64] More recently, political scientist and former alderman Dick Simpson asserted, "Although Richard M. Daley is more enlightened and modern than his father in his attitudes and policies, he has not completely abandoned the machine politics that brought his father and him to power."[65]

My particular dissatisfaction with this framing of Daley is its assumption regarding the seemingly fixed categories of "machine" and "reform," neither of which offers especially acute insights on contemporary trends in municipal decision making. Richard M. Daley

is not a local party boss in the traditional sense. Apart from his es-
chewing the chairmanship of the Cook County Democratic Party
organization, the mainstays of the old Cook County machine—its
ward organizations—can barely get out the vote in contemporary
Chicago. This is why the Daley campaign operation had come to
rely on non-ward organization electoral groups such as the Hispanic Democratic Organization. And if "reform" denotes a normative vision of the physically commodious, smoothly run city, in that
particular sense Richard M. Daley can be considered a reformer. Although Terry Nichols Clark misreads the empirical substructure of
Richard M. Daley's electoral edifice by supposing that individual favors and preferential treatment have vanished from a contemporary
Chicago transformed by a "new political culture," he is correct in
discerning the core of Daley's normative vision:[66] to preside over a
satisfied consumer's republic.

For a committed populist such as journalist David Moberg—even
conceding that Daley's administration deserves credit for its reimagining Chicago as a global city—the consumer's republic is not an
arena for civic engagement. Not only does the vaunted Daley campaign operation satisfy itself with winning large pluralities in low-
turnout elections, but in general, Chicago's local officialdom choose
to conduct much of their business out of public view. Consider, for
example, this 2006 account of the proceedings of the Joint Review
Board, an advisory group whose members represent local taxing
jurisdictions (such as the CPS) and which examines tax increment
finance (TIF) district proposals (a much-used development tool)
prior to their consideration by the city council:

> They ate doughnuts, drank coffee, and listened to Steven Friedman, a
> private consultant, read a summary of his own report endorsing the
> LaSalle Central TIF. When he was done, Friedman looked up and
> asked, "Any questions?" For a few awkward seconds the board mem-
> bers sat in silence. Then chairman Eric Reese called for a vote. And just
> like that they recommended the creation of the costly and controversial
> TIF district. From start to finish, the meeting took maybe ten min-
> utes—not a word of discussion, no questions asked.[67]

Contemporary Chicago may well be a physically vibrant city whose economy has made the industrial to postindustrial "turn," but to Richard M. Daley's populist critics, it is also a city in need of grassroots civic revival. For civic populists, key features of Daley's political hold on Chicago—in particular, the business and civic elite's lockstep admiration for the mayor, combined with the widespread political apathy manifest by rank-and-file Chicagoans—represent real barriers to their dream of a city in which an engaged public is the norm rather than the exception.

So who is Richard M. Daley, and can his record be judged in any unequivocal fashion? In the first instance, it seems to me that Chicago's current Mayor Daley cannot be understood apart from his identity as a sophisticated urbanite, an individual who has lived his entire life in a great city. This has involved an extended "apprenticeship" growing up in the old neighborhood of Bridgeport, a working-class urban village to this day. In recent years, Daley and his wife Maggie have resided in Central Station, an upscale enclave of architecturally traditional (though newly built) townhouses southeast of the Loop. Daley's local experiences and extended travels have impressed on him the grace of street-centered urban development, as well as the subtle efficiencies of mixed uses. Daley is a self-taught Jacobsian whose greatest contribution to contemporary Chicago has been his administration's restoration of the city's physical fabric.

Though Richard M. Daley's considerable ego does not allow for much acknowledgement of influences, he is a mayor who has learned from the practice of peers such as Rudolph Giuliani, Ed Rendell, and John Norquist. Whereas Daley's father by the late 1960s had become the self-conscious defender of an older urban order—a Chicago in which family and ethnic allegiances were presumed to be fundamental sources of identity, a city of Mike Royko's ethnic "nation states"—the second mayor Daley is self-consciously an innovator, catching the wave of new trends in city management and planning (even if the latter, like new urbanism, are themselves explicitly traditionalist). Of particular significance—for Chicago, and as an exemplar of the new form of urban governance that has taken shape across the United States in the last two decades—is how Richard M. Daley's administration has recast the aims of municipal administration. No longer the provider of the full slate of essential local services (including last-resort emergency assistance)—and with no aspiration whatsoever to equalize individual and family opportunity through redistributive means—Daley's municipal government *facilitates* economic entrepreneurship, neighborhood redevelopment, and privately devised policy innovation (for example, charter schools). This redirection of municipal policy has not produced an appreciably smaller municipal government—public works are expensive and over the years the Daley administration payroll has dipped only slightly—but it has substantially narrowed its aims. In effect, municipal government in Chicago has become an "entrepreneurial state," collaborating with major firms and key investors in advancing *their agendas*, promoting the city's overall image and, in particular instances, the fortunes of "promising" neighborhoods, and delivering a residue of traditional services such as police and fire protection, sanitation, and basic physical infrastructure.[68]

Viewed in this fashion, Richard M. Daley and his record as mayor do not fit very comfortably within the framing of Chicago's politics that is reflexively adopted by most commentators, that is, the war without end between "machine" and "reform." Daley is a mayoral innovator whose breaks with tradition share little with the older conventions of urban reform. He is a formidable campaigner whose electoral operation has outgrown the ward-based politics of his father, even as he has benefited from two parallel "de-mobilizations": the shrinking electorate of the 1990s and 2000s; the longstanding absence of a Chicago Republican Party. By aligning his reputation as mayor with a program of physical redevelopment that is so much more nuanced than the urban renewal era's "federal bulldozer," in the coming years Richard M. Daley is sure to become a touchstone for the country's next generation of ambitious municipal chief executives. Though the career of Richard M. Daley cannot be wholly extracted from the long line of his city's *local* politics, the sources of his agenda and the legacies of his administration reach well beyond Chicago.

East Garfield Park is one of the neighborhoods that suffered the most as the Second City wound down; it lost more than half of its population and housing units between 1960 and 1990.

THE CITY OF NEIGHBORHOODS

CHICAGO IS THE city of neighborhoods, or at least that is how it is so often described. Clicking on the "Exploring Chicago" link on the municipal government's Web site permits one to investigate neighborhood tours and download community maps.[1] In the summer of 2008, clicking on an icon entitled "Chicago Neighborhood Festivals" revealed that sixty-three such events were scheduled for the month of June alone. The municipal government's view of neighborhood celebrations is highly inclusive. In addition to characteristically locale-anchored events—such as the Bronzeville Cultural Fair and Jefferson Park Community Festival (both in June)—and ethnically inflected gatherings—such as the Croatian Fest, Ginza Holiday Festival, Serbfest, Taste of Greece, Taste of Polonia, and Ukrainian Festival (each presented in August)—there was an array of listings that substantially stretched the notion of "neighborhood festival." These included what might be considered problem-oriented events—"No Crime Day" (August 16) and the Annual Stay-N-School Picnic (August 30)—as well as celebrations reflecting emergent cultural trends. In August the upscale food retailer sponsored the "Whole Foods Market Flavor Fest." In the previous month Near West Side Union Park was the site of the Pitchfork Music Festival, an event bringing to Chicago nationally known rock, hip-hop, and alternative music performers. The Pitchfork Festival's connection to adjoining commercial and residential areas appears to be purely coincidental.

Some of the 2008 neighborhood festivals evoked a passing Chicago. For example, Shades of Riverview 13 recalled the long-demolished amusement park that once bordered the North Branch of the Chicago River. On August 17, the Altgeld Oldtimers Reunion returned former residents to a Far South Side public housing development. This event expresses a substantial irony. Since the Chicago Housing Authority's initiation of its "Plan for Transformation" in 2000 to redevelop its projects as "mixed-income communities," not only has the public housing agency demolished thousands of its apartments, it has typically renamed developments as a means of distinguishing the new CHA from the old, bad CHA. Nevertheless, there are current and past residents of the CHA's as-yet untransformed developments, among which are the Altgeld Gardens, who recall these residential communities with considerable fondness.

For visitors to Chicago, its status as "the city of neighborhoods" is unavoidable. In the third edition of *Fodor's Compass American Guide* to Chicago, author Jack Schnedler observes: "Visitors and residents amble Chicago to savor the celebrities, the architecture, the lakefront, the museums, the neighborhoods, the dining, the shopping, and the other obvious allures."[2] Very early in *Fodor's Chicago 2007* guide, on a page headed "Authentic Chicago," the reader is instructed to "visit an ethnic neighborhood." In this instance, "ethnic neighborhood" is defined expansively, for example, the characterization of North Side Andersonville as Swedish, Middle Eastern, and gay.[3] The current edition of *Time Out Chicago* includes a section entitled "What's in a Name?" that begins with these words: "Some say it's the City of Neighborhoods."[4] Journalist Alex Kotlowitz's *Never a City So Real*, a volume in Crown Publishers' Journeys Series, provides possibly the most encyclopedic introduction to Chicago's neighborhoods. Inside the front cover of his book is a map identifying 198 neighborhoods. Yet even this listing is incomplete. Kotlowitz's text notes that the number of neighborhoods is "over 200 if you count a few [the map] missed."[5]

But of course, all great cities are cities of neighborhoods. Consider how the English writer V. S. Pritchett explains the "muddle" of London's complicated geography, in *London Perceived* (1962):

Historically, London has grown not by planning, but by swallowing up the countryside village by village. It spread outside its medieval walls into the fields of Holborn, into the "liberties" of the East End, the ruralities of Southwark, the village of Charing—called that because there the Thames made a 'char' or bend—and eventually met the religious settlement of Westminister expanding eastward to meet it. The muddle is simply a muddle of villages that eventually surround the parks of kings . . . In the parks that stretch for many square miles from Westminister to Notting Hill and from Marylebone to Primrose Hill, and south of the river to Battersea—and to speak only of the centre and to leave out the greenery of Hampstead or Blackheath and the deer park of Richmond—one might be a hundred miles from London.[6]

A city of neighborhoods, indeed. Pritchett's Holborn, Westminister, Notting Hill, Hampstead, and Richmond are but a few entries from a roster of old villages that have long constituted well-known pieces of London's neighborhood mosaic.

New York's equally muddled network of neighborhoods also includes "absorbed" communities such as Greenwich Village, but notably, the city is distinguished by areas such as the Garment District and Wall Street, whose identities derive from their economic functions. The emergence of such local areas is not necessarily the result of organic forces. Historian Max Page has recounted the story of the Fifth Avenue Association: "founded in April 1907 by a small group of property owners, residents, and retailers with the motto 'to conserve at all times the highest and best interests of the Fifth Avenue section.'" During the 1910s and 1920s the association advocated zoning controls, street widening, and other infrastructure improvements with the aim of preserving Fifth Avenue above 59th Street as an elite residential enclave while promoting the avenue below 59th Street as an upscale commercial corridor. "The central idea behind the [Fifth Avenue Association's] advocacy was to retain an exclusive retail and residential area, where immigrants would be scarce and beggars absent, where the more flamboyant popular culture growing on Broadway would be held in check, and where a genteel, controlled commercial culture would hold sway."[7] In New York and elsewhere, as common as the neighborhood that "happens" is the neighborhood that is "made."

Merely by surveying the names of Kotlowitz's incomplete aggregation of 198 neighborhoods, one can pick out local areas whose identities spring from varying sources. There are the neighborhoods stamped by the work done there: Back o' the Yards (the exotic rendering of a locale I have never heard a Chicagoan enunciate any other way than "Back *of* the Yards") near the old Union Stock Yard site; Pullman, where the railroad sleeping car magnate founded his factory and worker housing complex; and Medical Center, a cluster of hospitals to the west of the Loop. Bronzeville, Chinatown, and Little Italy reflect the particulars of Chicago's diverse ethnic heritage. Unadorned location is the calling card of other neighborhoods in a city whose topography does not lend itself to descriptors such as "Heights" or "Hill" (but which has a celebrated lakefront): Near North, Near South Side, Near West Side, South Shore. My own experience confirms Kotlowitz's assertion that his neighborhood list is incomplete. Having for two decades lived in Uptown, a neighborhood renowned for its fiercely contested aldermanic elections, land use disputes, and arguably overconcentrated homeless population, I have noticed an emergent local designation, East Ravenswood, that is promoted by some realtors and evidently preferred by many of my neighbors just to the west. East Ravenswood is a sylvan image in its own right, and by so redesignating some of Uptown's western residential blocks, disconnects their identity from Uptown and its seemingly unending gentrification wars.

A defensible single-statement summary of *The Death and Life of Great American Cities* would be that "successful neighborhoods are the building blocks of successful cities," yet a reconsideration of Jane Jacobs's approach to neighborhoods reveals a perspective at some variance with the fluidity of sources and identities I have just sketched. Jacobs was a sufficiently acute empiricist to acknowledge that some neighborhoods were essentially residential in character (which in her view tended to be a negative attribute) while others were anchored by large-scale business enterprises or other institutions such as universities or hospitals. She also famously distinguished the small-scale, face-to-face environment of the "street neighborhood" from the "district," an aggregation of street neighborhoods whose "chief function" was "to mediate between the indispensable, but inherently politically powerless, street neighborhoods, and the inherently powerful city as a whole." And of course, Jacobs was the arch-exponent of neighborhood diversity: "Nor can districts be duplicates of one another; they differ immensely, and should. A city is not a collection of repetitious towns. An interesting district has a character of its own and specialties of its own."[8]

Yet as is revealed by Jacobs's specification of the district's role within the larger urban order, her organic conception of the city is also decidedly functionalist. The city is a very large and complicated organism. The fundamental unit within the city is the neighborhood, and the density of inter-neighborhood contacts ("cross use") and reciprocity of neighborhood ("district") / "city" (government) relations determine the degree of well-being achieved by the encompassing urban organism. Given these bedrock propositions, Jacobs's menu of remediation—"zoning for diversity," in-filling public housing developments, official recognition of districts as advisory planning jurisdictions, and so forth—represents an essentially generic set of policy practices.

The many and heterogeneous intellectual heirs of Jacobs, such as 1970s-era "neighborhood government" advocate Milton Kotler or contemporary new urbanist architects, however, have tended to defend and seek to protect neighborhoods in radically disparate ways.[9] Indeed, there is a long history of neighborhood conceptualization, remediation, and conflict that includes precursors to Jacobs—some of whose ideas she roundly excoriated—as well as subsequent parties to what might be called the "great neighborhood debates." Chicago—and Chicagoans—have made many contributions to these debates. Nevertheless, as I review and compare the many strands of

American neighborhood discourse, I will offer conclusive evidence that Chicago cannot be *the* city of neighborhoods. Chicago's neighborhood debates have shared far too many attributes with the neighborhood debates of other cities for its particular neighborhoods or even its network of neighborhoods to be unique. Yet there remains the paradox of why so many observers of Chicago have adopted this trope to distinguish this city. In part, this is surely a function of Chicago's tumultuous neighborhood history. Yet even more, the idea of neighborhood as it has evolved in Chicago and elsewhere has offered Chicagoans a way to reinterpret, or more to the point, to rationalize various persistent and inhospitable attributes of their city. By altering the popular perception of some of their city's least admirable traits, Chicagoans' sense of their city of neighborhoods can be sustained as a normative proposition. Yet Chicagoans, like Londoners and New Yorkers, bring myriad specific meanings to their definitions of neighborhood. Nor are Chicagoans unshakable in their commitment to neighborhoods. If circumstances dictate, they will indeed renege on their oft-repeated fealty to their city's local places and communal networks.

AN IDEA AS MUCH AS A PLACE

Americans discovered neighborhoods within their large cities in the middle decades of the nineteenth century. In 1800 the population of no American city exceeded 100,000, with Philadelphia's 81,000 residents comprising the country's largest urban agglomeration. Yet Philadelphia in the early years of the nineteenth century remained—like Boston, New York, Baltimore, and Charleston, South Carolina—a walking city of "substantial dwellings fronting on the major streets and alley dwellings for the poor crowded in behind," which were only a short distance from "workplaces remaining close to the older districts near the port." Robert Fishman explains how the actual physical growth of Philadelphia deviated from William Penn's late-seventeenth-century vision of a city rising between two roughly parallel river courses:

The city advanced slowly as a solid mass from the Delaware to the Schuylkill, advancing from east to west much the way contemporaneous New York City building was advancing from south to north along Manhattan Island. Only in the 1840s did the city reach the "Center Square" that Penn had laid out as the midpoint of his decentralized city of the 1680s.[10]

However, by midcentury, the gradual expansion of Philadelphia and New York alike had given way to a new, explosive phase of industrial growth, and the environmentally homogenous walking city would never again typify metropolitan urbanism. In 1850, New York's population exceeded 660,000, and Philadelphia, Baltimore, and Boston held 409,000, 169,000, and 137,000 residents, respectively.[11] Coinciding with this sudden burst in population growth, the internal structure of American cities began to differentiate. In the words of Sam Bass Warner Jr.:

> A special flavor pervaded the mixed downtown areas of the period. They were districts densely settled by unprepossessing offices and stores and factories of all kinds, and even by sugar refineries and slaughterhouses, side by side with the more genteel firms that dealt in banking, law, insurance, or cloth . . . Surrounding this characteristically mixed downtown section were two types of neighborhood, the slums and the streets of fashion.[12]

The emergent internal structure of the industrializing cities described by Warner produced two approaches to thinking about neighborhoods. The more renowned of these lines of thought and action confronted what was glibly termed the "immigrant problem." Yet the other approach, which one might say focused on the "streets of fashion," is also illustrative of how American cities were being reconceptualized. Historian David Schuyler argues that in the middle decades of the nineteenth century, figures such as architect Andrew Jackson Downing and landscape designer Frederick Law Olmsted promoted a hybrid vision intended to ameliorate the impacts of industrial urbanization by incorporating within cities restorative features of the countryside. Major cities' formation of municipal park systems during this era is an oft-told tale, but urban pastoralists such as Downing and Olmsted also promoted a strategy of neighborhood development that was both arcadian and—to apply a contemporary notion—modular.[13] Here is Schuyler's commentary on Downing's pamphlet, "Our Country Villages":

> It was a community that, by conscious design and allocation of public and private spaces, attempted to reconcile the family's desire for a home amid natural surroundings with the trenchant realities of urban growth and change. A house in such a suburb enabled a family to escape the congestion, disease, and "immoral influences" of the city and to rear children in more beneficial surroundings, while retaining ease of access to urban jobs and to the social and cultural attractions of the metropolis.[14]

Though Downing's country village placed the multiplying unpleasantnesses of the industrial city at a distance, it was situated to allow ready access to the urban center's business establishments, government offices, museums, and theaters. And of course, over the decades many such country villages and streetcar suburbs—like their London predecessors—were absorbed within expanding metropolises. Olmsted's vision of the commodious urban residential district derived from the analogy he drew between the well-designed home and city: "If a house to be used for many different purposes must have many rooms and passages of various dimensions and variously lighted and furnished, not less must such a metropolis be specifically adapted at different points to different ends."[15] A city was a house of many rooms, and from our standpoint, those many rooms constitute the network of neighborhoods to be found in any great city.

The main line of early neighborhood observation was pursued by Olmsted's younger contemporaries, settlement house pioneers such as Lillian Wald of New York, Robert Woods in Boston, and Jane Addams of Chicago. In his history of low-income housing provision in Boston, *From the Puritans to the Projects*, Lawrence Vale observes that "the settlement movement played a seminal role in establishing the neighborhood—rather than the individual building—as the appropriate unit for housing reform, and it consolidated the belief that such reform must encompass social and moral intervention as well as architectural design."[16] For the young, typically college-educated settlement residents, their choices of vocation and place of residence thrust them into what was, in many respects, an unknown city. Her most recent biographer, Louise Knight, reports that Addams and her close associate Ellen Gates Starr spent two months in early 1889 scouting locations—seeking, in Addams's words, a "low and dangerous neighborhood"—for the site of what would become Hull House. Knight adds: "The choice of the Nineteenth Ward was daring. People of Starr and Addams's class lived mostly on the North and South Sides and viewed the West Side as the exotic other, an unexplored, darkly threatening place, indeed, as a slum."[17]

The following is a portion of Jane Addams's description of the Hull House area presented in *Twenty Years at Hull House* (1910), reflecting on her early days in the neighborhood:

> The houses of the ward, for the most part wooden, were originally built for one family but now are occupied by several. They are after the type of the inconvenient frame cottages found in the poorer suburbs twenty years ago. Many of them were built where they now stand; others were brought thither on rollers, because their previous sites had been taken for factories. The fewer brick tenement buildings which are three or four stories high are comparatively new, and there are few large tenements. The little wooden houses have a temporary aspect, and for this reason, perhaps, the tenement-house legislation in Chicago is totally inadequate. Rear tenements flourish; many houses have no water supply save the faucet in the back yard, there are no fire escapes, the garbage and ashes are placed in wooden boxes which are fastened to the street pavements.[18]

One notes, of course, the careful detailing of housing features, which has been preceded by a similarly precise specification of which nationality groups lived within the district. Yet just as revealing is Addams's choice of designation for the Hull House area: not the Near West Side, not—given the area's ethnic heterogeneity—something like "Little Babel," not "Little Italy" given that group's local predominance, but rather, "the ward." Young Jane Addams was observing a perplexing and complex district within a rapidly expanding metropolis, and at this point in her experience of Chicago and her new neighborhood, she falls back on the local jurisdictional parceling of the city's space to designate the neighborhood.

Nor was Addams alone in struggling to typify just what constituted the working-class quarters that were the most numerous urban residential enclaves in this era. Jacob Riis, in his celebrated exposé of late-nineteenth-century slum conditions, *How the Other Half Lives* (1890), variously resorts to jurisdictional definitions (the Fourth Ward), physical features (for example, "the Bend"—the curving section of Mulberry Street along which the area's most degraded tenements were located—and "Five Points"), and resident identities ("Chinatown," "Jewtown") to designate locales within Manhattan's Lower East Side.[19] In sum, the emergence of the first broadly circulated conceptualization of neighborhood in the United States did not result from "ethnic communities" forming in the wake of mass immigration, nor did the settlement house progressives arrive in and find neighborhoods. Instead, the settlement house residents, various of their neighbors, pioneering social scientists (often collaborating with the settlement houses), and somewhat later, the emergent city planning profession, began to specify a set of local attributes that we now intellectually bundle as "neighborhood."

The scope of settlement house work was enormous, though in popular memory it is the "social service" activities that undoubtedly predominate: the formation of kindergartens and boys' and girls' clubs, children's art classes, adult education programs, and social "receptions" for various local nationality groups. There was also advocacy work. Louise Knight notes that Jane Addams and Ellen Starr "tracked down aid for women whose husbands had abandoned them, government insurance payments for widows, child support owed by husbands who had abandoned their wife and children, and damages for injured employees."[20] But in addition to hosting all manner of community activities within the Hull House complex and offering various forms of direct and indirect social support to the local population, Hull House residents researched the social, housing, and working conditions of the Near West Side. In 1893, the investigations of local sweatshops by one of Hull House's early residents, Florence Kelley, had earned sufficient public notice to result in her appointment as state factory inspector by Illinois governor John Peter Altgeld. Two years later, the *Hull-House Maps and Papers: A Presentation of Nationalities and Wages in a Congested District of Chicago, Together with Comments and Essays on Problems Growing Out of the Social Conditions* (1895), whose contributors included Addams, Starr, and Kelley, was published by Thomas Y. Crowell and Company.[21]

The breadth of the Hull House agenda was not unique. City planning scholar Daphne Spain describes the program of Boston's South End House in comparably expansive terms:

> The goals of South End House were educational rather than evangelical. Residents mapped conditions in the neighborhood and established the South End Improvement Association to carry out their recommendations. South End House was founded to "bring about a better and more beautiful life in its neighborhood and district and to develop new ways (through study and action in this locality) of meeting some of the serious problems of society." It also worked to create the "healthy corporate vitality [of] a well-ordered village"; to investigate local labor conditions; to "furnish a neutral ground where separated classes, rich and poor, professional and industrial, capitalist and wage-earner, may meet each other on the basis of common humanity"; and to take part in municipal affairs.[22]

Of particular note is the aspiration to achieve neighborhood conditions that could be likened to "a well-ordered village." Just such language was chosen by Andrew Jackson Downing to characterize his mid-nineteenth-century developments for the privileged. Although Progressive-era historian Allen F. Davis observes of settlement residents that "most grew up in pleasant residential neighborhoods in an urban environment far removed from the slum areas," the sense that a good neighborhood ought to be built on close interpersonal relations, the reduction of fundamental social cleavages (such as business ownership versus workers), and the formation of a collective ("corporate") identity—in short, would evoke the virtues associated with small town life—was a common impulse among reformers confronting the headlong urbanization of late-nineteenth-century America.[23]

Very nearly the antithesis of the settlement house leaders' neighborhood communalism was the brutal pragmatism of mid-twentieth-century urban renewal proponents such as Robert Moses of New York. In *The Power Broker*, Robert Caro relates a vignette passed on to him by one of Moses's principal assistants, Sid Shapiro. While inspecting a potential expressway route in Queens, Moses's entourage—inside an automobile and unrecognized—observed a demonstration whose leaders likened New York's Coordinator of Construction to Joseph Stalin and Adolph Hitler. To Shapiro's surprise, Moses was amused by the proceedings: "He laughed and laughed. RM really got a kick out of it." Such stories confirmed Caro's sense that Moses was personally gratified by decimating homes and neighborhoods as he pushed expressways across New York City. Moses's self-assessment was in equal measure blunt and panoramic: "You can draw any kind of picture that you like on a clean slate and indulge your every whim in the wilderness in laying out a New Delhi, Canberra, or Brasilia, but when you operate in an overbuilt metropolis, you have to hack your way through with a meat ax."[24]

Historian Joel Schwartz's careful account of post–World War II redevelopment initiatives in Moses's overbuilt metropolis, *The New York Approach*, offers an alternative interpretation of Moses's motives, characterizing him as a "loyal instrument" of liberal forces that had "continually campaigned for local improvements that had a stubborn tendency to reach fruition as middle-class apartments on broad boulevards. Pre–World War I hopes to gentrify the Lower East Side were the basis for the more scientific blueprints of the Regional Plan Association of New York to remove the working class for more desired residents."[25] It is Schwartz's contention that Moses's efforts from the late 1940s into the 1960s to equip New York City with a modern transportation network, eliminate slums, and produce new, desirable middle-class residential neighborhoods constituted an agenda that he shared with many mayors, business leaders, and city planners.

In the middle decades of the twentieth century most forward-thinking municipal leaders and planners presumed that older urban neighborhoods were in need of clearance—or at least, of significant physical upgrading—and that by rebuilding and modernizing such inner-city areas a new, functionally up-to-date metropolis could be produced. During this period the principal public policy tools for modernizing the American city were Title I of the 1949 U.S. Housing Act, which inaugurated federal government fiscal support for local redevelopment activity, and the Federal-Aid ("Interstate") Highway Act of 1956, which funded the metropolitan expressway networks built in the following decades. Title I urban redevelopment was a program whose aims were numerous and subject to highly selective emphasis:

> Downtown business interests saw it as a way to lure the well-to-do from the periphery to the center, a development, they believed, that would slow down decentralization and shore up the central business district. To other business interests, especially the building trades, it was a way to stimulate business enterprise; and to organized labor it was a way to generate employment. Big-city mayors viewed federal aid for urban redevelopment as an opportunity to replace low-income slums and blighted areas with middle- and high-income neighborhoods, a move, they thought, that would alleviate the growing fiscal problem. City planners viewed it as an opportunity to redesign the metropolis along more efficient lines.[26]

Robert Fogelson's cataloging of interests and their expectations of Title I redevelopment goes on to note the provisional support expressed by housing advocates, who without qualification applauded the public housing provisions (Title III) of the 1949 Housing Act and anticipated that Title I would be used to improve slum neighborhoods. Nevertheless, the Title I initiative's most prominent constituencies accepted—with Robert Moses—the view that thousands of acres of inner-city land, a sizable portion of which was occupied by poor and working-class urbanites, their dwellings, and neighborhood institutions, needed to be removed in order to promote urban revitalization, broadly defined. Across the United States, cities' experiences with carrying through Title I urban redevelopment—which, with the passage of the 1954 Housing Act, won its popular designation, urban renewal—was varied, though frequently acrimonious. In a host of cities, including Atlanta, Boston, Cincinnati, San Francisco, and Chicago, neighborhood activists claimed that urban renewal proponents, rather than aiming to improve inner-city living conditions, sought to clear strategically located residential areas in order to fortify downtown business districts.[27]

Chicago never produced a Robert Moses. Ceding to an appointee the metropolitan-spanning redevelopment power exercised by Moses was not Richard J. Daley's way. Nevertheless, Daley, in league with a team of planning technicians, reshaped Chicago's neighborhood map in the quest to fend off the "urban crisis" of the 1950s and 1960s. As historian Amanda Seligman explains: "Daley's administration envisioned renewing the city with a ring of clearance and redevelopment around the downtown. That buffer area would protect existing businesses and new government buildings in the Loop and also spread remedial effects outward into the city's residential neighborhoods."[28] The sense of extant neighborhoods as a resource to be manipulated in the interest of broader city advancement permeates the "Chicago 21" plan of 1973:

The structure of the Central Communities in the 21st Century should be determined by present and future transportation networks. Between the Lake and the River there is a high concentration of transportation systems which extend north, south and west from the major focal point of the City, its Central Business District. The accessibility network should be used as a spine for future development. Building intensity should vary directly with the accessibility of any given sites . . . The South Community area has limited residential development or community fabric. It has, however, extensive unused land ringed by older buildings and obsolete uses. The very low density and scattered nature of development is largely unrelated in value or function to the near-by Central Business District.[29]

To what degree Richard J. Daley personally subscribed to this highly mechanistic view of redevelopment and neighborhoods is the subject of considerable debate. One point of view on this matter is memorably encapsulated by the Daley contemporary who recalled him as having a "kind of worship for the pouring of concrete."[30]

In spite of Mayor Daley's unchallenged political leadership in the early 1960s, there were neighborhood objectors to his redevelopment plans. In the Near West Side Harrison-Halsted redevelopment area—otherwise known as Little Italy—which was slated for substantial clearance to make way for the construction of the University of Illinois at Chicago campus, between 1961 and 1963 a group of activists mounted a furious campaign to block demolitions.[31] A few years later, the leader of these neighborhood insurgents, Florence Scala, described what happened to the Harrison-Halsted area as an "uprooting":

> I lived on the same block for over forty-five years; my father was there before me. It takes away a kind of stability that big cities need. Lots of the people have moved into housing no better than the kind they lived in. Some have moved into public housing. The old people have really had it worse. Some have moved into "nicer" neighborhoods, but they're terribly unhappy, those I've spoken with.[32]

Nor were protests of this sort unique to Chicago. In early 1963, Boston Redevelopment Authority personnel organized a public meeting to describe their plans for the Charlestown neighborhood:

> For all the booing, catcalls, and what some described as complete chaos, the opposition on January 7 was for the most part precise, articulate, and concerned with the substantive issues of plan content and planning procedures. While Boston newspapers put a great deal of emphasis on rabble rousers with political motives who appeared from outside Charlestown, 36 of the 39 speakers were members of the Charlestown community . . . [T]he majority of the crowd, loud and rough in classic Townie style, wished not to throw renewal out of Charlestown but to bring about changes in the BRA's approach and in the content of its plan.[33]

The objections of the local "Townies" to "plan content and planning procedures" typified the reaction to renewal voiced in many neighborhoods. In the first instance, inner-city residents feared displacement from communities of long standing, especially given the redevelopment planners' penchant for posh high-rise redevelopment schemes. And often, neighborhood activists were just as aggrieved by the high-handedness of the redevelopment planners. The latter seemed to dictate rather than consult, often using public "hearings" to deliver scripted revelations of their designs for the neighborhood to come.

The early 1960s marked the birth of what a generation ago Harry C. Boyte called "the backyard revolution."[34] Federally funded urban renewal and interstate highway projects had disrupted many inner-city areas, and largely unrecognized at the time, deindustrialization was beginning to undermine the material prosperity of working-class neighborhoods in many northern cities. Widely noticed at the time was a third unsettler of central city neighborhoods: racial transition. In Chicago, the demographic profile of large portions of the South and West Sides shifted from white to African American between 1950 and 1980, a painful process that generated many varieties of contested community.

The backyard revolution coincided with a reassertion of European ethnic identity. Catholic priest, sociologist, and longtime Chicagoan Andrew Greeley forcefully articulated this line of thought in his book, *Neighborhood* (1977). An unusual amalgam of photographic documentation and social criticism, *Neighborhood* is a very telling reconsideration of the urban social upheavals of the 1960s. Greeley's themes include a paean to "the ethnic miracle" of immigrant upward mobility, as well as frequent, quasi-Jacobsian tributes to neighborhood life:

> The neighborhood, then, as a strong, powerful unit of urban society, is a postulate of the principle of the subsidiary function; if you believe in "no bigger than necessary" you have to believe in the neighborhood. Or, to put the matter somewhat differently, if you believe that human nature is the nature of the social animal, you have got to believe in the

neighborhood. The modernizers believe in neither, and it is therefore impossible to argue with them.[35]

Among the modernizers Greeley excoriates by name is Robert Moses, but *Neighborhood* is not a volume principally concerned with the threat posed to neighborhoods by city planning. Rather, Greeley views the neighborhood as a more fundamentally significant strand of the American social fabric: "the final justification for the neighborhood is that it is a guarantee and a protection for human freedom."[36] The neighborhood turmoil of the 1960s was not merely a contest pitting whites against blacks. It was a deeper conflict between modernizers and those reliant on dense interpersonal networks, anchoring local institutions, and neighborhood continuity. In Greeley's view, the old—and threatened—ethnic enclave is one of the principal bastions of the American way of life.

As if in counterpoint, another variety of backyard revolt seethed in urban America's African American neighborhoods. As the highwater mark of integrationist civil rights rhetoric ebbed after the mid-1960s, black activists in many cities began to call for the decentralization of municipal services and federal program implementation. But this agenda extended well beyond the mechanics of governmental operations. A friendly observer concluded, "They want to stop being colonized. They want their dependence on the benevolence of ruling outsiders (most of whom, in any case, are not very benevolent) to cease."[37] The persistent failure of local municipal and school district officials to deliver good services and meaningful integration to African American urbanites had engendered a reaction whose first premise was that if blacks were only left to themselves, they were perfectly capable of policing their streets, running local public schools, and otherwise sustaining their neighborhoods.

Yet there was more to demands for "Black Power" and "community control" than the rejection of failed integration. In his depiction of the aims of the black leadership of the insurgent Ocean Hill-Brownsville school district of Brooklyn—site of a bitter neighborhood school board–United Federation of Teachers conflict from the spring of 1968 into the following year—historian Jerald Podair describes the "threefold" challenge posed by local activists:

> First, it attacked the idea of the "culture of poverty" as an explanation for low black student achievement, and defended the validity of lower-class black culture against attacks by whites. Second, it questioned what it saw as the shallowness and fraud of the core "middle-class" values of the city—"race blind" individual merit, unbridled competition, and materialism—associating them specifically with whites. Finally, it rejected the moderate cultural pluralism that had come to prevail in New York by the mid-1960s—one which stressed the primacy of individual identity within a host of overlapping ethnic, racial, religious, class, and civic group affiliations—and sought to replace it with a radicalized version based almost exclusively on racial status.[38]

When the Ocean Hill-Brownsville school board turned its attention to the practical question of reshaping coursework within the neighborhood's schools, it proposed "a curriculum based on the glory and greatness of African American culture, history, and experience."[39] Ironically, just as cultural reappraisal and celebration animated the thinking of Catholic intellectuals such as Andrew Greeley, like impulses motivated the Black Power advocates of Ocean Hill-Brownsville. And in each instance, the urban neighborhood of the early- to mid-twentieth century was viewed as ground from which communal virtue sprang, and on which communal virtue could be sustained.

The backyard revolution's advocates typically spoke for communities experiencing some form of threat. By the 1970s, an interpretation of neighborhood that was at once more optimistic and instrumental emerged. Consider, for example, sociologist Sharon Zukin's account of Manhattan's resurgent SoHo in *Loft Living*. Predictably, SoHo's comeback—which was visible by the mid-1970s—was the result of a complicated sequence of events, notably, its mid-twentieth-century decline as a light manufacturing quarter, a subsequent plan to redevelop the area as an extension of the Wall Street business district, SoHo's unforeseen discovery by artists seeking large, inexpensive, well-lit studio space, and ultimately, the marketing of converted loft buildings as fashionable dwellings. Through her examination of how the new SoHo came to be, Zukin inferred a broader insight concerning shifting popular tastes, and relatedly, the shifting popular perception of older city districts:

> The cultural style that is associated with loft living—the "loft lifestyle"—shows a middle-class preference for open space and artistic modes of production, as well as a more general nostalgia about the "smaller past" of the great industrial era. The market in living lofts, along with the movement for the historic preservation of buildings that are not old, suggests how quickly these sentiments about space and time can be exploited for their commercial possibilities . . . So loft living takes its place—with "brownstoning," "parenting," and simply "Living," as a weekly section of the *New York Times* is called—among the cultural gerunds of our time.[40]

Formerly industrial SoHo's tightly built-up street grid, unadorned masonry and cast iron facades, and naturally illuminated interior spaces were redefined as aesthetically distinctive, and within a few years a new real estate trend had taken hold. Yet this linking of dwelling preferences to currents in popular taste as leavened by clever marketing is not unique to this neighborhood or era. Andrew Jackson Downing's "country villages" similarly aligned a cluster of aesthetic values to a particular constituency's dwelling preferences and, yes, sold a vision of community by defining a "lifestyle" associated with that physical ordering of community. In the late 1940s, Levitt & Sons also orchestrated just such a convergence of perceived dwelling need, aesthetics, and lifestyle in selling their iconic, eponymous Long Island suburban community, for as one real estate broker observed: "People don't buy a house. They buy a neighborhood. People will buy a back yard, they'll buy friendly neighbors who smile, they'll buy well-kept lawns."[41]

In retrospect it has become clear that among the serious miscalculations by mid-twentieth-century urban renewal planners was their enthusiasm for a seemingly unvarying, bargain-basement modernism: nondescript commercial and residential high-rise towers and low-rise, low-density residential developments in most respects indistinguishable from suburban counterparts. For myriad cultural, economic, and public policy reasons, the American middle class was not ready to return to cities in the 1960s and 1970s, but for even the minority that considered that prospect, the new central cities of the era offered little positive inducement.[42] How times— and American cities—have changed. In contemporary central Chicago, prospective residents can choose between loft developments and residential communities offering an array of historicist "looks" including prairie, Richardsonian romanesque, and even Georgian. Then there are the associated amenities: access to the Chicago River, health clubs, and if one chooses, gated security. The residential Chicago that is taking shape to the north, west, and south of the Loop is an amenities-rich, neo-romantic metropolis evoking the city's "great industrial era."

By thematizing neighborhood public spaces, Chicago's city government seeks to reinforce this real estate trend. In the 1990s, a pair of classically inspired pavilions were placed alongside major intersections at the north and south ends of the Greektown restaurant strip west of the Loop, and between these gateway structures, sidewalk improvements likewise featured Hellenic motifs. Coincidentally, the municipal government's proposal to visually specify a stretch of North Halsted Street as a gay commercial area generated heated debate. The main focus of attention was a pair of "massive, steel, flying saucer-like structures . . . ringed with a rainbow of lights in red, orange, yellow, green, blue, and purple" to be placed at the Grace Street and Belmont Avenue intersections with Halsted Street. While one proponent of the so-called Boystown streetscaping plans argued that the entry structures, streetside pylons, and sidewalk repaving would provide a "pedestrian friendly feel," a local merchant was concerned that the street improvements would contribute to the impression that this was a "gays-only community." Ultimately, city officials, local residents, and merchants compromised on a more subdued program of sidewalk improvements, which did not include the Belmont and Grace gateway structures.[43]

In a few instances, neighborhood thematization efforts have extended beyond public space and sidewalk improvements. Since the early 1990s, the City of Chicago has worked with community activists in several South Side neighborhoods to mount redevelopment initiatives derived from the vision of a revitalized Bronzeville, the once-commonplace designation for the northern end of the pre–World War II Black Belt. Joining the rehabilitation of several historic structures to a broader program of residential reinvestment and heritage tourism promotion, the Bronzeville initiative has, at the least, produced a substantial movement of middle-class African American families back to the Near- and Mid-South Sides.[44] More geographically and ethnically diffuse than the Bronzeville revitalization campaign is the Historic Chicago Bungalow Initiative (HCBI), which was inaugurated in 2000. The HCBI promotes the preservation of a very characteristic Chicago building type—the single-floor brick bungalow (constituting approximately one-third of Chicago's single-family homes)—that dominates the housing stock in many of the city's Northwest and Southwest Side neighborhoods. With the age of these structures typically exceeding three-quarters of a century, financial assistance for rehabilitation by bungalow owners serves both to stabilize neighborhood housing stocks and preserve one of Chicago's distinctive architectural types.[45]

It is also true that the development trends fueling the emergence of these new neighborhood identities can generate community contestation, which was clearly one component of the North Halsted streetscaping debate. In the summer of 2006, the *Chicago Tribune* reported that an organization in Humboldt Park called the Puerto Rican Agenda was seeking to recruit Puerto Rican professionals to settle in their neighborhood. A heavily Puerto Rican, poor- to working-class neighborhood since the 1960s, Humboldt Park has begun to experience a spillover of condominium development and artist relocation from Wicker Park on its eastern margin. As gentrification has swept Wicker Park, many of its younger artist residents have looked for housing in adjoining areas, and some Puerto

Rican activists in Humboldt Park fear an associated upsurge of high-end residential development in their neighborhood. Ironically, local groups in Humboldt Park have in the past sought to preserve its *working-class* Puerto Rican identity, but in the face of contemporary real estate forces, an amended vision of a multi-class Puerto Rican Humboldt Park has begun to form.[46]

So we see that one of the key words of the urban lexicon, "neighborhood," is in reality a fluid and much contested idea. Many are the ways that Americans have conceptualized neighborhoods: as frontiers of assimilation, providing village-like communalism for the weary newcomer; as strategic resources in campaigns to arrest physical decay and modernize the metropolis; as contested communities whose inherent virtues must be, at the least, defended, and if possible, amplified; as themed lifestyle options for a new generation of urban enthusiasts.

Quite like Ward Just's Famagusta—with "one civilization laid atop another"—contemporary Chicago reveals bits and pieces of each of these forms of neighborhood: pastoral residential enclaves dating from the early twentieth century, settlement houses that have evolved into neighborhood social service centers, Corbusian high-rise developments dating from the heyday of urban renewal, the belt of largely Mexican American neighborhoods running from just southwest of the Loop to the city's border with Cicero, Illinois (as such, an updated version of "ethnic Chicago"), themed commercial districts whose streetside markers speak of past artistic pioneers or African American strivers, and the array of upscale new neighborhoods (some willfully historicist and fitted out with Richardsonian or Sullivanesque flourishes, others crisply contemporary and loft-like) filling in the Near South and West Sides. However, even this layering of varied neighborhood forms is not a uniquely Chicago attribute. Analogous mixtures of place, institutions, and population can be found in many American cities. What distinguishes Chicago is the persistence of the idea that it is the city of neighborhoods.

BECAUSE CHICAGO IS THE CITY OF NEIGHBORHOODS . . . IT DOES NOT SEEM SO FLAT, DANGEROUS, OR MISGOVERNED

My first encounter with Chicago was brief and indirect: my older brother's wedding in Park Ridge, a suburban town just northwest of the city. I do not recall actually visiting Chicago during that weekend trip in the early 1960s, though I do recall that my brother and some of his friends spent the wedding eve touring the city's nightspots. I settled in Chicago in 1977 and remember quite vividly my first drive into the city from the south, having passed through Pennsylvania, Ohio, and Indiana. At that time Chicago's panoramic and street-level perspectives were jarringly contradictory. Viewed at a distance from the Dan Ryan Expressway in early evening, the downtown skyline was an exhilarating exclamation point to the many horizontal miles I had crossed in the preceding hours. Yet the next morning, as I began my apartment search on the North Side, the dull uniformity of the two- and three-story, asphalt siding-clad houses I passed was disturbingly reminiscent of New Brunswick, New Jersey, where I had lived a few years previously. At the time, I wondered why asphalt siding was such a hit in both places. I have since come to realize that a cluster of overlapping demographic and occupational attributes made for a not-so-surprising convergence in the domestic facade preferences expressed by residents of the faded college town and the Midwestern metropolis.

Notwithstanding the claims of local boosters—or the impressions of countless visitors who have hugged the lakefront while venturing no farther north than the Lincoln Park Zoo or farther south than McCormick Place—Chicago is neither a beautiful city nor, for the most part, even a visually distinctive city. Situated on an ancient lake bed, Chicago's topographic uniformity is reinforced by the regularity of its street grid. I must acknowledge that to some degree, my viewpoint is a function of having come to Chicago in the late 1970s. In those years fiscal crisis, bureaucratic indifference, and the flagging energies of Richard J. Daley yielded a legacy of unkempt city parks, pothole-strewn thoroughfares, and forlornly Dickensian public school buildings. Most of Chicago's residential areas were physically indistinguishable, and as urban design theorist Kevin Lynch would have it, the city's nondescript "paths" and "edges" further contributed to an overall sense of placelessness.[47]

Given Chicago's origins as a hastily erected depot of westward-grasping North American capitalism, its initial lack of physical amenity was to be expected. It speaks less well of Chicago's civic and municipal leaders that over the course of the twentieth century, many of their additions to the city—industrial complexes, its network of expressways, the huge public housing developments—often degraded an already-inhospitable urban environment. And yet—within the walls of those asphalt-sided houses, in residential districts constricted by its anonymous avenues and highways—Chicago's celebrators could ascertain a city of neighborhoods: places of family and ethnic conviviality, in which churches and local social networks bred a sense of belonging—"havens in a heartless world."

Beyond the putative safe havens represented by its neighborhoods, Chicago has been in many respects a heartlessly dangerous city. Historian Jeffrey Adler notes that "by the early 1920s, [Chicago's] homicide rate was nearly double that of New York City, Philadelphia, and San Francisco and more than triple that of Boston and Hartford."[48] For Chicagoans at work, the steel mill, packinghouse, and tractor assembly line offered perils nearly as grave. Historian Louise Carroll Wade describes the working conditions at the Union Stock Yard at the end of the nineteenth century:

> Packinghouse work was inherently dangerous because of the tools and the machinery. Defective equipment caused some of the accidents in Packingtown. Elevator cables snapped, and men stepped into open elevator shafts. An exploding lard tank at Armour's killed one and burned three others. On at least a dozen occasions in the 1880s newspapers reported deaths due to "getting in some machinery." Louis Schlovsk, for example, got tangled in a fertilizer dryer shaft, and the son of a pack-

inghouse owner caught his untied apron in the revolving wheel of the pig-hoist and was dashed against the ceiling.[49]

Chicago's many dangers have been fiscal as well as physical. Business downturns invariably followed the years of boom. For generations of marginal workers, every phase of the business cycle has meant low wages, limited hours, and infinitesimal prospects of advancement. Lizabeth Cohen's study of Chicago's working class between World War I and II, *Making a New Deal*, includes several Great Depression–era family profiles, such as the following:

> Steelworker George Patterson and his wife were unprepared for how hard the depression would hit them . . . [B]y 1932, Patterson was working at U.S. Steel's South Works plant only one day a month. To get more work than that was a game of "who you knew," whether or not you could win the foreman's favor. By the time his son was born later that year, Patterson and his wife moved in with his parents, and he "couldn't buy a bottle of milk." To make things worse for steelworkers like Patterson, the U.S. Steel stock they had scrimped to purchase as an investment in the future under the company's employee stock ownership plan, worth $259 a share in October 1929, had tumbled to fifty dollars within six months and continued to fall steadily until a share was worth less than $20.[50]

Among the trends that Cohen discerns during the 1930s was a growing public dissatisfaction with neighborhood-based, frequently ethnically oriented banks and merchants. Previously favored because of their "wealth and prestige" rather than "brains and experience," Chicago's ethnic banks experienced a very high default rate during the Great Depression.[51] Although the collapse of these banks and other local commercial concerns did not pull the curtain on Chicago's ethnic neighborhoods, Cohen argues that the 1930s represent a crucial transitional period in reference to working-class attitudes. From this point on, "national" institutions—including both chain retailers and the federal government—increasingly shaped the spending habits and political preferences of the city's neighborhood-rooted, working-class residents.

Following World War II, Richard J. Daley's Democratic Party machine exerted a powerful counterforce to this nationalizing of Chicagoans' political preferences. However, the city's predilection for localistic, client-oriented (and until the early 1930s, *two-party*) politics predated Richard J. Daley's ascendancy by several decades. As explained by political scientist Paul Kleppner, in a city of multiple, mutually wary ethnic groups, a pattern of ward-based and favor-distributing political practice had become the norm:

> The result was a brand of politics in which each party's coalition was composed of ethnically identifiable, and often personality-oriented, factions . . . Predominant strength within a ward provided the group with an opportunity to secure political representation and recognition by electing one of its members to the city council. This possibility encouraged the early development of ethnic-group political consciousness and then helped to maintain and reinforce it.[52]

Politicians represented their communities, and given access to governmental resources, took care of their own.

Over the long run, this approach to politics and the use of government produced widespread, though in most instances, tolerably minor corruption:

> It was an annoyance to have to slip a patrolman $10 to avoid a court appearance on a minor traffic infraction. To some it was an outrage. But it was part of the rules. One could denounce the rules or accept them, but nearly everyone understood them. They were a civic tradition.[53]

Journalist Alan Ehrenhalt further suggests that this mode of citizen / official interaction became a source of "perverse pride," and in his nostalgic evocation of Chicago in the 1950s, *The Lost City*, endows Mayor Daley with an otherworldly power to orchestrate personalities and events: "Richard J. Daley was a manager of sin, a decision maker who accepted the reality of sinful citizens and constant temptation, tolerated them up to a point, even took advantage of their presence to keep an organization functioning, but did his best to control the level of misdeeds and to prevent them from taking over and breeding chaos." As to the source of these esoteric skills, Ehrenhalt speculates that Daley's experience in "parochial school" was its foundation.[54]

In political scientist Milton Rakove's "insider's analysis," *Don't Make No Waves . . . Don't Back No Losers* (1975)—published just as the Richard J. Daley era was winding down—one reads an interpretation of Chicago's "civic tradition" that is saturated in perverse pride. Early in his book, Rakove observes, "Had Richard J. Daley been born in Russia, he would probably be the mayor of Kiev and chairman of the central committee of the Communist Party of the Kiev region."[55] Over the course of this volume, Rakove repeatedly returns to his analogy linking the workings of the Cook County Democratic and the Soviet Communist parties. Rakove's intent is more rhetorical than analytical, but his choice of analog to the Chicago Democrats is telling. Rakove proposes that intolerance of dissent, presumably ironclad organizational discipline, and cronyism are the building blocks of effective governance. How can such an ethically deficient politics be justified? Rakove's answer, once again, derives from an analogy. "The world is a Great Neighborhood made up of diverse peoples, each with their own customs and cultures to be respected, in which peace and prosperity can be best achieved by taking care of one's own problems at home, leaving others to do likewise in their respective neighborhoods."[56] As Alan Ehrenhalt would have it, the instrumental sinfulness of the Richard J. Daley machine mirrored the admirable clannishness of Chicago's neighborhoods.

THE RETURN OF THE EMBRACED

"Chicago—the city of neighborhoods" is the civic equivalent of a well-delivered card trick. As our eyes focus on some extravagant physical gesture that diverts our attention from the magician's right hand, the ace replaces the deuce, and the illusion materializes. As a city of neighborhoods, Chicago's physical dreariness, its multitude of hazards, the entrenched inequities of its politics are, at the least, removed from our attention. And in the hands of its more audacious intellectual gamesmen such as Milton Rakove, these various deficiencies are, at once, displayed and exonerated, because—in the end—Chicago's flaws are necessary to preserve its neighborhoods.

Though the uniqueness of Chicago's neighborhoods may be a civic conceit, countless Chicagoans have taken the conceit very seriously. Saul Alinsky's orchestration of the Back of the Yards Neighborhood Council at the end of the Great Depression incorporated church congregations, ethnic associations, and informal social networks into a politicized *neighborhood* organization.[57] During the 1950s and 1960s the most wrenching feature of Chicago's local civil rights revolution was the neighborhood racial transition that transformed much of the city's South and West Sides.[58] By the 1970s a new variety of neighborhood organization emerged, typically focusing on physical development efforts such as housing rehabilitation or neighborhood economic promotion. This new generation of community-based organizations reacted both to the shortcomings of preceding neighborhood mobilization strategies—notably, the Alinsky model's inability to produce community benefits when its municipal or corporate enemies were bankrupt or no longer present in the community—and emergent conditions—in particular, the deindustrialization of Chicago's economy—that were undermining neighborhood life across the city.[59]

Although the particular agendas of these post-1960s neighborhood organizations varied substantially, and their leaders were rarely given to linking local campaigns to broader ideological debates, one could say that most shared an underlying assumption of neighborhood salvationism.[60] By this I mean that the new generation of neighborhood activists reversed the causal logic of urban renewal, which proposed that citywide strategies were necessary to save particular neighborhoods. The post-1960s neighborhood activists—in part following Jane Jacobs, but just as frequently following insights derived from their own experience—acted on the proposition that the maintenance of viable neighborhoods was the means by which the larger city could be sustained.

Following the seemingly momentous Democratic Party mayoral primary of 1979, in which upstart Jane Byrne defeated the incum-

bent mayor of Chicago, Michael Bilandic—Richard J. Daley's successor—neighborhood activists across Chicago anticipated a new approach to local governance that would give heed to, indeed, would
affirmatively support their community-based initiatives. For the
most part, these expectations were dashed, and by late 1982—as a
serious challenge to Mayor Byrne by Congressman Harold Washington took life—many community activists committed themselves to
the Washington movement. As recalled by Doug Gills, one of neighborhood activists who joined the Washington campaign of 1982–83:

> The movement underpinning Harold Washington's campaign and his
> early administration was marked by aggressive, vocal, and independent
> action on the part of people associated with neighborhood organiza-
> tions and community action groups. These community activists had
> been isolated from meaningful political participation in prior re-
> gimes.[61]

Although Harold Washington's tumultuous four-and-a-half year
mayoralty, from the spring of 1983 until the autumn of 1987, is typically recalled as a period of ferocious black / white political contestation, just as seriously contested was the future of municipal development policy.[62] The Washington administration's Chicago Works
Together economic development blueprint emphasized a series of
policy commitments—job creation (as opposed to real estate development), neighborhood economic development, and industrial
retention—that had not been the priorities of mayors Byrne, Bilandic, or Daley. Members of the city council and various represen-
tatives of Chicago's corporate leadership objected to the change of
policy course, and ultimately, the Washington administration program often struck a pragmatic balance between continuity and innovation.[63]

One little-remembered Washington-era conflict marvelously illustrates the ambiguities of actual Chicagoans' (in this case, actual
Chicagoans with some degree of policy-making leverage) engagement with their "city of neighborhoods." In the middle months of
1985 the Chicago City Council considered a proposal from Mayor

Washington to authorize a $125 million general obligation bond issue for neighborhood infrastructure improvements: street resurfacing, sidewalk and sewer repairs, additional projects specific to particular neighborhoods. If there was an element of political misdirection driving the Washington administration's proposal, it was revealed by the distribution of funds, which favored the wards represented by the coalition of twenty-nine aldermen who had, for the preceding two years, repeatedly sought to stymie the mayor's initiatives. In effect, the Washington administration was challenging members of the majority opposition bloc to vote against a proposal funding needed physical improvements earmarked for their wards. For their part, Washington's opponents—many of them holdovers from the Richard J. Daley era—hesitated for more than a year before approving the neighborhood improvements proposal. During the standoff between mayor and city council, Alderman Richard Mell of the Thirty-Third Ward put it to journalist Gary Rivlin: "I will sacrifice a vote that probably won't be popular in my community for the good of the coalition."[64] In short, at that moment in the last half-century when Chicago's politics were most contested, a majority of the city's ostensible neighborhood tribunes—twenty-nine of its aldermen—were deeply reluctant to support a program of local improvements if credit for this initiative was to be shared with a despised political foe.

As I noted in the profile of Richard M. Daley in chapter 3, one of the chief points of debate concerning Chicago's current mayor is the degree to which his administration's program is a continuation of longstanding municipal policy. This debate is complicated by the monumentality of Richard J. Daley's legacy—though his mayoralty is now more than three decades past—even as the brief Washington administration of the 1980s seemed to mark such a sharp break with Chicago's early postwar policy consensus. Some Richard M. Daley observers accuse him of a return to machine politics; others find either substantial philosophical or specific programmatic carryovers from the Washington years. This much is certain. The idea of neighborhood salvationism persists. The most striking transformation of Chicago's physical environment that has been achieved during the Richard M. Daley years is the redevelopment of its near-Loop neighborhoods, and in particular, several of its huge public housing developments on the Near North, West, and Mid-South Sides. Not only are new physical neighborhoods emerging in these sections of Chicago, but a new variant of neighborhood salvationism seeks to create viable residential *communities* where once were high-rise public housing developments, industrial sites, and transportation infrastructure.

The Roosevelt Square neighborhood is emerging on the site of the old ABLA Chicago Housing Authority development. As promoted by this sign, it will be an "authentic" neighborhood.

FIVE

WRESTING THE NEW
FROM THE ONCE MODERN

CHAPTER

TWO MILES FROM the Loop in Chicago's Near West Side
is a residential development in progress called Westhaven Park.
Westhaven Park's northern margin is Lake Street, a major thoroughfare connecting Chicago's downtown to suburban Oak Park. Some
of Westhaven Park's new dwellings face not just Lake Street, but
also the Chicago Transit Authority (CTA) Green Line, whose support beams frame and whose tracks run above this section of Lake
Street. Westhaven Park's eastern border is another elevated railway,
the CTA Pink Line (so named by a poll of Chicago schoolchildren in
2006). As the Pink Line cuts north / south along Hermitage Avenue
it bisects an early post–World War II garden apartment complex,
the Hermitage Manor Cooperative. Though from a real estate agent's
perspective Westhaven Park may be an up-and-coming mixed-
income community, just a few years ago this was a low-income enclave wedged between light manufacturers and noisy rail lines.

Westhaven Park's architecture is a new urbanist pastiche of row
house minimalism trimmed with Industrial Age sheet metal and
ornamented by the occasional Victorian peaked roof. With the exception of Westhaven Park Tower (100 N. Hermitage Avenue), a
nine-floor structure running the length of the short block between
Washington Boulevard and Maypole Street, Westhaven Park's dwellings are of modest scale, standing two, three, and four floors high.
The facade materials and color shadings are vivid: variously painted
brick, concrete blocks, and built-in flower boxes. In what seems to
be a clever evocation of Chicago's characteristic building line (which
is not a line at all, but rather a sawtooth of similarly scaled but hap-
hazardly aligned house fronts), the facade lines and building heights

along Maypole Street jut in and out, up and down within the basic design parameters set for the larger development. In a nod to one of Mayor Daley's design preferences, low, black-painted, faux iron fencing borders the small yards fronting some of the dwellings along Maypole Street.

Westhaven Park is indeed a neighborhood in progress. In the summer of 2008, a very large open area ran west of Wolcott Street to Damen Avenue. A few large trees and a single basketball goal adorned this field. A well-worn footpath—an informal extension of Maypole Street—crossed the open space, connecting Westhaven Park with the built-up areas beyond Damen. At the back side of the commercial structures facing Lake Street, and to some degree camouflaged by the open field's prairie grasses, an outdoor drug market could be observed. As for legitimate merchants, that summer there was not a single coffee shop, restaurant, dry cleaner, pharmacy, or hardware store serving the one-third to one-half mile rectangle bounded by Hermitage, Damen, Lake, and Madison. However, just across from Westhaven Park at the intersection of Lake and Wood streets, Bark Chicago, Inc., which provides dog-walking and other pet services, had opened.

From 1957 until just a few years ago, most of this rectangle was occupied by the CHA's Henry Horner Homes, a 9-building complex (7 buildings of 7 floors, two reaching 15 floors) of 920 apartments completed in 1957. By 1961, with the construction of an extension west of Damen Avenue, the Horner development had grown to over 1,600 units of housing.[1] Like the CHA's other large high-rise developments—including Stateway Gardens and the Robert Taylor Homes on the South Side, the ABLA development within a mile of Horner on the West Side, and Cabrini-Green on the North Side—the decline of Horner Homes as a residential community was precipitous. In the spring of 1968, the Horner area's main commercial district along Madison Street was devastated by the rioting following Martin Luther King Jr.'s assassination.[2] In 1991, journalist Alex Kotlowitz observed of 1920 West Washington, the high-rise home of Lafeyette and Pharoah Rivers, the subjects of his *There Are No Children Here*:

Their building had no enclosed lobby; a dark tunnel cut through the middle of the building, and the wind and strangers passed freely along it. Those tenants who received public aid had their checks sent to the local currency exchange, since the building's first-floor mailboxes had all been broken into. And since darkness engulfed the building's corridors, even in the daytime, the residents always carried flashlights, some of which had been handed out by a local politician during her campaign.[3]

The Horner area's road to revitalization has, however, proceeded in a distinctive fashion. Unlike other CHA reconstruction efforts, which have been spurred by the federal government's HOPE VI public housing redevelopment program, the transformation of the Horner Homes property results from a civil suit filed by Horner residents in 1991. Finding that the CHA had willfully allowed the Horner buildings to deteriorate—to justify the agency's intention to demolish the development—a "consent degree" approved by U.S. district court judge James Zagel set in motion the removal of the Horner high-rises (with the exception of a single structure) and the development of a new, mixed-income neighborhood. But again, unlike the HOPE VI redevelopments at CHA projects such as the Robert Taylor and ABLA homes (the consolidated and adjoining Addams, Brooks, Loomis, and Abbott developments), the Horner decree mandates "one-for-one" replacement of demolished public housing units, in effect, giving Horner's incumbent residents a greater chance to resettle in the immediate neighborhood.[4]

In one striking visual respect, Westhaven Park does evoke an earlier phase of neighborhood formation in Chicago. Lying just south of Westhaven Park, beyond a labyrinth of fenced-in parking lots, is the huge United Center, home of the Chicago Bulls and Blackhawks, occasional host of the Rolling Stones, Cirque du Soleil, and Holiday on Ice. Yet unlike the neighborhood anchors of generations past such Wisconsin Steel Works or the Union Stock Yard, the United Center—according to Westhaven Park residents—barely registers as a local economic force. Few locals work at the United Center, and the restaurants and taverns catering to sports fans are east of Ashland Avenue, nearer to the Loop. But the United Center's presence in the neighborhood is not without consequence. Washington Boulevard, along Westhaven Park's southern margin, is a one-way thoroughfare permitting automobiles to speed from downtown to the United Center and beyond. As such, it represents quite a hazard for local youngsters as they wend their way to and from the Suder and Brown elementary schools.

In the daylight hours, Westhaven Park appears to be an African American neighborhood, but in the evenings—especially during the warm months as white condominium dwellers lead their pets on more expansive strolls—it is evident that the Near West Side is becoming more racially mixed. The future of Westhaven Park is highly uncertain. Vestiges of the Henry Horner era are everywhere: "home going" notices, that is, funeral announcements, for local residents taped to apartment entrances, and the evident physical deterioration of many of the structures west of Damen Avenue. Social interaction between new neighborhood arrivals and community holdovers is both infrequent and uneasy. Some low-income residents expect to be pushed out of Westhaven Park as it gentrifies. Many of the real estate agents and neighborhood newcomers undoubtedly worry that downtown Chicago, in the coming years, will not generate enough high-paying jobs to sustain further upscaling of the Near West Side. Such contradictory expectations are standard fare in the former public housing neighborhoods of central Chicago. How these areas reached this crossroads is, at once, a tale of past public policy failure and an invitation to consider how many central city neighborhoods in American cities are likely to evolve in the coming years.

ONE INSTANCE OF THE CRUMBLING OF THE NEW DEAL

The story of public housing transformation in contemporary Chicago begins many years ago, when local political leaders fell in line behind the visionary, Depression-era leadership of Franklin Roosevelt. From the outset, the Cook County Democratic Party and the New Deal were a star-crossed pairing. Before Roosevelt captured the Democratic presidential nomination in 1932, Chicago mayor and Cook County Democratic chair Anton Cermak had supported Al Smith's aspirations for a second run against Herbert Hoover. In February 1933, while in Miami to mend fences with FDR, Cermak was mortally wounded by gunfire directed at the president-elect.[5] Cermak's successor, Edward J. Kelly, capitalized on Roosevelt's New Deal to promote the local political realignment that made Chicago, by midcentury, a one-party city, even as his municipal administration only haltingly accepted the progressive tenets of Roosevelt's more ardent followers. During the 1930s Chicago's Democratic precinct captains became skilled "credit-claimers" as their constituents rushed to sign up for relief jobs or enroll in the new Social Security program.[6] Among African Americans—a constituency that Mayor Kelly courted much more ardently than did his fellow ethnic Democrats—the job-rich Works Progress Administration was an especially popular New Deal initiative. In *Black Metropolis* (1945), St. Clair Drake and Horace Cayton report the following blues lyric:

> Please, Mr. President, listen to what I've got to say:
> You can take away all of the alphabet, but please leave that WPA.
> Now I went to the poll and voted, I know I voted the right way—
> So I'm asking you, Mr. President, don't take away that WPA![7]

Ed Kelly was also a friend of public housing. Within months of Congress authorizing the public housing program in 1937, the Illinois General Assembly created the Chicago Housing Authority. The CHA's chief administrator from its founding until 1954 was Elizabeth Wood, a Vassar College graduate who had previously been director of a local civic organization, the Metropolitan Housing Council. The Wood years are widely recalled as the CHA's golden age. Writing in the mid-1950s, Martin Meyerson—who had served in various planning capacities at CHA—asserted of Wood: "It was she, more than any other individual, who had given the Authority its special character and standing, a character and standing which made it a widely acknowledged leader among the several hundred local housing authorities in the United States."[8]

A recent account of the CHA's early years is entitled *When Public Housing Was Paradise*, though in truth a more sober assessment of the Wood years would characterize the CHA's dwellings as passable.[9] The newly formed agency took over the management of a number of housing complexes that had been built by the federal Public Works Administration. These included the Jane Addams Houses on the Near West Side and the Julia Lathrop Homes overlooking the Chicago River five miles northwest of the Loop. Each of these low-rise developments featured imaginative site plans, and for many years, attractive landscaping. Yet as the CHA turned to the planning and construction of public housing complexes in the 1940s, it often settled for resolutely spartan building designs and skimpy public space provision. For example, both the Frances Cabrini Homes—the kernel of the subsequently expanded Cabrini-Green project—and the Robert H. Brooks Homes were cramped, monotonously aligned row house developments, as such, one aesthetic notch removed from military barracks.[10]

Nonetheless, Elizabeth Wood and her staff were animated by a progressive social vision that emphasized the uplifting effects of decent housing and also included a measured commitment to racial integration. In reference to integration, Wood's CHA adhered to the "neighborhood composition rule" initially mandated by the Public Works Administration—that is, individual developments' population mix should mirror that of the surrounding neighborhood—which also, so the CHA staff presumed, would reduce resistance in white neighborhoods to the proximate siting of new developments.[11] By the late 1940s, the CHA's portfolio of residential properties thus included all-white, all-black, and mixed (though predominantly white) developments. However, during the same years Chicago's African American population was increasing rapidly, which in turn began to shift the racial composition of many South and West Side neighborhoods. In the aftermath of World War II the CHA also endeavored to offer transitional housing to returning military veterans, among whose numbers there were many African Americans. Beginning in 1946, the CHA's efforts to settle African Americans in both temporary and conventional residential developments set off a series of nasty racial conflicts spanning Chicago's South and Southwest Sides.

The violent confrontations that followed the CHA's placement of the Howard family in the previously all-white Trumbull Park Homes in 1953 carried on for years. Historian Arnold Hirsch recounts one of the Trumbull Park melees, during the summer of 1954:

> Blacks entered Trumbull Park late in the afternoon on July 10 and occupied the diamond in the northwest corner of the park. Park district police surrounded the playing field while Chicago police encircled the entire park; patrol cars sat on the grass on all sides of the outfield. As the Blacks who lived in the project entered the park, the whites who lived on the east side of Bensley came out of their homes and began shouting abuse. Hostile whites then took positions along the left field foul line to watch the game. Estimates of the crowd ranged from two hundred to five hundred; approximately four hundred police massed as a counterforce . . . Once the fighting began, police rapidly replaced Blacks as the objects of the mob's anger. The captain in charge of the Trumbull Park detail was well known to the crowd, and his arrest of the white who precipitated the fight made the gathered whites "go wild." Shouts of "kill the dirty nigger loving bastard" came from the mob, and the captain had to fight his way to safety as his fellow officers, in a display of dissension, left him unassisted.[12]

Predictably, the white majority on Chicago's city council—oriented to serving constituents by means of helpful interventions with city agencies, little league sponsorships, and kind words at funerals, and wary of social discontent that might destabilize routine precinct captain / constituent transactions—was deeply suspicious of the CHA's incursions into their communities. In 1948, via state legislative enactment, the Chicago City Council won the unconditional authority to review, and if so inclined, reject the public housing agency's siting choices. During the next several years the city council and the CHA regularly squabbled over the latter's ambitious program of new construction. In their efforts to prevent the CHA from undercutting the city's prevailing racial geography, the aldermen were emboldened, in part, by Ed Kelly's retirement in 1947, and as recalled by CHA staff members, did not hesitate to make the McCarthyist charge that the public housing agency's racial progressives were left-wing subversives. In just such fashion, one of Elizabeth Wood's principal aides, Milton Shufro, was forced to resign in 1948. In 1954, the long-embattled Wood was finally ousted as CHA executive secretary.[13]

The CHA built the majority of its residential units—more than 20,000—between 1950 and the late 1960s, largely in high-rise structures. Moreover, in developments such as Robert Taylor, Cabrini-Green, and ABLA, the number of dwellings exceeded 3,000. These projects were not just tall. The provision of extensive grounds at developments such as Robert Taylor (whose site covered ninety-five acres) and in the Cabrini Extension and William Green Homes segments of Cabrini-Green meant that these public housing communities physically dominated their surrounding neighborhoods. A series of factors worked to produce the CHA's expansive neighborhood "footprint." Given the disinclination of white aldermen to accept public housing in their wards—and the City Council's statutory mandate to review public housing siting—the agency abandoned any pretense of distributing its dwellings across the city and proposed development sites only in African American or racially changing neighborhoods. And following the passage of the 1949 Housing Act, the CHA was further pressured to offer relocation housing for individuals and families displaced by urban renewal.[14]

For a time, Elizabeth Wood herself found virtue in the swelling architectural enthusiasm for "tower-in-the-park" residential design. Historian D. Bradford Hunt reports that Wood rather quickly reconsidered the proposition that high-rise design permitted planners "to achieve a more attractive use of the land . . . wide-open spaces, larger playgrounds, and a general effect of a park." Nevertheless, another of Wood's commitments—to use public housing developments as a slum removal tool—reinforced the idea that large residential developments were desirable. Building less extensive public housing communities would produce "islands in a sea of blight."[15] In effect, public housing developments needed to be large enough to turn back the insidious encroachment of neighborhood blight. Many years later, Wood acknowledged:

> The thing I feel most ashamed about is that the high-rises we began planning were not really experiments. They went up, and they were pretty much copied when we moved to the next project. We didn't know what to be concerned with in designing them.[16]

One of the sad ironies of the CHA's long decline after the early 1950s is that some of the seed yielding that decline had been planted during its so-called golden age. Yet even following Elizabeth Wood's departure from the CHA, the public housing agency attempted to build new low-rise developments. Ultimately, the federal Public Housing Administration's insistence that the CHA adhere to its per-unit construction cost ceiling forced the local agency to build tall. D. Bradford Hunt reports that as late as 1959, Richard J. Daley appealed to the U.S. Congress to prompt the Public Housing Administration to reconsider its position. Daley's effort failed, and it bears mentioning that there were local sources for Chicago's prohibitive low-rise public housing construction costs that the mayor chose not to address, in particular, union work rules and the city council's unwillingness to accept decentralized, vacant, and as such, comparatively inexpensive sites for public housing.[17]

In the last years of the 1950s and the first few years of the 1960s, the CHA rolled out its mammoth high-rise developments such as Robert Taylor, Stateway Gardens, Henry Horner, and, with the construction the Cabrini Extension and William Green Homes, the completed Cabrini-Green. Within a very short span of time things fell apart in many of these high-rise communities. Just three years following the opening of Robert Taylor Homes, the *Chicago Daily News* ran a seven-article series on the Taylor development entitled "Chicago's $70 Million Ghetto." The series author, M. W. Newman, chronicled the development's physical grimness: "humble concrete brick . . . painted a deadening battleship gray" (April 14, 1965) and "atrocious" vandalism (April 10), tellingly coupled with administrative indifference. One of Newman's informants described the CHA's fear of civil rights activity among the Taylor residents. A second commented, "The CHA management seems to discourage any of its employees who can work with the people, or it transfers them out of Taylor."[18]

Making only a brief appearance in the Newman series is Charles Swibel, a young real estate entrepreneur who at age twenty-nine had been appointed to the CHA Board of Commissioners in 1956, and in 1963 assumed the chairmanship. Swibel would hold this post until 1982, and it was during his tenure that public housing in Chicago jettisoned its remaining links to the spirit of the New Deal. Swibel ran a property management firm that banked with the same institution holding non-interest-bearing CHA accounts, received free personal services from CHA vendors, and intervened in the resident-selection process for CHA senior citizen buildings.[19] Apart from Swibel's personal improprieties, during his nearly two decades leading the public housing agency intractable budgetary problems emerged, maintenance operations in the high-rise developments collapsed, and local management became highly politicized. The staff at individual CHA developments routinely manipulated the provision of services to deflect tenant discontent, and access to apartments in many developments was contingent on good relations with one's Democratic Party precinct captain.[20]

By the late 1960s, past policy choices were devastating Chicago's public housing. Nearly 80 percent of the more than 4,400 apartments at the Robert Taylor Homes were three-, four-, or five-bedroom units, and as a result, the development's 20,000 children overwhelmed playgrounds and other public areas.[21] Across the CHA's developments, elevator breakdowns were unrelenting. In 1974, the CHA revealed that there were 1,200 pending repair orders at Cabrini-Green, and that more than two months were required to prepare an apartment for occupancy by new tenants.[22] Congressional action in 1969 and 1970—the Brooke Amendments to the 1937 U.S. Housing Act, so named for Republican senator Edward Brooke of Massachusetts—had sought to ease the housing burden of very poor families by instituting an income-graded rent system in public housing developments. The effect on the CHA was to reduce rental income even as maintenance expenditures hemorrhaged.[23]

On August 9, 1966, a group of African American public housing residents sued the agency, claiming that the CHA's siting practices since the mid-1950s and its continuing tenant assignment procedures were willfully discriminatory. Federal district court Judge Richard Austin's original *Gautreaux v. Chicago Housing Authority* ruling in mid-1969 in favor of the plaintiffs initiated an incredibly complex sequence of political maneuvers, subsequent litigation, and policy adjustments that profoundly influenced the CHA's future course and, more generally, has continued to shape inner-city development patterns in Chicago. As attorney Alexander Polikoff's memoir, *Waiting for Gautreaux*, amply illustrates, for several years following Judge Austin's 1969 ruling, much of the CHA's executive energy—initially as directed by Charles Swibel, with the evident support of Richard J. Daley—aimed to *avoid* compliance with the judge's mandate to begin distributing public housing across Chicago.[24] In large part, the CHA avoided building scattered-site public housing by not building any new public housing whatsoever, a tactic that was abetted by the federal government's diminishing fiscal support for such construction. A subsequent *Gautreaux* consent decree in 1981 inaugurated the Gautreaux Assisted Housing Program, a nearly two-decade initiative—that was not administered by the CHA—permitting approximately 7,000 low-income families (using federally funded housing vouchers) to access housing in outlying Chicago and suburban neighborhoods. The Gautreaux Assisted Housing Program's aims and implementation structure, as well as the research that monitored it, have made a substantial contribution to the current enthusiasm among some urban policy experts for "poverty deconcentration" and "mixed-income housing."[25]

In 1982, pressure from the federal Department of Housing and Urban Development (HUD) forced Charles Swibel to resign as head of the CHA Board. In many respects the agency's history since the Swibel era is a long, tortuous epilogue. Throughout the 1980s and into the 1990s, mayoral interest in the CHA's miserable situation fluctuated, and at various points federal officials sought to impose some degree of order on the public housing agency's clearly chaotic affairs. The climax of this *danse macabre* between federal and local officials was HUD's takeover of the CHA from 1995 to 1999. One additional factor, whose effects bridged the Swibel era and the years thereafter, sealed the fate of the CHA and its residents. This was the inner-city economic collapse—as the broader Chicago economy deindustrialized—that laid waste to many of the areas adjoining the CHA's developments.

I can illustrate the gravity of this economic disaster by presenting a few demographic and economic figures for the South Side Grand Boulevard community area, a large rectangle running from 39th to 51st streets north to south, and Cottage Grove Avenue to the Dan Ryan Expressway east to west. From the early 1960s until just a few years ago, the western portion of Grand Boulevard was dominated by the most populous of the CHA developments, Robert Taylor Homes. Between 1970 and 1990 Grand Boulevard's population halved, from slightly more than 80,000 to less than 36,000. During the same 20-year span, local unemployment more than tripled, from 9.5 percent to 34 percent. Throughout this period Grand Boulevard was one of Chicago's poorest areas, but even so, the degree of local impoverishment climbed to an astounding level: from 31.4 percent of local families in 1970, to 64 percent in 1990.[26] Though the late-century decline of Grand Boulevard was especially pronounced, similar economic catastrophes struck the Near South Side (and the CHA's Ickes and Dearborn developments), as well as the band of neighborhoods running west of the Loop in which developments such as Henry Horner, ABLA, and Rockwell Gardens were located.

It would be impossible to demonstrate precisely the degree to which neighborhood decline contributed to the erosion of communal life in the CHA developments, as opposed to the clearly plausible alternative proposition that the collapse of the big public housing communities spilled over into their surroundings. These processes were surely mutually reinforcing. What is indisputable, however, is that Elizabeth Wood's dream of employing large public housing developments to arrest inner-city blight had come to naught. During the 1980s and early 1990s the intractability of the "CHA crisis" produced a variety of local political maneuvers. In response to the deteriorating situation at Cabrini-Green, for a few weeks in early 1981 Mayor Jane Byrne, presuming that her magnetic presence would energize local public housing staff and police, actually took up residence in the North Side CHA development.[27] Probably the least admirable element of Byrne successor Harold Washington's mayoralty was his unwillingness to take decisive action at the CHA. In 1988, Eugene Sawyer—Washington's decidedly overmatched successor as mayor—appointed a private real estate entrepreneur, Vincent Lane, to head the beleaguered public housing agency.

Lane was a curious champion of public housing, approximately half visionary and half Charles Swibel redux. From 1988 until his removal as CHA chair in mid-1995, Lane used aggressive surveillance and building search techniques to weed out miscreants, successfully accomplished a much-applauded rehabilitation of two South Side high-rise buildings that were redubbed Lake Parc Place, and became a fervent advocate for mixed-income redevelopment. He also managed—as if reincarnating Charles Swibel—to mix CHA and his personal business affairs and to permit some egregious administrative breakdowns within the public housing agency.[28] From 1995 until 1999, the CHA was directed by Joseph Shuldiner, a HUD official delegated to clean up public housing in Chicago. During Shuldiner's tenure a congressionally mandated exercise called Viability Assessment determined that approximately half of the CHA's 40,000 units of housing were in structures whose renovation costs would be fiscally unacceptable.[29] Shuldiner's CHA was also a persistent applicant for federal HOPE VI funding to seed local demolition and redevelopment efforts.

In late 1999 the CHA was restored to local control, and since that time the public housing agency's initiatives have been closely linked to the broader program of central city redevelopment pursued by Richard M. Daley's municipal administration. The CHA's Plan for Transformation, announced in early 2000 shortly after the return to local control, proposes to reduce the public housing property portfolio to 25,000 units (approximately 10,000 of these reserved for senior citizens)—with all units either renovated or newly constructed—and to turn over day-to-day property management to private firms. The cost of the Plan for Transformation was initially set at $1.5 billion, with a projected completion date of 2010.[30] Ultimately, the price tag for the Plan for Transformation will substantially exceed this initial estimate, and the completion deadline has been officially pushed back to 2015.[31] As I write, the vast majority of the high-rise buildings at developments such as Robert Taylor, ABLA, and Cabrini-Green have been demolished, and at each of these complexes—though at widely varying paces—mixed-income residential redevelopment has begun.

Public housing in contemporary Chicago retains little of the "character and standing" that Martin Meyerson associated with Elizabeth Wood's regime. These days, as the CHA reviews the work, criminal, and residency records of both new and returning tenants, its animating vision is nearly the antithesis of the Wood-era effort to recruit "good" tenants. Rather than seeking out worthy residents who might be expected to make a positive contribution to a public housing community, in the CHA's new mixed-income developments the aim is to exclude troublemakers likely to antagonize their neighbors or management. More fundamentally, the idea of "public" housing residences—provided by the state to ensure decent housing for all, as such, considered a collective asset beyond their utility as dwelling spaces for particular individuals and families—is absent from the rhetoric of mixed-income community advocates. To the extent that social uplift will be accomplished, the assumption is that neighborly mentoring will be the means to that end. It is further assumed that the physical management of residential properties and the provision of basic services will be best accomplished if left to the private sector.

LIBERALS AT WAR

In a manner distinctly reminiscent of the University of Chicago ethnographers' coming to terms with early-twentieth-century Chicago neighborhoods via the terminology and conceptual apparatus that has come to be known as human ecology, an expansive theoretical vocabulary has emerged to describe how Chicago's public housing communities failed, and in turn, how new neighborhoods can be formed in their place. What does seem to distinguish the current era of neighborhood formation and analysis is the political contentiousness of the efforts both to direct this process and to anticipate how it will play out. By surveying the main lines of this debate we will observe a striking irony. Nearly everyone who has engaged intellectually with the fall of Chicago's public housing and its rebirth via mixed-income development sides with the public housing residents. Ultimately, what these liberals at war are contesting is how best to recover what was admirable in the Rooseveltian ideal of the benevolent state committed to universal citizen well-being, even as the basic tools that had been applied to that task—well-funded and rationally directed public bureaucracies, and "public servants" dedicated to helping those most in need—have succumbed to disrepute.

The participants in this debate fall into three not entirely separable camps—the analysts, the ethnographers, and the advocates—whose respective approaches to the questions of what went wrong with Chicago's public housing communities and how they should be reborn determine some part, though not all, of the main lines of disagreement. It is the analysts who have provided most of the theoretical architecture around which the various interpretations and arguments pivot. The dean of the analysts is sociologist William Julius Wilson, whose book *The Truly Disadvantaged* (1987) offers the concepts of "social isolation" and "concentration effects" to explain the gravity of neighborhood decline in areas such as Chicago's public housing developments.[32] The former notion pertains to what Wilson argues is the extreme disconnection between the day-to-day experiences of very poor inner-city residents and the social mainstream. As for concentration effects, by this Wilson has in mind the seemingly exponential increase in social pathologies (for example, single-parent families, juvenile crime, academic failure) in neighborhoods whose populations are overwhelmingly poor.

Like the other analysts I will discuss, Wilson's methodological approach has been mainly quantitative, interpreting census data and numerical indicators derived from social surveys. The subjects of *The Truly Disadvantaged* were not, in particular, public housing residents, nor is the book a study of Chicago neighborhoods. Nevertheless, as Wilson's arguments circulated among academic researchers and policy-making elites, soon enough they attached themselves to the local program of public housing rejuvenation. Consider, for example, this excerpt from the CHA's initial HOPE VI application, to support redevelopment at Cabrini-Green:

> The dense concentration of very low income and racially-homogeneous (94% African-American) residents in a geographically isolated area establishes a basic condition of distress, hopelessness and lack of opportunity for the Cabrini population. The monolithic nature of the population deprives the community of valuable role models, strong community and family supports and creates insurmountable obstacles to the socio-economic mainstream. This isolation, over time, is also reflected in an absence of external public, private and social service resources available to the community. Like many of Chicago's public housing and low income communities, the Cabrini-Green area and families are chronically underserved.[33]

For the local Chicagoan, especially the *North Side* Chicagoan, the one notably jarring feature of this depiction of the old Cabrini-Green is its assertion of geographical isolation. In those days, the early 1990s, the Cabrini-Green development was certainly an expansive and forbidding place, but it was not "geographically isolated" in the conventional sense of the expression, adjoining as it did a very busy commercial district to the south, the high-income Gold Coast neighborhood on the east, and the comfortably gentrified Old Town area to the north. Interviewing Cabrini-Green residents at the time, I found that they typically deplored the physical condition of their dwellings even as they prized where their development was located.[34]

The HOPE VI application's characterization of Cabrini-Green also deploys the prescriptive vocabulary—what to do with the residents of high-poverty neighborhoods—that has become joined to

Wilson's diagnosis of the problem. In mixed-income communities, more prosperous residents, who as such are fully integrated with the social mainstream, will serve as "role models" for their poor neighbors. In the more evangelistic scenarios describing this relationship, the better-off will actively engage with—"mentor"—their poor fellow residents. In the work of James Rosenbaum, a social psychologist at Northwestern University who has devoted years to studying families who found housing via the Gautreaux Assisted Housing Program, analysis drifts very near to evangelism. In 1998 Rosenbaum coauthored a study of Lake Parc Place, Vince Lane's great triumph as CHA commissioner: two renovated high-rise towers on the Near South Side lakefront whose residents were balanced between "very poor" and "working poor" individuals. Rosenbaum and his co-authors, Linda Stroh and Cathy Flynn, surveyed the residents of the recently reoccupied Lake Parc Place buildings to determine the quality of communal relations. They sought in particular to discern just how the two classes of residents interacted.

The Rosenbaum team's research strategy and findings typify what might be termed the analysts' consensus: mixed-income communities can work (given the favorable assessment of Lake Parc Place as expressed by its residents); the main engine of this success is the presence of better-off tenants. One of the principal findings of the Rosenbaum team was that the "nonproject" (that is, working poor) residents were more supportive of the development manager's house rules than were the "project" (very poor) residents. Rosenbaum, Stroh, and Flynn's interpretation of this point follows:

> Nearly all nonproject residents . . . strongly support the rules and insist on enforcement (rule enforcement is the most important factor in determining their satisfaction). A person considering violating a rule may realize that there is a 30 percent chance that a project observer will not care [the percentage of very poor residents who felt the rules were too strict], but a 95 percent chance [the percentage of working poor residents approving the rules] that a nonproject observer will care a lot. Because nonproject residents are scattered all over Lake Parc Place, there is a near certainty that violators will be reported. Therefore, the

knowledge that nonproject residents unanimously support rules and are scattered throughout the Lake Parc Place probably discourages crime and vandalism.[35]

Curiously, Rosenbaum, Stroh, and Flynn's respondents did not seem to *behave* in accordance with the researchers' explanation. The very poor residents engaged in neighborly socializing ("watching neighbors' children, having a meal, spending more than 10 minutes talking, loaning things, letting a neighbor use their phone, greeting a neighbor in the street or hallway") fully as much as the working poor residents, and there was very little difference (52 percent versus 49 percent, respectively) in the rate of volunteering reported by very poor and working poor respondents. Moreover, in a footnote, the researchers report that several residents classified as very poor took offense when interviewers sought to raise the issue of role modeling and its possible influences![36]

Although the Rosenbaum team findings, in company with quite a number of other studies, do not quite square with the expectations of the mixed-income uplift scenario, the staying power of this perspective is formidable.[37] A recently published account of the "theoretical basis" for anticipating that the urban poor will benefit from residence in mixed-income neighborhoods devotes a lengthy discussion to "social control," "the behavioral proposition" (that "the actions and routines of more affluent families are observed at a distance and emulated by others"), "social networks," and the "political economy of place" ("collective leveraging of external resources" due to the presence of more prosperous local residents).[38] The authors of this article, Mark Joseph, Robert Chaskin, and Henry Webber, to their credit, are careful to describe this check list as a series of propositions. Many advocates of mixed-income neighborhoods unreflectively tilt toward the acceptance of regulation, emulation, network activation, and the bourgeois squeaky wheel as eternal verities.

Most analysts of public housing redevelopment in Chicago are inclined to seek out signs of resident benefit in the ongoing processes of planning, development demolition, and new construction. Given the unrelenting degradation that came to be day-to-day reality in the big CHA projects, it is to be expected that a prime motivator of many analysts' research is the wish to shape policy action that will improve the lives of the CHA resident population. Nevertheless, one of the local analysts, Paul Fischer of Lake Forest College, has pinpointed a troubling flaw in Chicago's program of public housing rejuvenation. Beginning in the late 1990s with the CHA's big push to move ahead with building demolitions, the public housing residents who have relocated from CHA dwellings using federal Section 8 vouchers (subsequently renamed Housing Choice Vouchers) have, for the most part, found new apartments in overwhelmingly African American neighborhoods that, from an economic standpoint, are but a short step up from "the Projects."[39] As the CHA has scaled back its housing portfolio and moved out thousands of residents, it has deconcentrated poverty only slightly and advanced racial integration hardly at all.

It is, however, the group of observers that I call the ethnographers who—by focusing on the *processes* of public housing redevelopment and mixed-income community formation—have more directly challenged how Chicago's new cluster of inner-city neighborhoods is being formed. Among these ethnographers is sociologist Mary-ann Mason, whose 1998 doctoral dissertation is a careful examination of daily life in Lake Parc Place. Mason's most general finding was that the good quality of life at Lake Parc Place was due more to the collective action of tenants (irrespective of income level)—in particular, by demanding effective services from the private property management firm, thereby "managing management"—rather than the working poor population's uplifting the very poor through role modeling. As she conducted her research, Mason was especially struck by residents' tendency to find the working poor / very poor distinction illusory. As one resident told her:

> Let me tell you something about the relocatees [previous public housing residents] that moved here. All the relocatees that moved in here were not on fixed income (very low income). A lot of us were em-

ployed. That's a misconception . . . As it turned out, a lot of those who were working when they came in, they're now on fixed income. A lot of us (relocatees) that wasn't working are working now.[40]

An analogous point, the extremely permeable boundary between the law-abiding and the criminal, is one of Sudhir Venkatesh's principal themes in *American Project*. In *Off the Books*, Venkatesh's recently published ethnography of Maquis Park (a fictive designation), a South Side neighborhood adjoining several of the large CHA developments, he expands on this idea:

> The underground economy is known to mainstream America . . . as a criminal sphere, the den of drug dealers and prostitutes, of pimps and con artists, of welfare mothers and indigents, of those who are unable, or unwilling, to work as "normal" Americans do. Most of us would be shocked to find that many local preachers are often intricately involved in this world. Or that the local gang leader may hold the respect of many residents, even as they decry the drugs he brings into the neighborhood. Or that a member of the underground economy is as likely to be a middle-aged mother who cooks lunches for the local hospital staff as to be a teenage criminal. Indeed, figuring out exactly what is and isn't "criminal" can be very hard in the ghetto.[41]

The front in the war among the liberals that is opened up by ethnographers' research forces us to consider the *ethics* of public housing redevelopment and new neighborhood formation. In the first instance, the ethnographers question key sociological presumptions as deployed by most analysts, such as the abnormality of the public housing population. Secondly, they have observed planning and neighborhood formation processes that systematically underestimate the contributions to community-building that public housing residents can make, and that have additionally subordinated considerations such as the availability of affordable housing in favor of the arguably more compelling goals of poverty deconcentration and inner-city neighborhood revitalization.[42]

It is, nonetheless, the advocates—attorneys such as Alexander Polikoff of Business and Professional People for the Public Interest

(BPI) and William Wilen of the Sargent Shriver National Center on Poverty Law—who have most explicitly clashed over the future of public and subsidized housing in Chicago. Polikoff is a mythic figure in Chicago legal circles: he represented Dorothy Gautreaux and her fellow plaintiffs in the original *Gautreaux* legal action, and across the four decades since that 1966 filing, has pressured the CHA to build scattered-site public housing, accept the ambitious Gautreaux Assisted Housing Program, and demolish its high-rise developments. For Polikoff, the lesson of these four decades of legal combat with the CHA is that high-rise public housing must go: "Even for the 'worst case' families who suffer 'net losses' from involuntary relocation, I conclude that—quite apart from the societal benefits—we would be doing them no favor by preserving the high-rise shelter they now have." Elsewhere in his memoir, *Waiting for Gautreaux*, Polikoff asserts, "Society should not be forced to choose between Taylor [the Robert Taylor Homes development] and homelessness for any family. But of the two, a rebuilt Taylor seems the poorer option."[43]

For Wilen, who has represented residents at the Horner and ABLA developments, typically seeking to restrain CHA demolition activity and preserve public housing dwellings, the most pernicious consequence of Chicago's seemingly unending public housing crisis has been its contribution to the "huge shortfall in affordable housing units for the poor." As to the corrective measures that Alexander Polikoff has advanced—relocation of public housing families to white-majority communities, the break-up of the big CHA developments—Wilen has observed:

> By forcing African-Americans to leave their communities in order to revitalize them, integrationists are destroying the social networks, the friendships, and the service providers on which residents have come to rely. Forced integration of public housing residents presumes that, in a society free from discrimination, blacks would choose to live dispersed among whites . . . The choice of some African-Americans to remain in their neighborhoods may be born not out of knee-jerk sentiment but out of valid cultural preferences.[44]

Apart from the singular collapse of the Chicago Housing Authority, the transformation of public housing in Chicago and, in turn, the rebuilding of its inner-city public housing neighborhoods have been principally driven by national policy trends, and quite explicitly, by the local redevelopment program of Mayor Richard M. Daley. The analysts, ethnographers, and advocates have fleshed out the policy justifications and objections to this course of action, as well as some of the ambiguities intrinsic to any visionary program of community formation. Various institutional parties—including the CHA, non-profit legal offices such as BPI and the Shriver Center, and the main CHA residents' advocacy group, the Coalition to Protect Public Housing—have navigated the judicial and political arenas that have ultimately endorsed the approach to neighborhood formation typifying Chicago's new, inner-city communities.[45] And, a decade into the implementation of the CHA's Plan for Transformation, the evolution of these neighborhoods has proceeded to the point at which we can begin to discern what their characteristic, long-term features are likely to be.

THE NEW NEIGHBORHOODS

Though it has been more than a decade in the making, a very specific physical template has come to characterize Chicago's new inner-city, mixed-income neighborhoods. By way of our previous tour of Westhaven Park, we have touched on some of the principal components of the template. The great majority of residential buildings are limited to two, three, and four floors and have "traditional" architectural detailing like pitched roofs, double-hung windows, front stoops or porches, which further humanize the structures. Brick facades are also favored. This physical pattern, in addition, incorporates some more subtle elements. One is the commitment to building groups of residences "in which public housing units will be indistinguishable from those selling at market rates."

The designers of the new communities have virtually fetishized the idea of breaking up public housing superblocks by reinserting links to Chicago's predominant street grid. As architecture critic Blair Kamin has put it, the new neighborhoods will be "seamlessly rejoined to the rest of the city."[46] Ironically, this feature of the new design template is not always a corrective to what preceded it. For example, at Cabrini-Green, the three sections of the development were separated by one major thoroughfare, Division Street, and south of Division there was, in fact, an "internal" street system that connected to the surrounding grid. Within the Cabrini-Green development there were church buildings, public schools, and smaller structures occupied by social service agencies. In its later years, Cabrini-Green was a decidedly bleak area, and along its streets there were no permanent, legitimate business enterprises. Nonetheless, Cabrini-Green, in company with several other CHA developments, only loosely conformed to the tower-in-the-park isolation that has come to be the popular image of U.S. public housing.

As Kamin anticipated more than a decade ago, the physical template for public housing redevelopment in Chicago draws heavily on the new urbanist design menu. The new urbanists, in turn, have linked their vision of urban rejuvenation to various of Jane Jacobs's prescriptions, such as sidewalk- and street-oriented development, as well as mixed building types and uses. In reality, Chicago's new inner-city neighborhoods depart in some substantial ways from Jacobs's favored neighborhood form. In the first instance, their residential densities fall well below the hundred units per acre advocated by Jacobs. At Roosevelt Square—the former ABLA development— the density ratio of twenty-seven units per acre approaches what Jacobs dismissed as "semi-suburban."[47] Nevertheless, the private developers of areas such as Roosevelt Square have their reasons, notably the per-unit square footage expectations of "market-rate" purchasers and the need to provide ample parking. The latter consideration gives some of the new neighborhoods a Potemkin Village–like quality. At Westhaven Park, three sides of the street block formed by Lake, Hermitage, Maypole, and Wood are lined with residential structures. On the Lake Street side one finds the entrance to the large parking area that occupies most of the space within the four street lines. What from several points of view appears, in terms of building coverage, to be a dense city block, is not at all what it seems to be.

Similarly, Roosevelt Square's site plan sets aside a small number of commercial storefronts, which are typically assigned to the edges of the residential areas. However, as new construction has proceeded south of Roosevelt Road—where the larger portion of ABLA was located—there is no sign of commercial establishments. Again, one must assume that the middle-class preference for land-use segregation has trumped a key recommendation of the new urbanists' sacred text, Jacobs's *The Death and Life of Great American Cities*.

Beyond "the look" of the new neighborhoods, the profile of their residents also conforms to a template. In each mixed-income development a portion of the units, typically falling between one-fifth and one-third of the total, is set aside for public housing residents. A second category of "affordable" subsidized units—some rental, some for sale—may constitute as much as a quarter of the dwellings. The remainder, 50 percent or more of the units, are market rate and mainly for sale. To illustrate, the mellifluously designated Jazz on the Boulevard development facing South Side Drexel Boulevard (137 units total) includes 30 public housing units, 36 subsidized "affordable" units, and 71 for-sale, market-rate units. At North Town Village (261 units), built on the western fringe of Cabrini-Green, the public / affordable / market-rate housing proportions are 30 percent, 20 percent, and 50 percent, respectively.[48]

The occupants of the public housing units in these developments may or may not have relocated from a demolished CHA building on site or nearby. In the case of Westhaven Park, "local" relocatees are more prevalent due to the legal settlement accepted by the CHA in the mid-1990s. In any event, these public housing residents will have "passed" a formidable screening process to establish that adults are working, attending some form of training program, seeking employment, or disabled; to determine that the family is not in arrears of rent or utility bills; and to verify individual rectitude via criminal record checks and drug testing. In addition to meeting these entrance qualifications, public housing residents may be subject to community rules that do not apply to their fellow residents. At North Town Village, for example, tension has been produced by a ban on children (who overwhelmingly come from the households of the public housing residents) playing in the development's common areas.[49] In 2003, at nearby Orchard Park, a small development including public housing units that adjoined a CHA senior citizen high-rise, the Flannery Apartments, resident strife erupted when fencing was added within the development. A number of the public housing residents assumed that the fence was intended to isolate their units from the market-rate condominiums.[50]

In some of the mixed-income developments, governance arrangements may also amplify resident cleavages. In Westhaven Park, a Horner Residents Council continues to function, even as unit owners in the mixed-income 100 North Hermitage building convene a separate condominium association. In neither North Town Village nor Jazz on the Boulevard do the public housing and subsidized dwelling residents participate in the owners' associations, though in each, the property developer retains representation. North Town Village's developer, Peter Holsten, sometimes designates nonowners to attend the homeowners' association meetings in his stead.[51]

Among the striking discordances between mixed-income theorizing and the reality of these neighborhoods is the array of motivations that seem to bring higher income residents to them. In its July–August 2005 issue, the *Chicago Reporter* profiled a group of home purchasers in mixed-income developments. "Social mission" was not typically evident in the calculations yielding their choice of residence:

> New homeowners near changing public housing developments say they've moved there to be close to the Loop or other established areas and because the areas offered good opportunities to buy early when prices were low. Many realized that these neighborhoods would improve, as would property values, once nearby public housing high-rises were torn down.[52]

Without exception, the home purchasers profiled in this article had relocated from elsewhere in the city. Age-wise, most were in their thirties; for several it was their first purchase of a residential property. At Jazz on the Boulevard, Mark Joseph of Case Western Reserve University interviewed twenty-three purchasers and renters, with only one mentioning the development's mixed-income character as a factor influencing choice of neighborhood. This, by the way, was not due to an absence of information. All but one of Joseph's informants reported that they were aware of Jazz on the Boulevard's mix of housing types.[53] But in all likelihood, as the national housing market has deflated between 2007 and 2010, sales personnel at some of the mixed-income developments have downplayed social mission—or even the details of housing type variations—in an effort to sustain buyer interest in their projects.

In some cases, mixed-income developers have introduced community-building exercises as a means to stimulate resident cohesion. At North Town Village—completed in 2002 and, as such, one of the more longstanding mixed-income communities—Peter Holsten initiated a "story-telling" project which invited the newly arrived residents to gather and discuss their backgrounds and how they had come to be neighbors. This experiment, however, was short-lived: market-rate condominium and townhouse purchasers were not enthusiastic participants, and after a few meetings the story-telling exercise was discontinued.[54] At other mixed-income developments, resident-organized social gatherings have likewise failed to reach a cross-section of the households. In reference to owners and renters at Jazz on the Boulevard, Mark Joseph reports that "each group has hosted social events that were not attended by the other group."[55] In Westhaven Park, public housing residents have told me that only one or two local condominium purchasers have attended the "meet and greet" gatherings they have organized.[56]

Of course, it is a fine line that separates community-building efforts from intrusive neighboring, and most neighborhoods function perfectly well in the absence of social missionaries committed to multiplying interpersonal contacts, or more zealously, uplifting their fellow residents. Mary Pattillo's recently published study of North Kenwood–Oakland on Chicago's South Side, *Black on the Block*, illustrates the ambiguities of the black middle class seeking to do well, from the standpoint of shrewd real estate investment, while also doing good. Pattillo observes that many of the newcomers to North Kenwood–Oakland "[preach] the need to bring in higher income neighbors in order to create the ripple effect of better supported schools, a greater variety of businesses, and infrastructural improvements." In practice, interactions between North Kenwood–Oakland's newcomers and its public housing population are often fractious, which leads some of the newcomers to conclude that "the quick fix . . . is to drive out what is seen as the offending class."[57] In other instances, prosperous new arrivals to the mixed-income neighborhoods project more sweeping scenarios of neighborhood rebirth. In 2006, a *Chicago Tribune* reporter who had interviewed opponents of a proposed high-rise condominium project near Cabrini-Green noted that "one reason the first homeowners . . . decided to take a chance on the area was the idea that, once the public housing towers were gone, it would eventually offer a slice of suburban living minutes from downtown." Indeed, one of Antonio Olivo's sources flatly asserted that by settling in the Cabrini-Green area, the newcomers embodied neighborhood improvement: "We're actually concerned about the area. We moved in to transform it."[58]

In spite of such frictions and discordant visions of the neighborhood rejuvenation, at least until the real estate downturn of 2007–10, the mixed-income property development process was advancing briskly. For example, in mid-2005 the *Chicago Reporter* estimated that there was $281 million in residential property sales in the Cabrini-Green area during the preceding 18 months. Buying fever has been less pronounced in the other mixed-income neighborhoods, though newcomers to these communities have clearly begun to reshape the local family income profiles.[59] There are also signs of significant quality-of-life improvements. Crime levels have remained manageable in the mixed-income neighborhoods, in part due to intensive police patrolling. In 2004, the *Chicago Tribune*'s

Mary Schmich wrote of North Town Village: "You don't have to call the cops. They're everywhere already, their blue-and-white cars skimming past the sidewalks or parked on the perimeter, as conspicuous as stoplights to Cabrini kids tempted to walk the few steps across Scott Street into the prim new 'village.'"[60] My own experience on visits to the Cabrini-Green area, Westhaven Park, and Roosevelt Square confirms Schmich's perception. The improvement in public facilities serving the mixed-income neighborhoods is also striking. Amidst the high-rise clearance and townhouse development that is the most visible sign of change at Cabrini-Green, there is also a new police station, elementary school, and public library. At the corner of Orleans and Division streets, Seward Park—a visual gateway to Cabrini-Green—has been thoroughly renovated.

In the fifteen years between the renovation of Lake Parc Place and the marketing of the current generation of mixed-income neighborhoods, the meaning of "mixed-income" has shifted decisively. Not only has the "income spread" that encompasses the public housing population widened—due both to federal HOPE VI specifications and local public housing agency rules—but market-rate residential development in and adjoining the old public housing sites has imported very affluent neighborhood newcomers. In this particular respect, the ambiguous lessons of Lake Parc Place—as very poor residents interacted with poor *but not quite so poor* fellow residents—are irrelevant. A sense of the income and lifestyle disparities between public housing residents and the most prosperous of their new neighbors can be illustrated by reciting some of the features of the Kingsbury Park development just west of the Cabrini row houses: according to the development's promotional materials, the world's largest rooftop running track; a riverside marina; residential units selling for as much as $1 million.[61]

The longstanding residents of these neighborhoods—including those who have not occupied publicly subsidized dwellings—are quite aware of the income/lifestyle gulf separating them from a goodly share of their new neighbors. A Cabrini-Green area homeowner of many years, Larry Burns, explained to a reporter in 2005:

"Once you see the dogs coming in, then you know the neighborhood is gone . . . I don't know if it's going to get better. It's going to happen. It's a flow. It's like when the pioneers came to the West and moved the Indians out."[62] The bitterness expressed by Burns's final comment was more directly articulated by one of the Cabrini-Green resident leaders, Carol Steele: "The school is here, the stores are here, the new library is here. You done fixed up the streets and sidewalks . . . Now you're telling us, 'Go away and come back, maybe, when we build new housing.'"[63] Observing the specifics of local neighborhood change from very nearly the opposite social vantage point, Steele's comment exactly mirrors the expectation of the Cabrini-area newcomer who has "moved in to transform it." What Burns and Steele have to say about the new Cabrini-Green area touches on a conspicuously neglected point. Future neighborhood relations are likely to be, in part, an outgrowth of past neighborhood events. For the individuals and families who have long lived in the new mixed-income neighborhoods—public housing residents, homeowners and "private" renters alike—the wrenching *processes* of neighborhood transformation may well poison their approach to neighborliness for some time to come.

So far, the new mixed-income neighborhoods have not become lively street neighborhoods. In part, this may be a function of commercial development trailing residential development, though their relatively low residential densities will, in all likelihood, continue to impede the formation of extensive local merchant networks. Ultimately, the urban *look* of these neighborhoods disguises an automobile-oriented land-use model: low residential densities; the ample provision of parking space. The notable exception among the mixed-income neighborhoods is at the intersection of Clybourn Avenue and Division Street, just north of the old Cabrini Extension site, where a supermarket anchors a busy strip mall. The Dominick's grocery has become a neighborhood hub, drawing a clientele from the prosperous neighborhoods to the east and north, as well local shoppers of all incomes.[64] In the other mixed-income neighborhoods, the scarcity of such nearby merchants is a leading resident concern.[65] Indeed, one of the promises of mixed-income neighborhood development has been that it would spark entrepreneurial and job opportunities for the less prosperous local residents. At this time, Chicago's new neighborhoods are not being built in a manner that will enable them to deliver on this expectation.

PANORAMIC AIMS, A LESSON FROM HUDSON STREET

Less noted than the Jacobsian rhetoric of the mixed-income neighborhoods' developers is the panoramic vision of public housing deconcentrater Alexander Polikoff. Polikoff's Chicago is the metropolitan region, whose innumerable suburban communities offer a plenitude of housing choices, as well as education and job mobility opportunities for relocated public housing residents. From this perspective, the campaign to eradicate inner-city poverty is just as dependent on suburban relocation—assisted with federal government-supported housing vouchers—as it is on the creation of inner-city mixed-income neighborhoods. In practice, many suburban communities—particularly those whose local leaders are keen to protect property values and the school revenues derived from property taxation—use the power of land use control to limit the settlement of renters and the less prosperous. Given this reality, poverty reduction through suburban relocation appears to be a strategy subject to built-in limitations: workable if limited to highly motivated families, whose "access points" will be that portion of suburban towns whose municipal leaders, like Alexander Polikoff, hold to an inclusive, panoramic sense of metropolitan community.

Whether or not Polikoff's panoramic regionalism is also an anti-urban vision is another matter. Certainly, the promotion of most contemporary "outer-ring" suburbs—very low-density, highly auto-dependent places—as the antidote to poverty appears to be willfully naive. This, then, returns us to the promise of the mixed-income neighborhoods within Chicago and other cities, which purport to provide a density of interpersonal contacts that will nurture *urbanity* in its classic sense, the ability to navigate diverse people and situations, and concurrently, provide a density of persons that can build local *commercial* as well as *residential* neighborhoods.

As my preceding account has emphasized, one of the principal problems—up to this point in time—with mixed-income neighborhood development in Chicago has been its mistaking the look of the city for the underlying processes that can sustain busy, congenial neighborhood life. The new urbanist builders of the mixed-income neighborhoods talk the Jacobs talk, but walk the upscale residential developers' walk. More deeply, how the new urbanists violate some of Jane Jacobs's precepts forces one to reconsider the relationship between contemporary urban culture and various of Jacobs's assumptions regarding city life in the 1950s. The healthy street neighborhoods of New York, Boston, and Philadelphia that are documented in *The Death and Life of Great American Cities* occupied metropolises—indeed, occupied a nation—whose engrained egalitarianism is a world apart from the contemporary United States. Residing on Jacobs's Hudson Street were mechanics, attorneys, Wall Street executives, and at least one journalist. Their choice of street did not follow from a conscious commitment to mixed-income living; nor did they choose Hudson Street in order to share a lifestyle with others much like themselves. Rather, working in a city whose income spread was far narrower than what we now take for granted, and—possibly just as important—in which respect for a wide array of occupations was the stuff of everyday life, Hudson Street permitted them, in the main, to live the lives of their choice. Hudson Street's built form, in combination with its residents' openness to experience and their matter-of-fact egalitarianism, made for a workable, satisfying street neighborhood. Chicago's contemporary mixed-income neighborhood builders aim to reach a population of purchasers whose assumptions about themselves, their neighbors, and their city are radically different.

The United Airlines Terminal at O'Hare Airport, which is one of the Third City's main economic drivers.

SIX

CHICAGO AND AMERICAN URBANISM

THE PERVASIVENESS of Jane Jacobs's intellectual legacy can be illustrated by considering how her thinking has shaped two widely praised books that were published during the last decade. Richard Florida's *The Rise of the Creative Class* (2002) has been described as "extraordinary," "a revolutionary idea," and "revelatory." This success has made Florida a sought-after public speaker and advisor to municipal governments. He has also written a series of follow-up volumes elaborating themes initially presented in *The Rise of the Creative Class.*[1] Douglas E. Rae's *City: Urbanism and Its End* (2003) has not experienced the scholarly-to-general readership crossover of Florida's work, but it has been widely discussed by urban studies experts. For example, the January 2005 issue of *Urban Affairs Review* devoted a four-contributor "Review Symposium" to Rae's book.[2] At this point in time, that Jane Jacobs's ideas should be a primary influence on two such books is quite unremarkable. In this instance, what is striking about the intellectual pull of Jacobs's thinking are the sharply divergent analyses of American cities offered by Florida and Rae.

Richard Florida is the evangelist of the creative class: "people who add economic value through their creativity," an occupational cohort including "a great many knowledge workers, symbolic analysts and professional and technical workers." Their rising numbers and enthusiasm for urban spaces and experience promise to rejuvenate American cities.[3] The principal Jacobsian thread running through *The Rise of the Creative Class* is the appeal of street-oriented, mixed-use urban spaces for members of this group:

A vibrant, varied nightlife was viewed by many as another signal that a city "gets it," even by those who infrequently partake of nightlife. Interestingly, one of the biggest complaints of my focus groups had to do with cities where nightlife closes down too early. The reason is not that most of these people are all-night partyers, but with long work hours and late nights, they need to have options around the clock.[4]

Many of Florida's informants are younger professionals whose preference for such urban "scenes" reflects the turn in cultural style and popular preference noted by Sharon Zukin in *Loft Living*. However, Florida discerns deeper sources of the creative class's affinity for diverse neighborhood environments. Deriving his insight from a *New Yorker* essay in which Malcolm Gladwell linked "new office design" to Jacobs's interpretations of neighborhood vitality, Florida proposes that at-work environments tapping "the productive efficiencies that come from concentration and co-location" are not only analogous to stimulating street neighborhoods, but in addition, model the spatial characteristics the creative class seeks in leisure environments.[5]

Addressing the governmental and civic elites who shape economic development action at the municipal level, Florida argues that outmoded redevelopment techniques—such as "underwriting big-box retailers, subsidizing downtown malls, recruiting call centers and squandering precious taxpayer dollars on extravagant stadium complexes"—must be jettisoned in favor of "softer" approaches to urban rejuvenation.[6] Among the latter, Florida's preferences include government and foundation support for start-up and innovative arts organizations, mixed-use neighborhood development strategies, and more broadly, the promotion of social tolerance. A portion of Florida's program—mixed-use development, for example—seems already to have achieved broad popular approval, though it seems less clear how local elites can, in any direct or concerted fashion, induce public appreciation of provocative art or tolerance of sexual nonconformity. In Florida's view, among the principal barriers to innovative urban development is the afterglow of past triumphs, which tends to reduce contemporary cities' adaptive powers:

Cities like Detroit, Cleveland and Pittsburgh were the stars of that [bygone organizational] age. The cultural and attitudinal norms that drove their success became so powerful that they have prevented the new norms and attitudes of the Creative Age from becoming generally accepted. This process stamped out much of the creative impulse, causing talented and creative people to seek out more congenial and challenging places.[7]

Nevertheless, according to Florida creative-class demographics and experiential preferences are trending in favor of urban places, and the physical environments of even Detroit, Cleveland, and Pittsburgh are crammed with industrial-age structures ripe for conversion to galleries, coffeehouses, and "new economy" workspaces. As such, one of the main planks in Florida's program of urban revitalization is the return to the socially heterogeneous, mixed-use Jacobsian streetscape.

Richard Florida is a panoramic normativist. In chapter 16 of *The Rise of the Creative Class*, his broad stroke profiles of cities that have either mastered or lagged in mastering the logic of creative age economic development—Austin, Pittsburgh, and Dublin—span the Atlantic. His tabular rankings of urban creativity offer numerical assessments of 276 U.S. metropolitan areas! In various ways, it is difficult to imagine a volume more unlike *The Rise of the Creative Class* than *City: Urbanism and Its End*. Douglas Rae's book is the methodical account of economic, neighborhood, and political trends in a single city: New Haven, Connecticut. It is a chronology that extends more than 150 years. Nor are these books merely divided by focus and analytical strategy. Rae's title reveals the *tone* of his analysis, which is at once elegiac and regretful (having served as advisor to past New Haven mayors, he intimates some degree of complicity in the playing out of events).

At the core of Rae's history of New Haven's rise and fall is an economic / technological argument that "centering technologies," principally coal-powered manufacturing facilities and railroads, caused a rush of capital and population to settle in New Haven in the middle decades of the nineteenth century. The forces of economic centralization that anchored industrial-age New Haven, in turn, produced a "dense civic fauna" of nongovernmental institutions, both city-wide and within particular neighborhoods, that provided communal aid in times of stress and, day-to-day, enlivened the city's streets, shops, and workplaces. The ultimate expression of this convergence of forces was a political order based on limited municipal powers, but that coincidentally offered a reasonable degree of citizen responsiveness and an attractive stage for the exercise of benevolent civic leadership by New Haven's business barons. This day in the sun was not to last: "New Haven was . . . a cost-competitive environment for manufacturing as it had never been in previous history—and would cease to be a few generations hence."[8]

The principal movements in Rae's elegy to a lost city highlight empirical matters such as the demise of corner grocery stores (as chain merchants drained their customer base), the withdrawal of business leaders to New Haven's suburban periphery (and the consequent reduction in their centered civic energies), and the failure of New Haven's greatest mayor, Richard Lee, to counter decentering trends in spite of his aggressive application of federally funded urban renewal. What New Haven lost, as the intertwined centering tendencies of the nineteenth- and early-twentieth-century city gave way, was the particular variety of *urbanism* that had made it a prospering and congenial community. Rae defines this quality of urbanism in explicitly Jacobsian terms: "The dense fabric of enterprise, with perhaps three thousand retailers holding down street-corner and mid-block sites throughout the working-class neighborhoods and the downtown, was at once a normative force ('eyes on the street' as Jane Jacobs would say) and a major layer of opportunity for each generation of workers and their families."[9] *City: Urbanism and Its End* is an empirical account of New Haven's decline, emphasizing the street-level manifestations of that decline. Enveloping Rae's empirical analysis, and the source of its elegiac character, is his perception that a particular variety of normative city—generally inclusive, widely prosperous, and self-regulating—has been lost and will not be recovered.

Richard Florida's Day-Glo optimism, Douglas Rae's learned bleakness, coursing through each the Jacobsian appreciation of dense, mixed-use street environments: is it possible to reconcile these discordant interpretations of the contemporary American city? I think it is, if we consider the sea change in urban development trajectories and fortunes that has occurred during the last half-century. Just as Jane Jacobs chronicled a mid-twentieth-century New York cityscape whose formative elements were Gotham's centrality as a commercial hub, specialized industrial center, and leading cultural site—all the foregoing coinciding with the latter years of the epoch demarcated by America's ascendancy as the global leader in mass industrialization—Douglas Rae painstakingly describes the ebbing of this economy's reach in one of the New York region's satellite cities. By contrast, Richard Florida's gaze is firmly directed at a new variety of urbanism that can be inferred by considering the workplace experiences and leisure preferences of what he presumes to be the modal American of the oncoming decades. Rarely will this emergent, modal American labor in long production-line factory assembly; the characteristic day-to-day physical environment in the American city to come will owe but little to the Fordist factory and office environments that typified Jacobs's beloved New York and Rae's departed New Haven. In effect, Rae and Florida have analyzed, respectively, the winding down of one form of urbanism and the emergence—at this point in time, with many of the details still to be clearly articulated—of another type of American city. As such, Florida's enraptured normative projections and Rae's normatively despairing retrospection draw upon the same intellectual wellspring.

CHICAGO'S FIRST, SECOND, AND THIRD CITIES

It was early in that spring of 1834 that I found myself standing at the crossing of Dearborn and Lake streets looking west; and for the first time I could see where the street was by the line of buildings on either side of it. This was the first time I ever noticed a street in Chicago made perceptible by the buildings on both sides of it. Then for the first time I could fully realize that our little settlement was assuming the appearance of a town.[10]

John Dean Caton's recognition that Chicago was "assuming the appearance of a town" occurred three years before the frontier settlement at the southwestern corner of Lake Michigan was incorporated as an Illinois municipality. Chicago's First City—the industrial powerhouse spanning the decades between the Civil War and the Great Depression—would begin to take shape within just a few years. In *City of the Century*, Donald L. Miller dates the emergence of the First City quite unequivocally:

> Modern Chicago was born in 1848. In January of that year, the first telegraph line reached the city, and in succeeding months the Illinois and Michigan Canal opened, the first oceangoing steamship arrived from Montreal, Cyrus Hall McCormick, the future "Reaper King," moved to the city from the Shenandoah Valley, and construction began on Chicago's first railroad and on its first wooden turnpikes over mud and marsh to grain farms and young market towns on the prairie. To promote and give direction to the city's exploding economy, merchants and commission men established the Chicago Board of Trade in rooms over a flour store near the river.[11]

Other moments of converging incident might be selected to mark the birth of the First City. For instance, William Cronon, more than Donald Miller a historian of processes and trends, notes that "between 1850 and 1854, the net eastward movement of freight shipments via the Great Lakes finally surpassed shipments out of New Orleans. No place was more important than Chicago to this redirection of agricultural trade."[12] By the end of the Civil War, Chicago's transition from frontier settlement to First City was clearly under way. Between 1860 and 1870 its population nearly tripled from 109,000 to just under 300,000. Speaking of Chicago and the adjoining upper Midwest, Cronon comments, "Whether to meet the enormous demand of the Union Army or to purchase goods from booming eastern wholesale centers, the commerce of the region turned ever more thoroughly away from its old channels."[13] Notable among these "old channels" was the Mississippi River and its waterborne commercial traffic, which was disrupted by the war and subsequently overtaken by Chicago's expanding network of railroads.

In 1870 Chicago's meatpackers consolidated their operations with the opening of the Union Stock Yard. That year, three million animals were slaughtered.[14] And, as evoked by Upton Sinclair's famous description, the city was provided with an iconic image: "There is over a square mile of space in the yards, and more than half of it is occupied by cattle pens; north and south as far as the eye can reach there stretches a sea of pens. And they were all filled—so many cattle no one had ever dreamed in the world." Sinclair's portrait, of course, moves beyond the holding pens to describe a site of elemental transformation:

> There were groups of cattle being driven to the chutes, which were roadways about fifteen feet wide, raised high above the pens. In these chutes the stream of animals was continuous; it was quite uncanny to watch them, pressing on to their fate, all unsuspicious—a very river of death . . . [T]he hogs went up by the power of their own legs, and then their weight carried them back through all of the processes necessary to make them into pork.[15]

The First City—industrial powerhouse—has been succinctly, if less graphically characterized as a metropolis of "large firms and long production lines."[16] This essence was initially fused at the Union Stock Yard.

From the Civil War years until the onset of the Great Depression, Chicago was a boomtown. Having experienced a population increase of 68 percent between 1870 and 1880, a pace of growth probably reduced by the Great Fire of 1871, the number of city residents more than doubled in the following ten years. Across the five census decades spanning 1880 to 1930, in only one ten-year period— from 1900 to 1910—did Chicago add fewer than 500,000 residents. During the half-century preceding the Great Depression, New York City and Chicago were America's principal destination points for European immigrants. Indeed, by 1890 approximately three-quarters of Chicago's 1,099,000 residents were either foreign-born or had at least one foreign-born parent.[17] Chicago's allure was embodied by its "diverse, balanced, and rapidly expanding manufacturing base" and the job opportunities promised not just in leading "export" industries, such as meatpacking and railway car assembly, but also in many varieties of consumer product fabrication, "from washbowls and bathtubs to books, clothes, boots, and shoes."[18]

In this era the First City's mosaic of ethnic neighborhoods took shape, as did its longstanding politics of ward-level mobilization, ethnic identification, and patronage. Interethnic conflict was commonplace, and in addition to the "horizontal" sources of social strife, Chicago's huge working population frequently clashed with the city's big employers. Within a decade of the Haymarket Incident of 1886, the bitter Pullman strike of 1894 generated labor / owner conflict across the United States. At the Union Stock Yard, large-scale labor walk-outs occurred in 1904 and 1921. But surely the greatest instance of social disruption experienced by the First City was the nearly weeklong race riot of late July 1919, a roiling series of pitched battles whose death toll reached thirty-eight.[19]

Given the First City's array of "superlatives"—explosive population growth, industrial innovation, searing social conflict—it is easy enough to forget that even as Chicago the industrial powerhouse flourished, the seeds of its transformation were also taking root. For example, William Cronon notes that as early as the 1880s Chicago's meatpackers "could already see that Chicago's advantages—its transportation facilities, its concentrated market, its closeness to western supplies of cattle—were by no means unique. Conditions at the Union Stockyards were crowded, there was little room for expansion, and the city was not as close to the chief grazing regions of the country as were certain other cities that lay still farther to the west." As a result, the meatpackers began to build new facilities to Chicago's south and west, at East St. Louis, Kansas City, and Omaha. "It was the beginning of the end," though the winding down of Chicago meatpacking would take decades, with the Union Stock Yard officially ceasing operation on July 30, 1971.[20]

Nor were the First City's ethnic neighborhoods stable repositories of timelessness. As Lizabeth Cohen repeatedly demonstrates in *Making a New Deal*, the pleasures and discomforts of neighborhood life were, to a great degree, determined by the economic health and day-to-day practices of nearby job centers: the Union Stock Yard, the Hawthorne Works (Western Electric), and International Harvester on the West Side; the steel mills on the South Side. In the two decades between the first and second world wars, technological developments enabled the managers of these facilities to substantially increase worker output, which typically translated to shrinking workforces. Coincidentally, chain retailers such as Woolworth's, A&P, and J.C. Penney began to dot Chicago's neighborhood commercial strips. The benefits to consumers offered by the chain stores—lower prices and standardized products—exacted a substantial local cost. Neighborhood merchants frequently failed. Having related how emerging entertainment media—notably radio and Hollywood films—further "eroded local and ethnic institutions," Cohen concludes, "Workers in the 1930s were more likely to share a cultural world, to see the same movies and newsreels in the same chain theaters, shop for the same items in the same chain stores, and listen to the same radio shows on network radio, a situation very different from that of 1919 when workers lived in isolated cultural communities."[21]

The transition from Chicago's First to Second City—the exemplar of urban decline—coincided with the Great Depression and World War II. At the 1930 census point, Chicago's huge decade-by-decade population increases came to an end. Across the next two census periods the city added just under 250,000 residents; from 1950 to 1990 Chicago lost residents during each census decade, a proportional decline representing nearly one-quarter of the city's peak 1950 population figure of 3,620,962. The years of transition between the First and Second Cities were marked by a sequence of essentially contradictory developments. Chicago's economy, its residents, and its neighborhoods were battered by the Great Depression, but World War II and the early years of the postwar boom seemed to rejuvenate the city's industrial economy. It is not a coincidence that Alan Ehrenhalt's nostalgic evocation of a socially coherent Chicago, *The Lost City*, recalls just this period.[22] Crucial features of the First City, such as the network of ethnic neighborhoods, still retained some of their vitality; the most devastating attributes of the Second City, notably the withering of the industrial economy and the emergence of intense racial conflict, were still some years in the future.

Among the Chicagoans who did recognize something new in the 1950s—even if their diagnosis deviated in crucial respects from this account—were the city's governmental, business, and civic leaders. At the dawning of the Second City, major redevelopment initiatives began on the Near South Side and, at the University of Chicago's behest, in Hyde Park.[23] The "Development Plan for the Central Area of Chicago," released by the city government in 1958, is a significant document precisely because of the postindustrial Chicago that it imagines.[24] The irony of this plan, and more generally, of Chicago's Loop-oriented and neighborhood-directed redevelopment activity in the early years of the Second City, was the tendency of these initiatives—as they were carried through—to accelerate processes of neighborhood decline and the erosion of local economic networks.

To return briefly to population dynamics, from 1950 to 1960 Chicago's population dropped by a modest 70,000 residents (that is, 2 percent of the 1950 figure). However, during this decade, the African American population residing in Chicago grew by nearly 300,000. The white population, in turn, declined by approximately 350,000. As amply demonstrated by histories of the period such as Arnold Hirsch's *Making the Second Ghetto* and Amanda Seligman's *Block by Block*, the principal arena for the playing out of Chicago's racial crisis of the 1950s and 1960s was the city's neighborhoods.[25] With many near-Loop residential areas under pressure from redevelopment, African Americans pressed "out" across the South and West Sides, where in most cases they encountered—and were not welcomed by—ethnic whites who themselves had, in just the last generation, gained a foothold in the American middle class. Chicago's racial / neighborhood wars were also the ultimate source of the political crises of Richard J. Daley's latter years as mayor.[26]

The statistic that most tellingly defines the trajectory of the Second City is Chicago's loss of manufacturing employment, from 668,000 industrial workers in 1947 to 277,000 in 1982. But just as revealing are the proportions of the metropolitan total represented by these raw numbers. At the end of World War II, industrial employment within Chicago's city limits constituted two-thirds of such jobs across the metropolitan area. By the early 1980s Chicago was accounting for approximately one-third of the manufacturing employment in its metropolitan area.[27] The Second City stagnated even as its metropolitan region spread and prospered.

The Second City's duration can be considered a short two generations. A more specific temporal boundary can be set at 1950, when the city's population count peaked, and 1990, the census point at which Chicago's population began—following forty years of decline—a decade-long recovery. The emergent Third City is a postindustrial business and cultural node. Its economic strong suits include transportation facilities serving travelers and handling freight, business services (notably law, accounting, and advertising), commodities and securities trading, and "hosting," that is, both tourists and visitors to the city attending conventions and trade shows. Lacking major banks that are locally controlled, Chicago is not a financial center in the traditional sense. It is the Chicago metropolitan region—much more than the central city—that can be considered a significant corporate headquarters nexus. Vestiges of Chicago's industrial economy remain, although the "long production lines" have, for the most part, vanished. For instance, each of the half-dozen major industrial complexes profiled by Lizabeth Cohen in *Making a New Deal* shut down many years ago.

Certainly the most visible sign of the Third City's emergence is the boom in residential development that began to fill in the tangle of warehouses, railroad lines, factories, and Chicago Housing Authority developments that for decades bounded the Loop, especially to the west and south. Preceding the real estate downturn that began in 2007, Chicago's near-Loop neighborhoods had experienced years of intensifying residential and commercial development. For example, residential sales in the Loop and its adjoining neighborhoods exceeded 3,000 units in every year between 1998 and 2005.[28] As recently as 1980, the number of Loop residents totaled only 6,462. This figure had more than doubled by 2000. Recent population trends in the two community areas directly north and south of the Loop are especially striking: both the Near North Side and the Near South Side lost population in each census decade from 1950 until 1990, but from 1990 to 2000 both community areas added residents. The more populous Near North Side's proportional increase was 16 percent. The number of Near South Side residents jumped from 6,828 to 9,509, an increase of 39 percent.[29]

Is the Third City's economic foundation little more than "bread and circuses"? This is a conclusion some observers have reached, in particular, by noting the longstanding decline in unionized manufacturing employment coupled with the rise in service sector jobs.[30] Nevertheless, the scale of contemporary Chicago's leisure and hospitality economy is remarkable. By the late 1990s a half-dozen of the city's arts and recreation attractions reported annual attendance figures in excess of a million. These included venerable cultural institutions such as the Art Institute, the Field Museum, and the Museum of Science and Industry. But topping the list was the then recently redeveloped Navy Pier, a festival marketplace whose attendance figure approached eight million in 1999. There are also the "special events."[31] The Air and Water Show, Taste of Chicago, the Blues Festival, the Country Music Festival, and Venetian Night—all annual summer festivals—each report attendance figures surpassing half a million.[32] With the exception of the Air and Water Show, these events take place in Grant Park and generate billions of dollars of spillover spending directed to downtown restaurants and retailers.

Finally, the emergence of the Third City has coincided with the mayoralty of Richard M. Daley, whose administration in various ways—by supporting near-Loop development activity, directly sponsoring new tourist magnets such as the Millennium Park complex, and more broadly, by initiating a series of major policy redirections in the Chicago Public Schools and the Chicago Housing Authority—has redefined Chicago's image. As such, Mayor Daley's role in producing the Third City has been more nimbly reactive than visionary. Nevertheless, by managing the city with a seemingly steady hand and by pursuing a strategy of municipal governance that is aligned with local norms of official accountability, current notions of desirable governmental innovation, and a pragmatic approach to public sector/private sector interactions, Richard M. Daley's record and reputation have contributed much to the articulation of the Third City's distinctive features.

THE THIRD CITY: CAUSES, CONSEQUENCES, SERENDIPITY

"Chicago is a global city. Once the industrial powerhouse of the mid-continent, Chicago has transformed itself into one of the handful of cities—two or three in America, twenty or thirty in the world—that define and direct the global economy."[33] In this rendering of the Third City as a "command and control" center—offered in 2007 by the Chicago Council on Global Affairs—the emergent Chicago has "transformed itself," in effect reasserting its place as a leader among American metropolises. The local boosters of cities everywhere are prone to advancing such claims of inherent, self-regenerating virtue, though in this instance the Chicago Council on Global Affairs indeed does describe a real change in fortune for the former "industrial powerhouse of the mid-continent." Yet just as plausibly, one can identify a cluster of interrelated external trends whose cumulative impact has spurred Chicago's transition from Second to Third City. In the following pages I seek to connect these broad trends with local agency and, in addition, offer some comments concerning whether or not Chicago's Third City is likely to become the *kind* of city one might wish to call home.

Sociologist Saskia Sassen, the leading intellectual explorer of the "global cities" concept, initially used this idea to characterize the corporate management and finance functions that, by the 1980s, three cities—New York, London, and Tokyo—had come to dominate. Sassen subsequently expanded the notion of global cities by contending that, in addition to her original trio of preeminent global centers, "there is a powerful second tier of some twenty cities that command many of the resources and services that define global hubs."[34] Sassen places Chicago in this second tier of global cities, accompanied by, among others, Hong Kong, Zurich, Amsterdam, Milan, Toronto, and Sydney.

The specific links between the broad trend of economic globalization and Chicago's particular circumstances are as follows. At the midpoint of the twentieth century, that is, as the hardships of the Second City began to unfold, Chicago was nonetheless blessed with a significant concentration of major headquarters firms, as well as a complementary cluster of leading financial institutions. Even as deindustrialization, corporate restructuring, and local bank failures thinned out the Second City's economic bedrock, a dense "entrepreneurial fauna" of business services firms flourished. Coincidentally, Chicago's innovative commodities and securities exchanges attracted significant flows of capital, and Chicago's hosting infrastructure— O'Hare Airport; the McCormick Place convention complex; leading cultural attractions including the Art Institute, Chicago Symphony Orchestra, and Lyric Opera; and the Loop's hotels and restaurants— made the city an important venue for conventions, trade shows, and both business and leisure travel. Further contributing to Chicago's competitiveness in the globalizing economy has been its concentration of research universities, notably the University of Chicago, Northwestern University, and the University of Illinois at Chicago. In short, an array of attributes carried over from the First and Second Cities, coupled with the development of new business niches and exploitable pools of skilled human capital, from the viewpoint of global cities formation have produced the Third City.

The Sassen perspective, however, explains but one trend, albeit the encompassing external force that has given shape to the Third City. In no way contradictory to the global cities explanation, even as it focuses on distinctive consumer preferences, is Sharon Zukin's "cultural style" interpretation of inner-city revitalization.[35] From this standpoint, the proliferation of well-paying new economy jobs in cities such as New York, Los Angeles, Boston, San Francisco, Washington, D.C., and Chicago would have but a limited impact on commercial and residential revitalization were it not for the middle class's renewed appreciation of historic architecture, lively streets, and in general, the metropolitan ambiance. Contemporary Chicago retains many physical legacies of the First City, one of the handful of metropolises that embodied America's "great industrial age."

Chicago is also awash in university students, including many with substantial training in the arts. Since the 1990s, young artists, hipsters on the make, and the merchants serving these populations have contributed mightily to the transformation of near-Loop neighborhoods such as Pilsen, West Town, Wicker Park, and Logan Square. Both neighborhood observers and social scientists typically view artists as the first wave of gentrification, which in fact, would not have a second wave unless there were far greater numbers of accountants, commodities traders, and lawyers with the itch to live in accessible, architecturally distinctive, restaurant-rich residential districts. What the first wave of artists and their retinues in particular have brought to Chicago's belt of hip neighborhoods running from Logan Square down through Pilsen is the sidewalk busyness, storefront distinctiveness, and cosmopolitan aura that attract members of Sassen's managerial class. Chicago's cosmopolitan "Neo-Bohemia," as described by sociologist Richard Lloyd, also links the city to the arts world on the coasts and abroad in a particular way. The cheap rents that can still be found on the fringes of neighborhoods such as Wicker Park, in tandem with relatively low production costs for mounting various kinds of theatrical and musical presentations, have made Chicago a significant training ground for artists and performers who eventually will move on to Los Angeles or New York.[36]

The ravages of the Second City's decline also must be given their due. As Chicago lost residents in the second half of the twentieth century, and simultaneously, as the coherence of its neighborhood mosaic and the density of economic networks diminished, real estate values—other than those in the Loop and a few of the lakefront residential neighborhoods—plummeted. By sometime in the 1980s, as Chicago's emerging role in the global economy solidified, and given the cultural shift toward appreciation of things urban, real estate investment in downtown and near-downtown Chicago once more became attractive:

> Disinvestment in urban real estate develops a certain momentum that gives the appearance of being self-fulfilling. Historical decline in a neighborhood's real estate provokes further decline, since the ground rent that can be appropriated at a given site depends not only upon the level of investment on the site itself, but on the physical and economic condition of surrounding structures and wider investment trends . . . The opposite process, sustained neighborhood reinvestment, appears equally self-fulfilling, for it is obviously irrational for a housing entrepreneur to leave a building in dilapidated condition amidst widespread neighborhood rehabilitation and recapitalization.[37]

The Second City was not locked in an unyielding spiral of decline—what political scientist Edward Goetz has dubbed the "Detroit Scenario"—and the broad outlines of the emergent Third City were becoming apparent to property owners, developers, and financiers.[38] In the oblique terminology of real estate analysis, Chicago's inner-city areas were "revalorizing." More dramatically, as Robert Beauregard has put it in *When America Became Suburban*: "By the end of the twentieth century, westward expansion had been exhausted and the cities of the northeast—wild, untamed, and ripe for rediscovery and reinvestment—had become the country's new challenge."[39]

Apart from the inner-city neighborhood revitalization that provides residential quarters for Sassen's global management cadre and Florida's creative class—and is a hallmark of the Third City—the global economy's accelerating business and leisure travel patterns have contributed to new forms of commercial development. Political scientist Dennis Judd coined the term "tourist bubble" to describe the upscale, inner-city commercial districts that have been planned and built around the globe: "Tourist and entertainment facilities coexist in a symbiotic relationship with downtown corporate towers, often with a substantial spatial overlap: shopping malls, restaurants, and bars cater to tourists as well as daytime professionals who work downtown and weekend suburban commuters. In many cities, however, a well-defined perimeter separates the tourist space from the rest of the city."[40]

On the one hand, global and domestic travel opens up opportunities for cities to "import" visitors and their discretionary spending. On the other hand, innovative commercial developments such as the Rouse Company's much-analyzed "festival marketplaces" are among the characteristic architectural features of twenty-first-century cities.[41] Chicago has not hesitated to enter the tourist bubble sweepstakes: in the 1970s North Michigan Avenue's Water Tower Place was a pioneering "vertical shopping mall"; since the 1990s Navy Pier—a very sophisticated, multipurpose Rouse project—has become a leading tourist destination; in just the past few years Millennium Park has, in a fashion some have likened to the Eiffel Tower's embodiment of *Belle Époque* Paris, "rebranded" the Third City for international visitors.

Some boosters will assert that the design creativity clearly in evidence at Millennium Park is one more instance of a resurgent Chicago that has transformed itself. I would respond that the design breakthroughs visible at Water Tower Place, Navy Pier, and Millennium Park reflect broad, indeed globe-spanning architectural innovations whose emergence has both contributed to the expansion of business and leisure travel, and more fundamentally, come to define what is conventionally understood as rewarding urban tourism. Yet in some respects—though the "how" and "to what effect" of these local projects are surely subject to debate—the boosters must also be given their due. Since the 1980s, Chicago has become a much more urbanistically appealing city. Apart from the much-discussed Navy Pier and Millennium Park, major thoroughfares such as Lakeshore Drive, LaSalle Street, and Ashland Avenue have been attractively landscaped, and across the city new, stylishly dignified branch libraries, rebuilt "vest-pocket" playgrounds, and dedicated bicycle lanes grace neighborhoods and their streets. Much of the credit for these urban planning improvements—both large- and small-scale—belongs to Richard M. Daley, who clearly has absorbed many of Jane Jacobs's "micro-planning" insights.

Of course, to return to Dennis Judd's notion of the tourist bubble, beyond these visitor- and consumer-friendly zones one can expect to find "crime, poverty, and urban decay," a cluster of infirmities that is still amply expressed in Chicago's geography.[42] A belt of neighborhoods running west from the Loop—including West Garfield Park, North Lawndale, and Austin—and then to the south and east—including West Englewood, Englewood, Washington Park, and Woodlawn—have experienced little of the economic boom associated with the emergent Third City. In some of these areas, public infrastructure improvements, such as park renovations and new school construction, reflect a municipal commitment to neighborhood improvement, but the private sector has not responded to this cue by seeding these neighborhoods with well-paying jobs or substantial commercial or residential investment. The Daley administration's "entrepreneurial state" has focused public investment—as well as programmatic innovation (for instance, in local schools)—in portions of the South and West Sides adjoining the lakefront and Loop, areas within the Third City that have flourished since the 1990s. Mike Royko's "Loop versus the rest of the city" trope no longer quite holds, because prosperous Chicago now extends for several miles along Lake Michigan both north and south of the Loop, and to the west gentrification reaches beyond Ashland Avenue. Yet apart from this boundary realignment, Chicago's longstanding spatial divide between the rich and poor endures.

Even from the standpoint of city planning and architecture, the Third City's designers walk a thin line between evocative historicism and grandiose self-parody. For many years the city government's planners have encouraged street-oriented residential construction, and most dramatically, the redevelopment of the public housing neighborhoods has coupled demolition of high-rise towers with low-rise, frequently row house–style new construction. Nonetheless, as often as not, Chicago's new neighborhoods for the very prosperous fail both aesthetically and urbanistically. In Dearborn Park on the Near South Side just below Roosevelt Road, the builders of faux prairie style mansions have crudely squeezed showy single-family dwellings onto postage stamp lots. Few pedestrians will not ponder the threat of physical dismemberment as they are squeezed on both sides by these top-heavy brick and concrete cupcakes. But worse, Dearborn Park is very nearly a single-use gated community. Though entrance to the neighborhood does not require negotiating a checkpoint, its internal street system is minimally connected to the adjoining grid, pedestrian "through traffic" is virtually nonexistent, and storefronts are entirely absent. When they shop, Dearborn Parkers use their automobiles to reach the supermarket or boutique.

The most surprising aspect of the Third City's public discourse has been the emergence of the metropolitan vision promoted by the Chicago Metropolis 2020 organization. The panoramic normativeness of the *Chicago Metropolis 2020* plan offers a compelling intellectual counterpoint to the very real prospect of the Third City's becoming a dual metropolis of jewel-like enclaves set amidst pervasive social deprivation. In promoting governance, planning, and public finance reforms that would give more coherence to the idea of the Chicago region, while simultaneously advocating the redirection of resources to poorer communities and underfunded public services, *Chicago Metropolis 2020* advances what is admittedly a conservative social justice program. For example, the plan's ready acceptance of market-based educational reforms is more reflexive than deeply considered.[43] Nevertheless, the "equal opportunity" premise anchoring much of the ongoing work of Chicago Metropolis 2020 represents a more progressive view of Chicago *as a metropolitan community* than the gentrification-aligned real estate boosting that often passes for planning in City Hall. Moreover, the civic and business leadership that has promoted the Chicago Metropolis 2020 program, in the coming years, is more likely than the city's political class to seriously engage with policy innovations that may be forthcoming from the metropolitan area's more progressive grassroots organizations.

Unanswerable at this time is the question of whether an organic creativity—by virtue of which contemporary Chicago can "imagine itself and its place in the larger global imaginary, openly construct-ing a distinctive way of life"—or a variant of Chicagoans' longstand-ing proclivity for self-consciousness, will be the principal ground-ing for efforts to fill in the details of the Third City in-the-making.[44] Chicago is rich in its architectural, political, and communal heritage, yet, as I have sought to demonstrate, the city's "literatures" are so iconic and intertwined as to sometimes obscure the beam of con-temporary opportunity. Mistaking vision for another sortie to the attic of prairie style design, endlessly recycling the lexicon of reform-ism versus "The Machine," or holding fast to Mike Royko's view of the *real* Chicago are not strategies that will produce a broadly hospi-table Third City for future generations. Chicago's self-consciousness, so deployed, will only reinforce another staple of local conventional wisdom: the ways of Chicago are so ingrained that fundamental change is impossible. Equally foolish, however, would be a quest for urban reinvention that wholly discounts the cultural riches carried over from the First and Second Cities. Innovation in contemporary Chicago must also avoid the modernist trap of rejecting everything that has come before.

RENEWING THE NORMATIVE CITY

The contemporary intellectual influence of Jane Jacobs towers above that of her fellow urbanists in much the way New York, London, and Tokyo exceed the economic reach of the second-tier global cities. New urbanist architects invariably cite Jacobs as a principal influ-ence. Many of the most admired planning initiatives of the Rich-ard M. Daley administration have reflected the street-conscious, micro-planning tenets initially articulated by Jacobs in the 1950s. Nevertheless, contemporary Jacobs worship routinely suppresses the considerable gap between the particulars of her vision and those of "Jacobsian" planning as currently executed. Even by the 1950s Jacobs's model metropolis, Manhattan, was an outlier among

American cities. Contemporary new urbanists *never* propose developments that approximate mid-twentieth-century Manhattan's population density, mass transit dependence, or neighborhood-level mixed uses.

Apart from and of considerably greater importance than the "density gap" between Jacobs and the new urbanists is a more subtle "contextual gap." As discussed in the conclusion to the preceding chapter, the residents of Jacobs's block on Hudson Street may not have hungered for social intimacy, but as a matter of course—so various of Jacobs's local narratives demonstrate—they assumed a rough equality of local statuses, if not of incomes. As recognized members of an unobtrusive street neighborhood community, individually self-interested behavior was attuned to collective considerations. This version of "self-interest properly understood" was an outgrowth of the block's collective norms even as it reinforced these norms through efficacious, typically noncoercive practice.

Jacobsian design precepts implemented in the absence of these underlying social assumptions and behavioral prompts will not reproduce the Hudson Street of the 1950s. This, in turn, reveals the particular flaw in Richard Florida's neo-Jacobsianism. While correctly perceiving the attractions of Jacobs's urban design menu—and just as correctly observing how many young, middle-class Americans have internalized these design preferences—Florida fails to apprehend the limits of Jacobs's urbanism in the context of contemporary social realities. In the absence of a physically decentralized retail economy (baldly put, a shopkeeper's consumer economy)—and given the highly stratified income structure of the contemporary United States—the "lively streets" philosophy of urban design will, at best, produce Jacobsian enclaves in the vicinity of universities, bohemian districts, and historic neighborhoods. For contemporary Chicago, as well as a number of other American cities, Jacobsian neighborhood development of this sort can, in fact, make a substantial mark, but only in the rarest of cases will it be sufficient to jump-start economic rejuvenation on a city- or region-wide scale.

Jane Jacobs's New York of the 1950s was still an "equality-generating" city, which was a byproduct of its decentralized manufacturing and retail economies and high-quality public schools. Coincidentally, Chicago as it moved from First to Second Cities was also for a time an equality-generating city, though for different reasons. Elementary and secondary education in Chicago never achieved the level of excellence found, for a few decades, in New York, but during the very "short American century"—from the end of World War II until the early 1970s—its highly unionized industrial economy lifted many assembly line workers and their families into the prosperous working class. Contemporary Chicago, just like contemporary New York and the other first-, second-, and third-tier global cities, is an "opportunity-generating" rather than an equality-generating metropolis. For every immigrant to Chicago from, say, Michoacán in southern Mexico, who successfully starts and sustains a family enterprise, ten of his fellow arrivals to the Third City spend years upon years clearing tables, landscaping, or questing for day-labor opportunities. The backdrop to equality-generating New York and Chicago of the 1950s was an economy that distributed incomes in a much less stratified manner than at present and a national government whose social welfare commitments further equalized economic fortune.[45] In order for the Third City to become an equality-generating metropolis, the national government must enact a fiscal and regulatory regime explicitly committed to reducing the economic inequality that has grown so markedly since the early 1970s.[46]

The Jacobsian city cannot simply restore itself, and there remains the task of finding a workable communalism in the era of the Third City. In reference to the latter challenge, the thinking of Jacobs's overshadowed colleague and sometime antagonist, Lewis Mumford, merits serious reconsideration. Mumford's panoramic normativeness—anchored by its twin commitments to social justice and environmental sustainability—offers an urban vision that can be usefully grafted onto Jacobsianism. In effect, it is a merging of Jacobs and Mumford that has been attempted by Chicago Metropolis 2020: a regional vision emphasizing equal economic opportunity, the pooling of localized resources in order to more equitably and rationally direct public expenditure, and innovative planning techniques. The latter give primacy to pedestrianism and mass transit accessibility, compact and mixed-use physical development, reduced fossil fuel consumption, and preservation of open space. Although their dream of achieving equal opportunity is contingent on complementary policy action by the national government, the contemporary Chicago regionalists have taken the necessary initial steps toward specifying the content of an inclusive Third City. By promoting dialogue in reference to how crucial public services, notably education, can be reinvented, and by seeking to enrich, indeed to *urbanize* the experience of living in suburban Naperville, Woodstock, and Harvey—and yes, in the central city's devastated South and West Side neighborhoods as well—the regionalists are engaging with the fundamental civic task of defining just what kind of metropolis it is that we wish to inhabit.

An urbanism that joins Mumford's panoramic communalism to Jacobs's street-level sensibility is especially attractive as Americans confront the daunting challenges posed by global climate change. In countless ways we will need to scale back the materialist America of the twentieth century, but Jacobsian communities nested within Mumfordian regions represent an urbanism that is in every way an enhancement of American cities as we know them. Achieving this truly new urbanism will require much planning, debate, and persuasion. It will further require a formidable reallocation of material resources. Nevertheless, the context of looming social, economic, and technological imperatives surely undercuts the idea of an "end to urbanism." Cities are not simply the byproduct of inexorable economic and technological processes, and the quality of life achieved in the emergent Chicagos, New Yorks, and San Franciscos—as well as the Austins, Burlingtons, and Savannahs—can provide the experiential grounding necessary to build popular enthusiasm both for the new Mumfordian / Jacobsian metropolis *and* an America prepared to reassert its egalitarian heritage.

NOTES

CHAPTER ONE

1. William Cronon, *Nature's Metropolis* (New York: W. W. Norton & Co., 1991).

2. Thomas S. Hines, *Burnham of Chicago* (Chicago: University of Chicago Press, 1979), 123. In Sullivan's words, the Columbian Exposition was an "appalling calamity," the source of a "violent outbreak of the Classic and Renaissance in the East, which slowly spread westward, contaminating all that it touched" (Louis H. Sullivan, *The Autobiography of an Idea* [1924; New York: Dover Publications, 1956], 321, 324). But is it possible that Sullivan's animus was, more than he cared to acknowledge, a matter of envy? See Garry Wills, "Chicago Underground," *New York Review of Books*, October 21, 1993, 15–22.

3. Robert E. Park, Ernest W. Burgess, and Roderick McKenzie, *The City* (1925; Chicago: University of Chicago Press, 1967), 1–46.

4. Frederic M. Thrasher, *The Gang* (Chicago: University of Chicago Press, 1927); Louis Wirth, *The Ghetto* (Chicago: University of Chicago Press, 1929); Clifford R. Shaw, *The Natural History of a Delinquent Career* (Chicago: University of Chicago Press, 1931).

5. Mary P. Ryan, *Civic Wars: Democracy and Public Life in the American City during the Nineteenth Century* (Berkeley: University of California Press, 1997).

6. The idea of two Chicagos—one a city of direct action unencumbered by ethics or even rational thinking, the second a place of elevating ideals—was frequently addressed by Saul Bellow, for example, "I was aware, in a word, that if the post-realists of my youth, in describing white-knuckle Chicago, thought they were representing human types as simple as Fabre's insects or Hudson's birds, they were badly mistaken. It was, then, in blacktop Chicago, among the white knuckles, that an apprentice novelist was reading refined and exquisite poets and grave philosophers, while he sat on park benches or in the public libraries" (*It All Adds Up* [New York: Viking, 1994], 131). I thank Carl Smith for bringing this point to my attention.

7. Douglas Bukowski, *Big Bill Thompson, Chicago, and the Politics of Image* (Urbana: University of Illinois Press, 1998); Harold F. Gosnell, *Machine Politics Chicago Model* (1937; Chicago: University of Chicago Press, 1968); Steven Erie, *Rainbow's End* (Berkeley: University of California Press, 1988), 126.

8. Milton Rakove, *Don't Make No Waves . . . Don't Back No Losers* (Bloomington: Indiana University Press, 1975); Roger Biles, *Richard J. Daley: Politics, Race, and the Governing of Chicago* (DeKalb: Northern Illinois University Press, 1995); Adam Cohen and Elizabeth Taylor, *American Pharaoh* (Boston: Little, Brown, 2000).

9. Biles, *Richard J. Daley*, 119–85; David Farber, *Chicago '68* (Chicago: University of Chicago Press, 1988).

10. Paul Kleppner, *Chicago Divided: The Making of a Black Mayor* (DeKalb: Northern Illinois University Press, 1985); William Grimshaw, *Bitter Fruit: Black Politics and the Chicago Machine, 1931–1991* (Chicago: University of Chicago Press, 1992).

11. Pierre Clavel and Wim Wiewel, eds., *Harold Washington and the Neighborhoods* (New Brunswick, NJ: Rutgers University Press, 1991); Barbara Ferman, *Challenging the Growth Machine: Neighborhood Politics in Chicago and Pittsburgh* (Lawrence: University Press of Kansas, 1996).

12. Gary Rivlin, *Fire on the Prairie: Harold Washington and the Politics of Race* (New York: Henry Holt, 1993).

13. The Chicago Project report is discussed in Andrew H. Malcolm, "Study Portrays Chicago as a City That's Divided," *New York Times*, October 5, 1986.

14. J. Linn Allen and Cindy Richards, "Making No Plans," *Chicago Tribune*, February 9, 1999.

15. Terry Nichols Clark, with Richard Lloyd, Kenneth K. Wong, and Pushpam Jain, "Amenities Drive Urban Growth," *Journal of Urban Affairs* 24 (2002): 493–515.

16. Ed Zotti, "Cityscape: Planning for Daley," *Reader* (Chicago), April 14, 1989.

17. A.J. Liebling, *Chicago, the Second City* (New York: Knopf, 1952).

18. This essay is reprinted (and somewhat more generously retitled) as "Home Remedies for Urban Cancer" in *The Lewis Mumford Reader*, ed. Donald L. Miller (New York: Pantheon Books, 1986), 184–200.

19. Jane Jacobs, *The Death and Life of Great American Cities* (New York: Vintage Books, 1961), 20.

20. Jane Jacobs, *The Economy of Cities* (New York: Vintage Books, 1970); and *Cities and the Wealth of Nations* (New York: Random House, 1984).

21. Robert Wojtowicz, ed., *Sidewalk Critic: Lewis Mumford's Writings on New York* (New York: Princeton Architectural Press, 2000).

22. The Jacobs/Mumford relationship is discussed by Donald L. Miller, *Lewis Mumford: A Life* (New York: Weidenfeld & Nicolson, 1989), 473–76. See also Anthony Flint, *Wrestling with Moses* (New York: Random House, 2009), 80–81, 156–57.

23. Mumford, "Home Remedies for Urban Cancer," 185.

24. Jacobs, *The Death and Life of Great American Cities*, 12.

25. For example, see Herbert Gans's review of *The Death and Life of Great American Cities*, reprinted in his *People and Plans* (New York: Basic Books, 1968), 25–33.

26. Jacobs, *The Death and Life of Great American Cities*, 60–62. Sociologist Mark Granovetter originated the concept of "weak ties," which is discussed by Ross Gittell and Avis Vidal in *Community Organizing: Building Social Capital as a Development Strategy* (Thousand Oaks, CA: Sage Publications, 1998), 19–20.

27. Jacobs, *Cities and the Wealth of Nations*, 212.

28. Lewis Mumford, "The Regional Framework of Civilization," in Miller, *The Lewis Mumford Reader*, 213, 215.

29. If there is currently a modest revival in Mumford's intellectual stock, it is due to a line of urban analysis sometimes called the new regionalism. See, for example, Peter Dreier, John Mollenkopf, and Todd Swanstrom, *Place Matters: Metropolitics for the Twenty-first Century* (Lawrence: University Press of Kansas, 2001), esp. 177–78. But the most prominent new regionalists, such as Myron Orfield (*American Metro Politics: The New Suburban Reality* [Washington DC: Brookings Institution Press, 2002]) and David Rusk (*Inside Game Outside Game: Winning Strategies for Saving Urban America* [Washington DC: Brookings Institution Press, 1999]), advocate a much more narrowly gauged regional agenda than Mumford's.

30. Richard Florida, *The Rise of the Creative Class* (New York: Basic Books, 2004); Douglas W. Rae, *City: Urbanism and Its End* (New Haven, CT: Yale University Press, 2003).

CHAPTER TWO

1. Burnham, quoted in Thomas S. Hines, *Burnham of Chicago: Architect and Planner* (Chicago: University of Chicago Press, 1979), 315.

2. Carlo Rotella, *October Cities: The Redevelopment of Urban Literature* (Berkeley: University of California Press, 1998), 49.

3. Carla Cappetti, *Writing Chicago: Modernism, Ethnography, and the Novel* (New York: Columbia University Press, 1993), 20.

4. My selection of topics reflects my particular interests, but also ranges widely enough, I think, to offer a representative account of characteristic modes of Chicago interpretation. Other possibilities for analogous exploration might include professional urban historians' work on Chicago, Chicago-focused documentary filmmakers, or particular varieties of journalism. Among the latter, Chicago crime reporting is, in all likelihood, a subject broad enough to encompass a book of its own.

5. Fred Matthews, *The Quest for an American Sociology: Robert E. Park and the Chicago School* (Montreal: McGill-Queen's University Press, 1997); Martin Bulmer, *The Chicago School of Sociology* (Chicago: University of Chicago Press, 1984), 89–128.

6. Robert E. Park, Ernest W. Burgess, and Roderick D. McKenzie, *The City* (1925; Chicago: University of Chicago Press, 1968), 47. The characterization of Burgess's diagram is by Mike Davis, *The Ecology of Fear* (New York: Vintage, 1999), 384. Davis, in turn, was paraphrasing historian Dennis Smith, *The Chicago School: A Liberal Critique of Capitalism* (Basingstoke, UK: MacMillan Educational, 1988), 28. Louis Wirth, "Urbanism as a Way of Life," *Classic Essays on the Culture of Cities*, ed. Richard Sennett (New York: Appleton-Century-Crofts, 1969), 143–64.

7. Robert E. Park, "The City: Suggestions for the Investigation of Human Behavior in the Urban Environment," in Park, Burgess, and McKenzie, *The City*, 1–46.

8. Park, Burgess, and McKenzie, *The City*, 51, 55.

9. Ernest Burgess, "The Growth of the City: An Introduction to a Research Project," in Park, Burgess, and McKenzie, *The City*, 47.

10. Bulmer, *The Chicago School of Sociology*, 61.

11. William Isaac Thomas and Florian Znaniecki, *The Polish Peasant in Europe and America*, 5 vols. (Chicago: University of Chicago Press, 1918–20). There is also a single-volume abridgement that was issued by the University of Illinois Press in 1984.

12. Upton Sinclair, *The Jungle* (1906; New York: Signet, 1960).

13. Alice O'Connor, *Poverty Knowledge: Social Science, Social Policy, and the Poor in Twentieth-Century America* (Princeton, NJ: Princeton University Press, 2001), 84.

14. Park, "The City," in Park, Burgess, and McKenzie, *The City*, 40, 43.

15. Harvey Warren Zorbaugh, *The Gold Coast and the Slum* (1929; Chicago: University of Chicago Press, 1976), 231–32.

16. Sudhir Venkatesh, "Chicago's Pragmatic Planners," *Social Science History* 25 (2001): 275–317.

17. St. Clair Drake and Horace Cayton, *Black Metropolis: A Study of Negro Life in a Northern City* (1945; Chicago: University of Chicago Press, 1993).

18. Zorbaugh, *The Gold Coast and the Slum*, 234.

19. Drake and Cayton, *Black Metropolis*, 635, 703.

20. Zorbaugh, *The Gold Coast and the Slum*, 13. Although Drake and Cayton can be likened to Zorbaugh as Chicago panoramists, their account of African Americans' circumstances persistently registers the impacts of racial subordination as a particular shaper of the Chicago African American life. As they bring their mammoth study to a close—and in particular—delineate the differences between the "foreign-born immigrant" and African American experience in Chicago, Drake and Cayton write: "People eventually forget the foreign antecedents of successful Americans. In the case of Negroes, however, the process stops just short of assimilation. A Job Ceiling limits them to unskilled and semi-skilled work and condemns them to relief rolls during depressions. Residential segregation results in a Black Ghetto. The color-line preserves social segregation and sets the limits of advancement in politics and other non-economic hierarchies" (*Black Metropolis*, 757).

21. Sam Bass Warner Jr., *The Urban Wilderness: A History of the American City* (New York: Harper & Row, 1972), 111–12; Zorbaugh, *The Gold Coast and the Slum*, 274–79.

22. Sanford D. Horwitt, *Let Them Call Me Rebel: Saul Alinsky—His Life and Legacy* (New York: Knopf, 1989), 10–33.

23. Horwitt, *Let Them Call Me Rebel*, 56–76; Robert A. Slayton, *Back of the Yards: The Making of a Local Democracy* (Chicago: University of Chicago, 1986).

24. In this and the following paragraph I focus on material in chapters 7–9 of Alinsky's *Reveille for Radicals* (1946; New York: Vintage, 1969).

25. Zorbaugh's assertion appears in *The Gold Coast and the Slum*, 271.

26. Herbert J. Gans, *The Urban Villagers: Group and Class in the Life of Italian-Americans* (New York: The Free Press, 1965).

27. Horwitt, *Let Them Call Me Rebel*, 303–449; Robert Bailey Jr., *Radicals in Urban Politics: The Alinsky Approach* (Chicago: University of Chicago Press, 1974).

28. Amanda I. Seligman, *Block by Block* (Chicago: University of Chicago Press, 2005).

29. Gerald Suttles, *The Social Construction of Communities* (Chicago: University of Chicago Press, 1972), 37.

30. For example, in New York City there were Sunnyside Gardens, built in the 1920s, and the huge Peter Stuyvesant Town, constructed in the 1940s, among others. See Roy Lubove, *Community Planning in the 1920's: The Contribution of the Regional Planning Association of America* (Pittsburgh: University of Pittsburgh Press, 1963), 58–61; and Joel Schwartz, *The New York Approach: Robert Moses, Urban Liberals, and the Redevelopment of the Inner City* (Columbus: Ohio State University Press, 1993), 84–107. In Chicago there was an influential group of "philanthropic" housing developments, notably the Michigan Avenue and the Marshall Field Garden Apartments, which had opened in the interwar period. See Thomas Lee Philpott, *The Slum and the Ghetto* (New York: Oxford University Press, 1978), 259–69.

31. Suttles, *The Social Construction of Communities*, 88.

32. Arnold R. Hirsch, *Making the Second Ghetto: Race and Housing in Chicago, 1940–1960* (New York: Cambridge University Press, 1983); Leonard S. Rubinowitz and James E. Rosenbaum, *Crossing the Class and Color Lines: From Public Housing to White Suburbs* (Chicago: University of Chicago Press, 2000), 19–24.

33. See William Julius Wilson, *The Truly Disadvantaged: The Inner City, the Underclass, and Public Policy* (Chicago: University of Chicago Press, 1987) and *When Work Disappears: The World of the New Urban Poor* (New York: Knopf, 1996); Douglas S. Massey and Nancy A. Denton, *American Apartheid: Segregation and the Making of the Underclass* (Cambridge, MA: Harvard University Press, 1993).

34. Mary Pattillo, *Black Picket Fences: Privilege and Peril Among the Black Middle Class* (Chicago: University of Chicago Press, 1999), 3.

35. Ibid., 117–45.

36. Ibid., 92–94.

37. Sudhir Alladi Venkatesh, *American Project: The Rise and Fall of a Modern Ghetto* (Cambridge, MA: Harvard University Press, 2002), 93–94.

38. Ibid., 173.

39. Eric Klinenberg, *Heat Wave: A Social Autopsy of Disaster in Chicago* (Chicago: University of Chicago Press, 2002), 22 (original emphasis).

40. Ibid., 79–128.

41. Ibid., 129–64, 185–224.

42. Mel Scott, *American City Planning* (Berkeley: University of California Press, 1971), 109. The most recent facsimile edition of Daniel H. Burnham and Edward H. Bennett's *Plan of Chicago* was produced by Princeton Architectural Press in 1993. Also see Carl Smith, *The Plan of Chicago* (Chicago: University of Chicago Press, 2006).

43. Thomas S. Hines, *Burnham of Chicago: Architect and Planner* (Chicago: University of Chicago Press, 1979), 341.

44. James Krohe Jr., "The Man with the Plan," *Reader* (Chicago), June 18, 1993. Carl Smith's discussion of the Burnham Plan's implementation does not resolve the debate over its ultimate impact on Chicago, but it does provide a close account of projects initiated and completed, those that were substantially modified in execution, and those left undone. See Smith, *The Plan of Chicago*, 130–50.

45. "Development Plan for the Central Area of Chicago" (Chicago: City of Chicago, Dept. of City Planning, August 1958); "Chicago Central Area Plan: Final Report to the Chicago Plan Commission" (Chicago: City of Chicago, June 2003).

46. Elmer W. Johnson, *Chicago Metropolis 2020* (Chicago: University of Chicago Press, 2001).

47. Smith, *The Plan of Chicago*, 132–33.

48. "Development Plan for the Central Area of Chicago," 1. The report's list of contributors appears on the inside back cover. Further page references to this plan will be given parenthetically in the text.

49. Joel Rast, *Remaking Chicago: The Political Origins of Urban Industrial Change* (DeKalb: Northern Illinois University Press, 1999), 29–30.

50. "Chicago 21: A Plan for the Central Area Communities" (Chicago: Chicago Dept. of Development and Planning, September 1973).

51. Carl W. Condit, *Chicago 1930–1970: Building, Planning, and Urban Technology* (Chicago: University of Chicago Press, 1974), 272–79.

52. Robert Mier and Kari J. Moe, "Decentralized Development: From Theory to Practice," in *Harold Washington and the Neighborhoods*, ed. Pierre Clavel and Wim Wiewel, (New Brunswick, NJ: Rutgers University Press), 67–68; Lois Wille, *At Home in the Loop: How Clout and Community Built Chicago's Dearborn Park* (Carbondale: Southern Illinois University Press, 1997), 48–52.

53. Paul Gapp, "Power Elite Drafts City Master Plan," *Chicago Tribune*, May 21, 1973.

54. "Chicago 21," 124–25. Further page references to this plan will be given parenthetically in the text.

55. Robert M. Fogelson, *Downtown: Its Rise and Fall, 1880–1950* (New Haven, CT: Yale University Press, 2001), 34–35.

56. Typically, this perspective views "Chicago 21," and in particular the development of the South Loop Dearborn Park residential area, as the Trojan horses of central Chicago residential gentrification. Lois Wille, in *At Home in the Loop*, both accepts this version of events and endorses the presumed outcomes. Some of the oppositionist groups she discusses in her fifth chapter adopted the same perspective on the train of the events but decried the likely outcomes.

57. "Chicago Development Plan 1984"(Chicago, City of Chicago, May 1984), 2. Hereafter, references to this plan will be given parenthetically in the text.

58. John McCarron and Thom Shanker, "Mayor's Economic Plan Stresses Poorest Areas," *Chicago Tribune*, April 22, 1984.

59. Barbara Ferman, *Challenging the Growth Machine: Neighborhood Politics in Chicago and Pittsburgh* (Lawrence: University Press of Kansas, 1996), 111–23; Clavel and Wiewel, *Harold Washington and the Neighborhoods*.

60. My citations of plan contents refer to the published version: Johnson, *Chicago Metropolis 2020*.

61. Larry Bennett, "Regionalism in a Historically Divided Metropolis," in *The New Chicago*, ed. John Koval et al. (Philadelphia: Temple University Press, 2006), 282–84.

62. Johnson, *Chicago Metropolis 2020*, 4–5.

63. Ibid., 72.

64. Ibid., 10.

65. "Chicago Central Area Plan: Final Report to the Chicago Plan Commission" (Chicago: City of Chicago, June 2003), 35. My page references to this document correspond to the online version, available at the City of Chicago Web site, http://egov .cityofchicago.org/city/webportal/home.do (accessed October 17, 2005). This is a seemingly inconsistent text in that the cover page identifies the document as "Final Draft Report" (May 2003) but in the remaining sections the bottom-page identifier is "Final Report" (June 2003). Further references to this document will be given parenthetically in the text.

66. See Carl S. Smith, *Chicago and the American Literary Imagination* (Chicago: University of Chicago Press, 1984), 20–21.

67. Asa Briggs, *Victorian Cities* (Harmondsworth, UK: Penguin Books, 1980), 56.

68. Arnold Lewis, *An Early Encounter with Tomorrow: Europeans, Chicago's Loop, and the World's Columbian Exposition* (Urbana: University of Illinois Press, 2001).

69. Smith, *Chicago and the American Literary Imagination*, 60–78.

70. Rotella, *October Cities*, 49–50.

71. Martin Amis, introduction to *The Adventures of Augie March*, by Saul Bellow (1953; New York: Knopf, 1995), x.

72. Nelson Algren, *The Man with the Golden Arm* (1949; New York: Seven Stories Press, 1990), 324–37.

73. Michael Raleigh, *In the Castle of the Flynns* (Naperville, IL: Sourcebooks, Inc., 2002).

74. Ward Just, *An Unfinished Season* (Boston: Houghton Mifflin, 2004), 115, 218, 250.

75. Bayo Ojikutu, *47th Street Black* (New York: Three Rivers Press, 2003).

76. Sara Paretsky, *Blood Shot* (New York: Dell, 1988), 1.

77. Sara Paretsky, *Burn Marks* (New York: Delacorte Press, 1990), 137–38.

78. Sara Paretsky, *Hard Time* (New York: Dell, 1999), 46.

79. Paretsky, *Blood Shot*, 370.

80. Sara Paretsky, *Killing Orders* (New York: Dell, 1985), 11.

81. Sara Paretsky, "Baptism in the Bungalow Belt," *Chicago Tribune*, August 29, 1996.

82. See Gregory D. Squires, Larry Bennett, Kathleen McCourt, and Philip Nyden, *Chicago: Race, Class, and the Response to Neighborhood Decline* (Philadelphia: Temple University Press, 1987); and Alan Ehrenhalt, *The Lost City: Discovering the Forgotten Virtues of Community in the Chicago of the 1950s* (New York: Basic Books, 1995), respectively.

83. Aleksandar Hemon, *Nowhere Man* (New York: Doubleday, 2002) 149–150, 7, 9.

84. Ibid., 90.

85. Studs Terkel, foreword to *One More Time: The Best of Mike Royko*, by Mike Royko (Chicago: University of Chicago Press, 1999), xv.

86. Lois Wille, "The Sixties," in Royko, *One More Time*, 3.

87. Mike Royko, "Daley Embodied Chicago," in *One More Time*, 103.

88. Mike Royko, *Boss: Richard J. Daley of Chicago* (New York: Signet, 1971), 30.

89. Royko, "He Can Dream, Can't He?" in *One More Time*, 34.

90. Royko, "Mike Royko—High-Rise Man," in *One More Time*, 155–58.

91. Royko, *Boss*, 21.

92. Ibid., 103.

93. For example, see Clavel and Wiewel, *Harold Washington and the Neighborhoods*.

94. Royko, "How This City Really 'Works,'" in *One More Time*, 81–84.

95. Royko, *Boss*, 23, 24.

96. Ibid., 134, 136.

97. Ibid., 141, 143.

98. Royko, "It Wasn't Our 'Clout' She Stole, But a Counterfeit," in *One More Time*, 17–18.

99. Mike Royko, "San-Fran-York on the Lake," in *I May Be Wrong, But I Doubt It* (Chicago: Henry Regnery Co., 1968), 3–6.

100. Royko, "Daley Embodied Chicago," 104.

101. Royko, *Boss*, 20, 28.

102. Royko, "The Welcome Wagon Didn't Come," in *I May Be Wrong*, 63–65.

103. Royko, "Kids Say the Darndest Things," in *I May Be Wrong*, 191.

104. Royko, "Give Washington a Break," in *One More Time*, 168.

105. Royko, "Daley the Elder and Daley the Younger," in *One More Time*, 200–2.

106. Terkel, foreword to *One More Time*, xvi.

107. Royko, "Daley Embodied Chicago," 104.

108. Royko, "Rostenkowski's Sin Was Not Changing with the Times," in *One More Time*, 266–68 (quotations, 267).

CHAPTER THREE

1. Mickey Ciokajlo and Robert Becker, "In Terms of Clout, City's 11th Ward Towers Above the Rest," *Chicago Tribune*, July 19, 2005.

2. Dan Mihalopoulos, "Defense Makes Point of Ethnicity in Politics," *Chicago Tribune*, June 5, 2006.

3. Rudolph Bush and Dan Mihalopoulos, "U.S., Defense Make Their Final Pitches," *Chicago Tribune*, June 28, 2006.

4. John Kass, "Boss' Son Rebuilt Machine in Own Image," *Chicago Tribune*, May 10, 2006.

5. See the Clout on Wheels series, coauthored by Tim Novak and Steve Warmbir, which ran in the *Chicago Sun-Times* on January 23, 25, and 26, 2004.

6. *United States of America v. Donald S. Tomczak, Gerald J. Wesolowski, Richard E. McMahon, Flenory S. Barnes Sr., Joseph S. Ignoffo, Leroy S. Peters, and Commelie R.*

Peters, Indictment filed in United States District Court, Northern District of Illinois, Eastern Division, December 16, 2004, http://www.ipsn.org/hired_truck_scandal/default.htm (accessed January 8, 2010).

7. Gary Washburn and Ray Long, "Daley Will Kill Scandal-torn Hired Truck," *Chicago Tribune*, February 9, 2005, 28.

8. Matt O'Connor and Mickey Ciokajlo, "Trucking Firm's Owner 16th Charged in Probe," *Chicago Tribune*, January 16, 2005. Consider this comment on the trial of Al Sanchez, a leading Hispanic Democratic Organization figure who was convicted on four criminal counts involving preferential city government hiring: "Sanchez also contended that his political efforts had the empowerment of Hispanics as their goal" (Jeff Coen and Dan Mihalopoulos, "Sanchez Denies He Rigged Hiring," *Chicago Tribune*, March 18, 2009).

9. Jon C. Teaford, *The Unheralded Triumph: City Government in America, 1870–1900* (Baltimore, MD: Johns Hopkins University Press, 1984), 15.

10. Martin J. Schiesl, *The Politics of Efficiency* (Berkeley: University of California Press, 1980), 46–67.

11. Jack Beatty, *The Rascal King* (Reading, MA: Addison-Wesley, 1993); Robert Caro, *The Power Broker* (New York: Vintage, 1975), 324–28; Douglas Bukowski, *Big Bill Thompson, Chicago, and The Politics of Image* (Urbana: University of Illinois Press, 1998).

12. Mark I. Gelfand, *A Nation of Cities* (New York: Oxford University Press, 1975), 30–39, 52–54; Sidney Fine, *Frank Murphy: The Detroit Years* (Ann Arbor: University of Michigan Press, 1975); Caro, *The Power Broker*, 444–57; Thomas Kessner, *Fiorello H. La Guardia and The Making of Modern New York* (New York: McGraw-Hill, 1989).

13. R. H. Salisbury, "Urban Politics: The New Convergence of Power," in *The City: Problems of Planning*, ed. Murray Stewart (Harmondsworth, UK: Penguin Books, 1972), 395. Salisbury's essay originally appeared in the *Journal of Politics* 26 (1964): 775–97.

14. Jeanne R. Lowe, *Cities in a Race with Time* (New York: Random House, 1967), 405.

15. Peter Eisinger, "City Politics in an Era of Federal Policy Devolution," *Urban Affairs Review* 33 (1998): 320.

16. Melvin G. Holli, *The American Mayor: The Best and Worst Big-City Leaders* (University Park: Pennsylvania State University Press, 1999), 19.

17. Douglas W. Rae, *City: Urbanism and Its End* (New Haven, CT: Yale University Press, 2003), 360.

18. E. S. Savas, *Privatization: The Key to Better Government* (Chatham, NJ: Chatham House, 1987).

19. David Osborne and Ted Gaebler, *Reinventing Government* (New York: Penguin Books, 1993), xviii, 19–20 (original emphasis).

20. David Osborne, "John Norquist and the Milwaukee Experiment," *Governing*, November 1992, 63; Rob Gurwitt, "Indianapolis and the Republican Future," *Governing*, February 1994, 24–28; Rob Gurwitt, "Detroit Dresses for Business," *Governing*, April 1996, 38–42.

21. James Lardner, "Can You Believe the New York Miracle?" *New York Review of Books*, August 14, 1997, 54–58.

22. Philadelphia's Ed Rendell is the subject of Buzz Bissinger's *A Prayer for the City* (New York: Random House, 1997). Rudolph Giuliani has been profiled by many journalists and scholars. Fred Siegel's *The Prince of the City* (San Francisco: Encounter Books, 2005) is both detailed and admiring. Giuliani's book, *Leadership* (New York: Hyperion, 2002), far more than the Goldsmith and Norquist books discussed below, can be considered an "advertisement for himself." For a more critical view of Giuliani, see Wayne Barrett, *Rudy! An Investigative Biography of Rudolph Giuliani* (New York: Basic Books, 2000).

23. Stephen Goldsmith, *The Twenty-First Century City* (Lanham, MD: Rowman & Littlefield, 1999), 173.

24. Ibid., 146.

25. John O. Norquist, *The Wealth of Cities* (Reading, MA: Addison-Wesley, 1998), 194, 206.

26. Siegel, *The Prince of the City*, 108. Another speaker at this event: David Osborne.

27. Raphael J. Sonenshein, *The City at Stake: Secession, Reform, and the Battle for Los Angeles* (Princeton, NJ: Princeton University Press, 2004), 65, 70.

28. A biographical essay on Richard M. Daley, a list of his honorary citations, and various of his public statements can be accessed as the City of Chicago Web site, http://www.ci.chi.il.us/city/webportal/home.do. Other profiles of Richard M. Daley include Thomas Hardy, "His Goal: Make His Own Name," *Chicago Tribune*, April 5, 1989; and James Atlas, "The Daleys of Chicago," *New York Times Magazine*, August 25, 1996, 37–39, 52, 56–58.

29. Henry Hansen, "Ten to Keep Around, Ten to Kick Around," *Chicago*, November 1977, 146–47.

30. David Moberg, "Can You Find the Reformer in this Group?" *Reader* (Chicago), February 18, 1983.

31. Thomas Byrne Edsall, "Black vs. White in Chicago," *New York Review of Books*, April 13, 1989, 21–23.

32. Alan Ehrenhalt, "Master of the Detail," *Governing*, December 1997, 22.

33. Larry Bennett, Michael Bennett, and Stephen Alexander, "Chicago and the 2016 Olympics: Why Host the Games? How Should We Host the Games? What Should We Accomplish by Hosting the Games?" (Chicago: Egan Urban Center, DePaul University, November 2008); Monica Davey, "Second City Absorbs Its Latest Defeat," *New York Times*, October 4, 2009; Dan Mihalopoulos, "Daley Returns Undaunted," *Chicago Tribune*, October 7, 2009.

34. Saskia Sassen, "A Global City," in *Global Chicago*, ed. Charles Madigan (Urbana: University of Illinois Press, 2004), 29. At a presentation by Sassen that I attended a number of years ago, she referred to these gentrifying areas of Chicago as the city's "glamour zone."

35. Anthony S. Bryk, David Kerbow, and Sharon Rollow, "Chicago School Reform," in *New Schools for a New Century*, ed. Diane Ravitch and Joseph Viteritti

(New Haven, CT: Yale University Press, 1997), 164–200; Dorothy Shipps, *School Reform, Corporate Style: Chicago, 1880–2000* (Lawrence: University Press of Kansas, 2006), 130–69; Tracy Dell'Angela and Gary Washburn, "Daley Set to Remake Troubled Schools," *Chicago Tribune*, June 25, 2004.

36. "The Plan for Transformation" (Chicago: Chicago Housing Authority, January 6, 2000); Larry Bennett, Janet S. Smith, and Patricia A. Wright, eds., *Where Are Poor People to Live? Transforming Public Housing* (Armonk, NY: M. E. Sharpe, 2006); Matthew F. Gebhardt, "Politics, Planning and Power: Reforming and Redeveloping Public Housing in Chicago" (PhD diss., Columbia University, 2009).

37. Paul Fischer, "Section 8 and the Public Housing Revolution: Where Will the Families Go?" (Chicago: Woods Fund, September 4, 2001), and "Where Are the Public Housing Families Going? An Update" (unpublished paper, January 2003); Susan Popkin and Mary K. Cunningham, "CHA Relocation Counseling Assessment" (Washington DC: The Urban Institute, July 2002); Dan A. Lewis and Vandna Sinha, "Moving Up and Moving Out? Economic and Residential Mobility of Low-Income Chicago Families," *Urban Affairs Review* 43 (2007): 139–70; Deidre Oakley and Keri Burchfield, "Out of the Projects, Still in the Hood: The Spatial Constraints on Public Housing Residents' Relocation in Chicago," *Journal of Urban Affairs* 31 (2009): 589–614; Thomas P. Sullivan, "Independent Monitor's Report No. 5 to the Chicago Housing Authority and the Central Advisory Council" (Chicago: January 8, 2003). Sullivan writes in reference to CHA relocation activities in summer and early fall of 2002: "In July, August and September 2002, the large number of HCV [housing choice voucher]-eligible families still in the CHA buildings, coupled with imminent building-empty dates, and the relatively small number of relocation counselors, caused a rush to place families in rental units. This in turn led inevitably to placing families hurriedly, and to relocating families into racially segregated areas already overwhelmingly populated by low income families. Housing quality was overlooked or given little attention" (22).

38. Wesley G. Skogan and Susan M. Hartnett, *Community Policing, Chicago Style* (New York : Oxford University Press, 1997); Wesley G. Skogan, Lynn Steiner, Jill DuBois, J. Erik Gudell, and Aimee Fagan, "Taking Stock: Community Policing in Chicago" (Washington DC.: National Institute of Justice, July 2002).

39. David Moberg, "How Does Richie Rate?" *Reader* (Chicago), February 19, 1999.

40. This characterization of the 1989 Daley campaign appeared in Hardy, "His Goal: Make His Own Name"; Richard M. Daley, inaugural address, April 24, 1989, http://www.chipublib.org/cplbooksmovies/cplarchive/mayors/rm_daley_inaug01 .php (accessed December 29, 2009).

41. John W. Kingdon, *Agendas, Alternatives, and Public Policies* (Boston: Little, Brown, 1984), 83, 93.

42. Paul Merrion, "City's Internet Project Becomes a Daley Double," *Crain's Chicago Business*, January 14, 2002, 9; Jon Van, "Broadband Picture Not Finished," *Chicago Tribune*, September 9, 2007; Joel Rast, *Remaking Chicago: The Political Origins of Urban Industrial Change* (DeKalb: Northern Illinois University Press, 1999), 132–57.

43. Amanda Seligman, *Block by Block: Neighborhoods and Public Policy on Chicago's West Side* (Chicago: University of Chicago Press, 2005), 63. By the mid-1960s, some local civic activists began to express the view that the aggressiveness of city government-initiated building demolition activity itself posed a threat to neighborhood stability.

44. Larry Bennett, "Downtown Restructuring and Public Housing in Contemporary Chicago," in Bennett, Smith, and Wright, *Where Are Poor People to Live?* 290.

45. Rast, *Remaking Chicago*, 149–50.

46. Skogan and Hartnett, *Community Policing, Chicago Style*, 138.

47. Clarence N. Stone, Jeffrey Henig, Bryan D. Jones, and Carol Pierannunzi, *Building Civic Capacity: The Politics of Reforming Urban Schools* (Lawrence: University Press of Kansas, 2001); Janet L. Smith, "Public Housing Transformation: Evolving National Policy," in Bennett, Smith, and Wright, *Where Are Poor People to Live?* 19–40, and Yan Zhang and Gretchen Weismann, "Public Housing's Cinderella: Policy Dynamics of HOPE VI in the Mid-1990s," in Bennett, Smith, and Wright, *Where Are Poor People to Live?* 41–67.

48. Dan Mihalopoulos, "Group Pays for Skyway Lease," *Chicago Tribune*, January 25, 2005.

49. Michael Oneal and Dan Mihalopoulos, "Midway Deal Breaks Apart," *Chicago Tribune*, April 21, 2009; Dan Mihalopoulos, "After Parking Goes Private, Aldermen Target Meter Deal," *Chicago Tribune*, April 23, 2009.

50. James M. Smith, "Special-Purpose Governance in Chicago: Institutional Independence and Political Interdependence at the Municipal Pier and Exposition Authority" (paper presented at the Annual Meeting of the Urban Affairs Association, Montréal, April 2006).

51. Robert A. Baade and Allen R. Sanderson, "Bearing Down on Chicago," in *Sports, Jobs, and Taxes: The Economic Impact of Sports Teams and Stadiums*, ed. Roger G. Noll and Andrew Zimbalist (Washington DC: Brookings Institution Press, 1997), 324–54.

52. Timothy J. Gilfoyle, *Millennium Park: Creating a Chicago Landmark* (Chicago: University of Chicago Press, 2006), 63–76.

53. Jeffrey Mirel, "School Reform, Chicago Style: Educational Innovation in a Changing Urban Context, 1976–1991," *Urban Education* 28 (1993): 116–49; Shipps, *School Reform, Corporate Style*, 130–69.

54. Gary Washburn and John Chase, "Daley Puts on a Press for Liquor Proposals," *Chicago Tribune*, October 22, 1998; Kathryn Masterson, "Gay-Marriage Backers Get Daley's Signature," *Chicago Tribune*, October 29, 2004; John Chase, "City to Put List of Sex Offenders On-line," *Chicago Tribune*, November 23, 1998.

55. David H. Roeder, "Mayor Daley as Conciliator," *Illinois Issues*, April 1994, 23. The brackets appear in Roeder's text.

56. Gary Washburn, "Daley Quick to Defend his Record," *Chicago Tribune*, May 10, 2006.

57. Charles Storch, "Vision for Park Grew Over Decades," *Chicago Tribune*, July 15, 2004. Storch's article appears in a special section of the *Tribune* devoted to the opening of Millennium Park.

58. Gary Washburn and Jon Hilkevitch, "Daley Rips Up Meigs Runways in Surprise Raid," *Chicago Tribune*, April 1, 2003.

59. Atlas, "The Daleys of Chicago," 56.

60. Terry Nichols Clark, with Richard Lloyd, Kenneth K. Wong, and Pushpam Jain, "Amenities Drive Urban Growth," *Journal of Urban Affairs* 24 (2002): 512.

61. Atlas, "The Daleys of Chicago," 52; Roeder, "Mayor Daley as Conciliator," 23.

62. Richard M. Daley, quoted in Shane Tritsch, "The Mystery of Mayor Daley," *Chicago*, July 2004, 63.

63. David Naguib Pellow, *Garbage Wars: The Struggle for Environmental Justice in Chicago* (Cambridge, MA: MIT Press, 2002); also see Dan Mihalopoulos and Gary Washburn, "City to Wave White Flag on Blue Bags," *Chicago Tribune*, October 25, 2006.

64. William Grimshaw, *Bitter Fruit: Black Politics and the Chicago Machine, 1931–1991* (Chicago: University of Chicago Press, 1992), 206–20.

65. Dick Simpson, *Rogues, Rebels, and Rubber Stamps: The Politics of the Chicago City Council from 1863 to the Present* (Boulder, CO: Westview Press, 2001), 287.

66. Clark, "Amenities Drive Urban Growth," 501–3.

67. Ben Joravsky, "Pass the Doughnuts," *Reader* (Chicago), August 18, 2006.

68. Eric Klinenberg, *Heat Wave: A Social Autopsy of Disaster in Chicago* (Chicago: University of Chicago Press, 2003), 139–44; Mary Pattillo, *Black on the Block: The Politics of Race and Class in the City* (Chicago: University of Chicago Press, 2007), 150, 179.

CHAPTER FOUR

1. "The Official Mayor's Guide to the City of Chicago," http://egov.cityofchicago.org/city/webportal/home.do (accessed July 19, 2008).

2. Jack Schnedler, *Fodor's Compass American Guide: Chicago* (Oakland, CA: Compass American Guides, 2001), 19.

3. *Fodor's Chicago 2007* (New York: Fodor's Travel Publications, 2007), 13.

4. *Time Out Chicago*, 4th ed. (London: Ebury Publishing, 2007), 24.

5. Alex Kotlowitz, *Never a City So Real* (New York: Crown Publishers, 2004), 19.

6. V. S. Pritchett, *London Perceived* (1962; Boston: David R. Godine, 2001), 16.

7. Max Page, *The Creative Destruction of Manhattan, 1900–1940* (Chicago: University of Chicago Press, 1999), 53, 54.

8. Jane Jacobs, *The Death and Life of Great American Cities* (New York: Vintage, 1961), 121, 133.

9. Milton Kotler, *Neighborhood Government: The Local Foundations of Political Life* (Indianapolis: Bobbs-Merrill, 1969); Philip Langdon, *A Better Place to Live: Reshaping the American Suburb* (Amherst: University of Massachusetts Press, 1994); Andres Duany, Elizabeth Plater-Zyberk, and Jeff Speck, *Suburban Nation: The Rise of Sprawl and the Decline of the American Dream* (New York: North Point Press, 2000).

10. Robert Fishman, *Bourgeois Utopias: The Rise and Fall of Suburbia* (New York: Basic Books, 1987), 139–40.

11. Adna Ferrin Weber, *The Growth of Cities in the Nineteenth Century* (1899; Ithaca, NY: Cornell University Press, 1967), 450.

12. Sam Bass Warner Jr., *The Urban Wilderness: A History of the American City* (New York: Harper & Row, 1972), 82.

13. Galen Cranz, The Politics of Park Design: A History of Urban Parks in America (Cambridge, MA: MIT Press, 1989).

14. David Schuyler, *The New Urban Landscape: The Redefinition of City Form in Nineteenth Century America* (Baltimore, MD: Johns Hopkins University Press, 1986), 156.

15. Ibid., 172.

16. Lawrence J. Vale, *From the Puritans to the Projects: Public Housing and Public Neighbors* (Cambridge, MA: Harvard University Press, 2000), 73.

17. Louise W. Knight, *Citizen: Jane Addams and the Struggle for Democracy* (Chicago: University of Chicago Press, 2005), 194-95.

18. Jane Addams, *Twenty Years at Hull House* (1910; New York: Signet, 1981), 82.

19. Jacob A. Riis, *How the Other Half Lives* (1890; New York: Dover Publications, 1971).

20. Knight, *Citizen*, 206.

21. Ibid., 274, 326.

22. Daphne Spain, *How Women Saved the City* (Minneapolis: University of Minnesota Press, 2001), 195-96.

23. Allen F. Davis, *Spearheads of Reform: The Social Settlements and the Progressive Movement 1890-1914* (New York: Oxford University Press, 1967), 34.

24. Robert Caro, *The Power Broker: Robert Moses and the Fall of New York* (New York: Vintage, 1975), 849.

25. Joel Schwartz, *The New York Approach: Robert Moses, Urban Liberals, and Redevelopment of the Inner City* (Columbus: Ohio State University Press, 1993), 297.

26. Robert M. Fogelson, *Downtown: Its Rise and Fall, 1880–1950* (New Haven, CT: Yale University Press, 2001), 377.

27. James Q. Wilson, ed., *Urban Renewal: The Record and the Controversy* (Cambridge, MA: MIT Press, 1973); Jon C. Teaford, *The Rough Road to Renaissance: Urban Revitalization in America, 1940–1985* (Baltimore, MD: Johns Hopkins University Press, 1990); Clarence N. Stone, *Economic Growth and Neighborhood Discontent: System Bias in the Urban Renewal Program in Atlanta* (Chapel Hill: University of North Carolina Press, 1976); Langley Carleton Keyes Jr., *The Rehabilitation Planning Game* (Cambridge, MA: MIT Press, 1973); Zane L. Miller and Thomas H. Jenkins, eds., *The Planning Partnership: Participants' Views of Urban Renewal* (Beverly Hills, CA: Sage Publications, 1982); John H. Mollenkopf, *The Contested City* (Princeton, NJ: Princeton University Press, 1983).

28. Amanda I. Seligman, *Block by Block: Neighborhoods and Public Policy on Chicago's West Side* (Chicago: University of Chicago Press, 2005), 70.

29. "Chicago 21: A Plan for the Central Area Communities," (Chicago: Chicago Department of Development and Planning, September 1973), 14, 25.

30. Milton L. Rakove, *We Don't Want Nobody Nobody Sent: An Oral History of the Daley Years* (Bloomington: Indiana University Press, 1979), 256. Rakove's source is Lynn Williams, a retired University of Chicago official.

31. George Rosen, *Decision-Making Chicago-Style: The Genesis of a University of Illinois Campus* (Urbana: University of Illinois Press, 1980), 94–111.

32. Studs Terkel, *Division Street America* (1967; New York: The New Press, 1993), 8.

33. Keyes, *The Rehabilitation Planning Game*, 122–23. Two analogous instances of neighborhood rebellion against urban renewal, in Atlanta and Chicago respectively, can be found in Stone, *Economic Growth and Neighborhood Discontent*, 107–12, and Larry Bennett, *Neighborhood Politics: Chicago and Sheffield* (New York: Garland Publishing, 1997), 82–88.

34. Harry C. Boyte, *The Backyard Revolution: Understanding the New Citizen Movement* (Philadelphia: Temple University Press, 1980).

35. Andrew M. Greeley, *Neighborhood* (New York: The Seabury Press, 1977), 134.

36. Ibid., 166.

37. Alan A. Altshuler, *Community Control* (Indianapolis: Pegasus, 1970), 15.

38. Jerald E. Podair, *The Strike That Changed New York: Blacks, Whites, and the Ocean Hill-Brownsville Crisis* (New Haven, CT: Yale University Press, 2002), 49.

39. Ibid., 67.

40. Sharon Zukin, *Loft Living: Culture and Capital in Urban Change* (Baltimore, MD: Johns Hopkins University Press, 1982), 81.

41. Real estate agent John Milligan of Needham, Massachusetts, quoted in Lois Craig, "Suburbs," *Design Quarterly* 132 (1986): 19.

42. Robert A. Beauregard, *When America Became Suburban* (Minneapolis: University of Minnesota Press, 2006).

43. Stephanie Banchero, "N. Halsted to Get $3.2 Million Face Lift," *Chicago Tribune*, August 18, 1997; Suzy Frisch, "Gay-Pride Theme on Halsted is Protested," *Chicago Tribune*, September 4, 1997.

44. Kristin Ostberg, "Here Comes the Neighborhood," *Reader* (Chicago), April 26, 1996; Mary Pattillo, *Black on the Block: The Politics of Race and Class in the City* (Chicago: University of Chicago Press, 2007); Michele R. Boyd, *Jim Crow Nostalgia: Reconstructing Race in Bronzeville* (Minneapolis: University of Minnesota Press, 2008).

45. Blair Kamin, "Chicago's Sweetest Home Gets Its Due," *Chicago Tribune*, November 6, 2001. The HCBI's Web site can be accessed at http://www.chicagobunga low.org/.

46. Antonio Olivo, "Edgy About 'Yuppies,'" *Chicago Tribune*, June 12, 2006; Ray Quintanilla, "Red, White and Blue Carries Own Meaning in West Town," *Chicago Tribune*, January 26, 2007.

47. Kevin Lynch, *The Image of the City* (Cambridge, MA: MIT Press, 1960), 46–90.

48. Jeffrey S. Adler, *First in Violence, Deepest in Dirt: Homicide in Chicago 1975–1920* (Cambridge, MA: Harvard University Press, 2006), 272.

49. Louise Carroll Wade, *Chicago's Pride: The Stockyards, Packingtown, and Environs in the Nineteenth Century* (Urbana: University of Illinois Press, 1987), 232.

50. Lizabeth Cohen, *Making a New Deal: Industrial Workers in Chicago, 1919–1939* (New York: Cambridge University Press, 1991), 216.

51. Ibid., 233.

52. Paul Kleppner, *Chicago Divided: The Making of a Black Mayor* (DeKalb: Northern Illinois University Press, 1985), 19–20, 21.

53. Alan Ehrenhalt, *The Lost City: The Forgotten Virtues of Community in America* (New York: Basic Books, 1995), 35.

54. Ibid., 54.

55. Milton Rakove, *Don't Make No Waves . . . Don't Back No Losers* (Bloomington: Indiana University Press, 1975), 5.

56. Ibid., 63.

57. Robert A. Slayton, *Back of the Yards: The Making of a Local Democracy* (Chicago: University of Chicago Press, 1986); Sanford D. Horwitt, *Let Them Call Me Rebel: Saul Alinsky—His Life and Legacy* (New York: Knopf, 1989), 56–76.

58. Arnold R. Hirsch, *Making the Second Ghetto: Race and Housing in Chicago, 1940–1960* (New York: Cambridge University Press, 1983), 171–211; John T. McGreevy, *Parish Boundaries: The Catholic Encounter with Race in the Twentieth-Century Urban North* (Chicago: University of Chicago Press, 1996), 92–101; Seligman, *Block by Block.*

59. Barbara Ferman, *Challenging the Growth Machine: Neighborhood Politics in Chicago and Pittsburgh* (Lawrence: University Press of Kansas, 1996), 66–75; Joel Rast, *Remaking Chicago: The Political Origins of Urban Industrial Change* (DeKalb: Northern Illinois University Press, 1999), 83–95.

60. Bennett, *Neighborhood Politics*, 11–14.

61. Doug Gills, "Chicago Politics and Community Development: A Social Movements Perspective," in *Harold Washington and the Neighborhoods*, ed. Pierre Clavel and Wim Wiewel (New Brunswick, NJ: Rutgers University Press, 1991), 35.

62. Thomas Byrne Edsall, "Black vs. White in Chicago," *New York Review of Books*, April 13, 1989, 21–23.

63. Larry Bennett, "Harold Washington and the Black Urban Regime," *Urban Affairs Quarterly* 28 (1993): 423–40.

64. Gary Rivlin, *Fire on the Prairie: Chicago's Harold Washington and the Politics of Race* (New York: Henry Holt, 1992), 266–67. There is also an earlier, fuller account of this conflict, in which the quotation from Alderman Mell appears: Gary Rivlin, "City Hall: How Low They Can Go," *Reader* (Chicago), July 26, 1985.

CHAPTER FIVE

1. Devereux Bowly Jr., *The Poorhouse: Subsidized Housing in Chicago, 1895–1976* (Carbondale: Southern Illinois University Press, 1978), 112–14.

2. David Farber, *Chicago '68* (Chicago: University of Chicago Press, 1988), 138–46.

3. Alex Kotlowitz, *There Are No Children Here: The Story of Two Boys Growing Up in the Other America* (New York: Doubleday, 1991), 8–9.

4. Cory Oldweiler, "Horner Moves at Faster Pace, But Much Work Remains," *Chi-*

cago Reporter, March 1998, 10–12; and "Horner Residents Negotiate Housing Redevelopment Plans," *Illinois Welfare News* (Sargent Shriver National Center on Poverty Law), December 2001, 3–4, 10.

5. Steven Erie, *Rainbow's End: Irish-Americans and the Dilemmas of Urban Machine Politics, 1840 to 1985* (Berkeley: University of California Press, 1988), 116.

6. Harold F. Gosnell, *Machine Politics, Chicago Model* (1937; Chicago: University of Chicago Press, 1977), 78.

7. St. Clair Drake and Horace R. Cayton, *Black Metropolis: A Study of Negro Life in a Northern City* (1945; Chicago: University of Chicago Press, 1993), 354. The likely composer is Jimmie Gordon. See John Solomon Otto, "Hard Times Blues (1929–1940): Downhome Blues Recordings as Oral Documents," *Oral History Review* 8 (1980): 77–78.

8. Martin Meyerson and Edward C. Banfield, *Politics, Planning, and the Public Interest: The Case of Public Housing in Chicago* (New York: The Free Press, 1964), 45. In reference to Mayor Edward Kelly's support of the CHA, see Roger Biles, *Big City Boss in Depression and War: Mayor Edward J. Kelly of Chicago* (DeKalb: Northern Illinois University Press, 1984), 135–37.

9. J. S. Fuerst, with the assistance of D. Bradford Hunt, *When Public Housing Was Paradise: Building Community in Chicago* (Westport, CT: Praeger, 2003).

10. Bowly, *The Poorhouse,* esp. the photographs on 36 and 40.

11. Arnold R. Hirsch, *Making the Second Ghetto: Race and Housing in Chicago, 1940–1960* (New York: Cambridge University Press, 1983), 14, 218–19.

12. Hirsch, "Massive Resistance in the Urban North: Trumbull Park, Chicago, 1953–1966," *Journal of American History* 82 (1995): 536–37.

13. Meyerson and Banfield, *Politics, Planning, and the Public Interest,* 84–86; Fuerst, *When Public Housing Was Paradise,* 17–18.

14. D. Bradford Hunt, *Blueprint for Disaster: The Unraveling of Chicago Public Housing* (Chicago: University of Chicago Press, 2009), 87–93; Hirsch, *Making the Second Ghetto,* 212–58.

15. Elizabeth Wood, quoted in D. Bradford Hunt, "Understanding Chicago's High-Rise Public Housing Disaster," in *Chicago Architecture: Histories, Revisions, Alternatives,* ed. Charles Waldheim and Katerina Rüedi Ray (Chicago: University of Chicago Press, 2005), 303, 305; also see Hunt, *Blueprint For Disaster,* 93–97.

16. William Mullen, "The Road to Hell," *Chicago Tribune Magazine,* March 31, 1985, 16.

17. D. Bradford Hunt, "What Went Wrong with Public Housing in Chicago? A History of the Robert Taylor Homes," *Journal of the Illinois State Historical Society* 94 (2001): 104–6; Hunt, *Blueprint for Disaster,* 137–38.

18. M. W. Newman's Chicago's $70 Million Ghetto series ran in the *Chicago Daily News* from April 10 through April 17, 1965 (the *Daily News* did not publish a Sunday edition). Newman's two sources are quoted in "The Ghetto Struggle for Livability," *Chicago Daily News,* April 16, 1965, 31.

19. Charles Swibel's murky oversight of the CHA is chronicled in a *Chicago Sun-*

Times series, The CHA Empire, that ran during the last two weeks of July 1975. In particular, see Edward T. Pound and Scott Jacobs, "Tell Swibel Ties to Bank Holding CHA Accounts," *Chicago Sun-Times*, July 20, 1975; Pound and Jacobs, "Firm Does Swibel Favor, Gets CHA Guard Contract," *Chicago Sun-Times*, July 21, 1975; Pound and Jacobs, "Swibel Favors Aged with Pull, " *Chicago Sun-Times*, July 25, 1975.

20. Sudhir Alladi Venkatesh, *American Project: The Rise and Fall of a Modern Ghetto* (Cambridge, MA: Harvard University Press, 2002), 35–36; Harold F. Baron, "Building Babylon: A Case of Racial Controls in Public Housing" (Evanston, IL: Northwestern University Center for Urban Affairs, 1971), 70; also see Nicholas Lemann's profile of Ruby Haynes in *The Promised Land: The Great Black Migration and How It Changed America* (New York: Vintage Books, 1992), 264.

21. Venkatesh, *American Project*, 22; Hunt, "Understanding Chicago's Public Housing Disaster, 310–11; Hunt, *Blueprint for Disaster*, 145–81.

22. Scott Jacobs and Edward T. Pound, "CHA to Put $21 Million into Cabrini," *Chicago Sun-Times*, July 28, 1975.

23. D. Bradford Hunt, "Anatomy of a Disaster: Designing and Managing the Second Ghetto" (paper presented at the American Historical Association Annual Meeting, Chicago, January 2000); Hunt, *Blueprint for Disaster*, 183–212.

24. Alexander Polikoff, *Waiting for Gautreaux: A Story of Segregation, Housing, and the Black Ghetto* (Evanston, IL: Northwestern University Press, 2006), esp. chap. 3.

25. Leonard S. Rubinowitz and James E. Rosenbaum, *Crossing the Class and Color Lines: From Public Housing to White Suburbia* (Chicago: University of Chicago Press, 2000).

26. The descriptive statistics for Grand Boulevard are drawn from the Chicago Community Fact Book Consortium's *Local Community Fact Book: Chicago Metropolitan Area*, 1990 edition (Chicago: Academy Chicago Publishers, 1995), and 1980 edition (Chicago: Chicago Review Press, 1984).

27. Hunt, *Blueprint for Disaster*, 176–77.

28. Sandy Banisky, "Chicago Housing Authority Watches Its Best Efforts Fail," *Baltimore Sun*, June 18, 1995; Michael Schill, "Chicago's Mixed-Income New Communities Strategy: The Future of Public Housing?" in *Affordable Housing and Urban Redevelopment in the United States*, ed. Willem van Vliet (Thousand Oaks, CA: Sage Publications, 1997), 135–57.

29. Harold Henderson, "There Goes Their Neighborhood," *Reader* (Chicago), May 29, 1998.

30. "Plan for Transformation" (Chicago: Chicago Housing Authority, January 6, 2000); see also Sharon Gilliam and Philip Jackson, letter to the editor, *Chicago Tribune*, February 2, 2000. The progress of the Plan for Transformation can be monitored at the CHA Web site, http://www.thecha.org/.

31. Jason Grotto, Laurie Cohen, and Sara Olkon, "Public Housing Limbo," *Chicago Tribune*, July 6, 2008.

32. William Julius Wilson, *The Truly Disadvantaged: The Inner City, the Underclass, and Public Policy* (Chicago: University of Chicago Press, 1987), esp. chap. 2, 6.

33. Chicago Housing Authority, "The Urban Revitalization Demonstration Program," May 5, 1993, 19.

34. Larry Bennett and Adolph Reed Jr., "The New Face of Urban Renewal: The Near North Redevelopment Initiative and the Cabrini-Green Neighborhood," in *Without Justice for All: The New Liberaliasm and Our Retreat from Racial Equality*, ed. Adolph Reed Jr. (Boulder, CO: Westview Press, 1999), 201-2.

35. James E. Rosenbaum, Linda K. Stroh, and Cathy A. Flynn, "Lake Parc Place: A Study of Mixed-Income Housing," *Housing Policy Debate* 9 (1998): 733.

36. Ibid., 732.

37. Edward G. Goetz, *Clearing the Way: Deconcentrating the Poor in Urban America* (Washington DC: Urban Institute Press, 2003), 67-85. The bulk of the research that Goetz reviews has monitored efforts to deconcentrate poverty by moving poor families into middle-class, often suburban, communities.

38. Mark L. Joseph, Robert J. Chaskin, Henry S. Webber, "The Theoretical Basis for Addressing Poverty Through Mixed Income-Development," *Urban Affairs Review* 42 (2007): 376-79.

39. Paul B. Fischer, "Section 8 and the Public Housing Revolution: Where Will the Families Go?" (Chicago: Woods Fund, September 4, 2001), and "Where Are the Public Housing Families Going?: An Update" (unpublished paper, January 2003). See also Dan A. Lewis and Vandna Sinha, "Moving Up and Moving Out? Economic and Residential Mobility of Low-Income Chicago Families," *Urban Affairs Review* 43 (2007): 139-70; and Deidre Oakley and Keri Burchfield, "Out of the Projects, Still in the Hood: The Spatial Constraints on Public Housing Residents' Relocation in Chicago," *Journal of Urban Affairs* 31 (2009): 589-614.

40. Maryann Mason, "Mixed Income Public Housing: Outcomes for Tenants and Their Community, A Case Study of the Lake Parc Place Development in Chicago, Illinois" (PhD diss., Loyola University of Chicago, 1998), 86. Over the longer run, conditions at Lake Parc Place seem to have deteriorated. See "The Third Side: A Mid-Course Report on Chicago's Transformation of Public Housing" (Chicago: Business and Professional People for the Public Interest, September 2009), 68.

41. Sudhir Alladi Venkatesh, *Off the Books: The Underground Economy of the Urban Poor* (Cambridge, MA: Harvard University Press, 2006), xviii-xix.

42. Sudhir Venkatesh's work has also included studies of the tenant relocation process that are highly critical of the CHA's support efforts. See "The Robert Taylor Homes Relocation Study" (Center for Urban Research and Policy, Columbia University in the City of New York, September 2002). Mary Pattillo's *Black on the Block: The Politics of Race and Class in the City* (Chicago: University of Chicago Press, 2007), an ethnographic study of the gentrifying Oakland / Kenwood area on the South Side, might have been subtitled "The Failures of Intraracial Mentoring."

43. Polikoff, *Waiting for Gautreaux*, 328, 325-26.

44. William P. Wilen and Wendy L. Stasell, "*Gautreaux* and Chicago's Public Housing Crisis: The Conflict Between Achieving Integration and Providing Decent Housing for Very Low-Income African Americans," in *Where Are Poor People to*

Live? Transforming Public Housing Communities, ed. Larry Bennett, Janet L. Smith, and Patricia A. Wright (Armonk, NY: M. E. Sharpe, 2006), 248–49.

45. Patricia A. Wright offers a detailed account of the Coalition to Protect Public Housing's activities in "Community Resistance to CHA Transformation: The History, Evolution, Struggles, and Accomplishments of the Coalition to Protect Public Housing," in Bennett, Smith, and Wright, *Where Are Poor People to Live?* 125–67.

46. This and the previous quotation are drawn from Blair Kamin, "Can Public Housing Be Reinvented?" *Architectural Record*, February 1997, 88, 84. The current civic myth attributing seemingly therapeutic powers to the street grid recalls nineteenth-century Bostonians' emotional projection onto their "sacred skyline." See Robert Fogelson, *Downtown: Its Rise and Fall, 1880–1950* (New Haven, CT: Yale University Press, 2001), 129–31.

47. Larry Bennett, Nancy Hudspeth, and Patricia A. Wright, "A Critical Analysis of the ABLA Redevelopment Plan," in Bennett, Smith, and Wright, *Where Are Poor People to Live?* 197.

48. Mark Joseph, "Early Resident Experience at a New Mixed-Income Development in Chicago," *Journal of Urban Affairs* 30 (2008): 231; "Working with Tenants: Peter Holsten Helps Rebuild Cabrini Green," *Network Builder* (newsletter of the Chicago Rehab Network), Winter 1999, 1, 22.

49. Mary Schmich, "Kids See Dogs, Life in New Light," *Chicago Tribune*, July 16, 2004.

50. Ray Quintanilla, "New Neighbors Draw the Line at Cabrini," *Chicago Tribune*, July 31, 2003.

51. Interview with Jackie Holsten, Kendra Jackson, and Lesley Kiferbaum, Holsten Development staff, December 5, 2007.

52. Amy Rainey and Whitney Woodward, "Rapid Change," *Chicago Reporter*, July/August 2005, 17.

53. Joseph, "Early Resident Experience," 239–40. Each of the market-rate purchasers that Joseph interviewed had previously lived in a Chicago neighborhood.

54. Holsten, Jackson, and Kiferbaum, interview.

55. Joseph, "Early Resident Experience," 247.

56. Interview with Sarah Ruffin and Annette Hunt, residents of the Horner Annex building, May 29, 2008.

57. Pattillo, *Black on the Block*, 133, 268.

58. Antonio Olivo, "New Cabrini Homeowners Fight to Keep Skyline View," *Chicago Tribune*, May 19, 2006.

59. Kimbriell Kelly, "Rising Values," *Chicago Reporter*, July/August 2005, esp. 10, 15.

60. Mary Schmich, "New Neighbors Settle in with High Hopes," *Chicago Tribune*, July 11, 2004.

61. Mary Schmich, "Invisible Line Separates 'Chic' from Real World," *Chicago Tribune*, June 8, 2003.

62. Kelly, "Rising Values," 9.

63. Ibid., 11.

64. Mary Schmich, "Everyone Equal in Cabrini-Green Supermarket," *Chicago Tribune*, June 4, 2000.

65. According to Mark Joseph, "The biggest limitation of the development [Jazz on the Boulevard] is the lack of retailing in the adjoining area. Homeowners are anxious to see amenities like a quality grocery store, restaurant, a drycleaner, and a gas station open nearby" ("Early Resident Experience," 244). Also see "The Third Side," 26–27.

CHAPTER SIX

1. These characterizations of Florida's book appear inside the front jacket of the paperback edition: Richard Florida, *The Rise of the Creative Class* (New York: Basic Books, 2004). Florida's "follow-up" books include *The Flight of the Creative Class* (New York: HarperCollins, 2005) and *Who's Your City?* (New York: Basic Books, 2008).

2. "Review Symposium," *Urban Affairs Review* 40 (2005): 402–11.

3. Florida, *The Rise of the Creative Class*, 68.

4. Ibid., 225.

5. Ibid., 125–27.

6. Ibid., 302.

7. Ibid., 303.

8. Douglas E. Rae, *City: Urbanism and Its End* (New Haven, CT: Yale University Press, 2003), 53.

9. Ibid., 203.

10. Wilson Smith, ed., *Cities of Our Past and Present: A Descriptive Reader* (New York: John Wiley & Sons, 1964), 53.

11. Donald L. Miller, *City of the Century: The Epic of Chicago and the Making of America* (New York: Touchstone, 1997), 89.

12. William Cronon, *Nature's Metropolis: Chicago and the Great West* (New York: W. W. Norton & Co., 1991), 110.

13. Ibid., 301.

14. Blair A. Ruble, *Second Metropolis: Pragmatic Pluralism in Gilded Age Chicago, Silver Age Moscow, and Meiji Osaka* (New York: Cambridge University Press, 2001), 53.

15. Upton Sinclair, *The Jungle* (1906; New York: Signet, 1960), 36, 37–38.

16. Sam Bass Warner Jr., *The Urban Wilderness: A History of the American City* (New York: Harper & Row, 1972), 92.

17. From 1900 to 1910, Chicago's population increase was 487,000, that is, not much less than the half-million figure surpassed in each of the two preceding and succeeding decades. A concise and highly informative overview of Chicago's late nineteenth-century immigration dynamics is found in Paul Kleppner, *Chicago Divided: The Making of a Black Mayor* (DeKalb: Northern Illinois University Press, 1985), 16–19.

18. Ruble, *Second Metropolis*, 54.

19. Paul Avrich, *The Haymarket Tragedy* (Princeton, NJ: Princeton University Press, 1984); Stanley Buder, *Pullman: An Experiment in Industrial Order and Community Planning 1880-1930* (New York: Oxford University Press, 1970), 147-201; Robert Slayton, *Back of the Yards: The Making of a Local Democracy* (Chicago: University of Chicago Press, 1986), 93-95; Allan H. Spear, *Black Chicago: The Making of a Negro Ghetto, 1890-1920* (Chicago: University of Chicago Press, 1967), 214-219; William M. Tuttle, Jr., *Race Riot : Chicago in the Red Summer of 1919* (Urbana: University of Illinois Press, 1996).

20. Cronon, *Nature's Metropolis*, 257.

21. Lizabeth Cohen, *Making a New Deal: Industrial Workers in Chicago, 1919-1939* (New York: Cambridge University Press, 1991), 325. Cohen discusses the rise of the chain retailers in chap. 3.

22. Alan Ehrenhalt, *The Lost City: The Forgotten Virtues of Community in America* (New York: Basic Books, 1995).

23. Arnold R. Hirsch, *Making the Second Ghetto: Race and Housing in Chicago, 1940-1960* (New York: Cambridge University Press, 1983), 100-170.

24. "Development Plan for the Central Area of Chicago" (Chicago: City of Chicago, Dept. of City Planning, August 1958).

25. Hirsch, *Making the Second Ghetto*; Amanda I. Seligman, *Block by Block* (Chicago: University of Chicago Press, 2005).

26. Larry Bennett, "Postwar Redevelopment in Chicago: The Declining Politics of Party and the Rise of Neighborhood Politics," in *Unequal Partnerships*, ed. Gregory D. Squires (New Brunswick, NJ: Rutgers University Press, 1989), 161-77; Roger Biles, *Richard J. Daley: Politics, Race, and the Governing of Chicago* (DeKalb: Northern Illinois University Press, 1995), esp. 84-185.

27. Gregory D. Squires et al., *Chicago: Race, Class, and the Response to Urban Decline* (Philadelphia: Temple University Press, 1987), 26.

28. Thomas A. Corfman, "Downtown Home Sales Heated," *Chicago Tribune*, February 10, 2005, and "Downtown Homes Could Set Record," *Chicago Tribune*, August 17, 2005.

29. Evelyn M. Kitigawa and Karl E. Taeuber, eds., *Local Community Fact Book: Chicago Metropolitan Area*, 1960 edition (Chicago: Chicago Community Inventory, 1963); Chicago Fact Book Consortium, *Local Community Fact Book: Chicago Metropolitan Area*, 1990 edition (Chicago: Academy Chicago Publishers, 1995); "Census 2000 General Profiles for the 77 Chicago Community Areas from Summary File 1," http://www.nipc.org/test/Y2K_SF1_CCA.htm (accessed January 7, 2010).

30. David Moberg, "Economic Restructuring: Chicago's Precarious Balance," in *The New Chicago: A Social and Cultural Analysis*, ed. John P. Koval et al. (Philadelphia: Temple University Press, 2006), 36-38.

31. Terry Nichols Clark, with Richard Lloyd, Kenneth K. Wong, and Pushpam Jain, "Amenities Drive Urban Growth," *Journal of Urban Affairs* 24 (2002): 504.

32. Costas Spirou, "Urban Beautification: The Construction of a New Identity in Chicago," in Koval et al., *The New Chicago*, 299.

33. "The Global Edge: An Agenda for Chicago's Future," (Chicago: The Chicago Council on Global Affairs, 2007), 7.

34. Saskia Sassen, "A Global City," in *Global Chicago*, ed. Charles Madigan (Urbana: University of Illinois Press, 2004), 17; also see Sassen, *The Global City: New York, London, Tokyo*, 2nd ed. (Princeton, NJ: Princeton University Press, 2001).

35. Sharon Zukin, "Urban Lifestyles: Diversity and Standardization in Spaces of Consumption," *Urban Studies* 35 (1998): 825–39; also see Zukin, *Loft Living* (Baltimore, MD: Johns Hopkins University Press, 1982).

36. Richard Lloyd, *Neo-Bohemia: Art and Commerce in the Postindustrial City* (New York: Routledge, 2006), 155–56.

37. Neil Smith, Betsy Duncan, and Laura Reid, "From Disinvestment to Reinvestment: Mapping the Urban 'Frontier' in the Lower East Side," in Janet L. Abu-Lughod et al., *From Urban Village to East Village: The Battle for New York's Lower East Side* (Cambridge, MA: Blackwell, 1994), 150; see also Neil Smith, *The New Urban Frontier: Gentrification and the Revanchist City* (New York: Routledge, 1996).

38. Edward G. Goetz, *Clearing the Way: Deconcentrating the Poor in Urban America* (Washington DC: Urban Institute Press, 2003), 105.

39. Robert A. Beauregard, *When America Became Suburban* (Minneapolis: University of Minnesota Press, 2006), 193.

40. Dennis R. Judd, "Constructing the Tourist Bubble," in *The Tourist City*, ed. Dennis R. Judd and Susan S. Fainstein (New Haven, CT: Yale University Press, 1999), 36.

41. For contrasting perspectives on "tourist bubbles," see the favorably disposed Bernard J. Frieden and Lynn B. Sagalyn, *Downtown Inc.: How America Rebuilds Cities* (Cambridge, MA: MIT Press, 1989) and the vigorously hostile contributors to Michael Sorkin, ed., *Variations of a Theme Park: The New American City and the End of Public Space* (New York: Noonday Press, 1992).

42. Judd, "Constructing the Tourist Bubble," 36.

43. Elmer W. Johnson, *Chicago Metropolis 2020* (Chicago: University of Chicago Press, 2001), 85–94.

44. Here I am reflecting the thinking of historian Thomas Bender, *The Unfinished City: New York and the Metropolitan Idea* (New York: The New Press, 2002), 252.

45. The great exception to this generalization was the exclusion of African Americans from the full benefits of the New Deal. See Ira Katznelson, *When Affirmative Action Was White* (New York: W. W. Norton & Co., 2005).

46. America's expanding income and wealth gap is a much-discussed topic. For an excellent survey of the many issues associated with this trend, see the collection of *New York Times* articles entitled *Class Matters* (New York: Times Books, 2005). As to the fiscal and regulatory innovations necessary to sustain a more progressive urbanism, that truly is a subject beyond the scope of the present text.

INDEX

Page numbers in italics refer to illustrations.

public housing developments
(*continued*)
VI program, 149; Ickes complex, 49,
158; Jane Addams Houses, 152; Julia
Lathrop Homes, 152; mixed-income
uplift scenario, 163–66; in Near
South Side Douglas community,
30–32; panoramic perspective, 176–
77; parking in, 169–70; poverty and
unemployment levels in, 158, 165–68;
racial composition, 152–54, 165; resident relocation services, 94, 149, 165,
170–71; Robert H. Brooks Homes,
152; Robert Taylor Homes, 34–35,
148, 149, 154, 155–56, 158, 160; Rockwell Gardens, 158; screening process,
170–71; as slum removal tool, 154–55;
spartan design of, 152; Stateway Gardens, 148, 155; street-grid restoration
in, 168–69; Swibel era, 156–57, 219–
20n19; Wood era, 151–55, 158–59, 160
Public Works Administration, 152
Puerto Rican Agenda, 135–36
Pullman strike of 1894, 186

Rae, Douglas E.: *City: Urbanism and
Its End*, 85, 179, 181–83
Rakove, Milton: *Make No Waves . . .
Don't Back No Losers*, 141–42
Raleigh, Michael: *In the Castle of the
Flynns*, 51–52
Ranney, George Jr., 106
Rast, Joel, 41, 100
real estate development: economic
disparities and, 76, 177; interracial
tensions exacerbated by, 30; market
downturn, 173, 194; market under
Richard M. Daley, 98; neighbor-
hood thematization, 134–36; Royko
on, 64, 66
recycling, 108
Regional Plan Association of New
York, 126

regionalism, concept of, 13–14, 200–1,
205n29
Reinventing Government (Osborne and
Gaebler), 86–87
Renaissance 2010, 93
Rendell, Ed, 82, 88–89, 110, 212n22
Reveille for Radicals (Alinsky), 28
Riis, Jacob: *How the Other Half Lives*,
65, 124
Riordan, Richard, 82, 88–89
Rise of the Creative Class (Florida),
179–81, 183
River North district, *18*
Rivlin, Gary, 144
Robert H. Brooks Homes, 152
Robert Taylor Homes (public housing
development), 34–35, 148, 149, 154,
155–56, 158, 160
Roberts, Alice and Charlie, 70
Rockwell Gardens, 158
Roe, E. P.: *Barriers Burned Away*, 49
Roeder, Richard H., 107
Roger and Me (film), 92
Roosevelt, Franklin Delano, 150–51
Roosevelt Square neighborhood, *146*,
169, 170, 174
Rosenbaum, James, 163–64
Rostenkowski, Dan, 72–73
Rouse Company, 195
Royko, Mike, 62–73; *Boss: Richard J.
Daley of Chicago*, 63, 64–65, 67–68,
69–71, 73; *Chicago Daily News*
articles, 62–64, 65–66, 68–69, 70–
71; as informed insider, 65–66; me-
morial columns, 71–72; *One More
Time: The Best of Mike Royko*, 71;
perspective of, 62–63, 68–69, 71–
72, 75, 110, 196, 198; Rostenkowski
viewed by, 72–73
Ruffin, Sarah, 222n56

Salisbury, Robert, 84
San Francisco, 69